Other books by Herbert S. Strean
published by Scarecrow Press, Inc.:

The Casework Digest.   1969
Crucial Issues in Psychotherapy.   1976.
The Experience of Psychotherapy: A Practitioner's Manual.
   1972.
New Approaches in Child Guidance.   1970.
Personality Theory and Social Work Practice.   1975
Social Casework: Theories in Action.   1971
The Social Worker as Psychotherapist.   1974

CONTROVERSY IN PSYCHOTHERAPY

edited by

Herbert S. Strean

The Scarecrow Press, Inc.
Metuchen, N.J., & London
1982

08840

Library of Congress Cataloging in Publication Data

Main entry under title:

Controversy in psychotherapy.

    Includes index.
    1. Psychotherapy—Addresses, essays, lectures.
I. Strean, Herbert S. [DNLM: 1. Psychotherapy. WM 420 C764]
RC480.C645   616.89′14   81–18490
ISBN 0–8108–1498–6   AACR2

To the discussants of this book, my friends and colleagues who gave so generously and energetically, this volume is affectionately and appreciatively dedicated.

CONTENTS

v

ACKNOWLEDGMENTS

I would like to thank the editors and publishers of the following for their kindness in permitting me to reproduce articles that originally appeared in their journals.

Clinical Social Work Journal for "A Critique of the Newer Treatment Modalities" and "A Psychosocial View of Social Deviancy."

Family Process for "A Family Therapist Looks at Little Hans."

Journal of Jewish Communal Service for "The Contemporary Family and the Responsibilities of the Social Worker in Direct Practice" and "A Clinician Looks at Intermarriage."

The Psychoanalytic Quarterly for "Extra-Analytic Contacts: Theoretical and Clinical Considerations."

Psychoanalytic Review for "The Extramarital Affair," "Some Reflections on Therapeutic Work With the College Dropout," "A Note on the Treatment of Schizophrenia," and "The Unanalyzed Positive Transference and the Need for Reanalysis."

PREFACE

During the last decade many controversies have arisen within the field of psychotherapy, and virtually all of them are still unresolved: behavioral therapy vs. dynamically oriented therapy; family treatment vs. one-to-one treatment; long term therapy vs. short term therapy and crisis intervention; dynamic reconsiderations of certain diagnostic groups—e.g. the psychopath, the college drop out; the dynamics of certain lifestyles such as intermarriage, extra-marital affairs, and homosexual and heterosexual cohabitation; the role of the therapist regarding his or her neutrality, activity, anonymity, etc.; and other diagnostic and therapeutic concerns.

Within the past several years I have addressed all of the aforementioned issues in various psychoanalytic, psychotherapeutic, and social work journals. My notions have sparked a great deal of response—sharp and intense disagreement, marked ambivalence, and unqualified endorsement. As I became more and more certain that most of my interests were shared by therapists in the mental health professions, I thought it would be helpful to them if I put together in one volume these position papers on controversial issues in psychotherapy. Inasmuch as I knew my positions were just one man's opinion, I further thought it would be a stimulating venture to locate experts in the areas I have written—particularly those experts who had strong opinions of their own and would not necessarily agree with me—and have them discuss some of the issues presented.

The twenty-four discussants in this book were chosen with several criteria in mind: 1) They had already taken a position on the subject that they have been asked to address; 2) they were considered experts in the area to be discussed; and 3) they would feel free to agree, or disagree with me and raise issues that I had overlooked.

As the reader peruses the discussants' remarks, he or she will note that with only one or two exceptions the writers have maintained the finest of professional standards by staying with the issues and not engaging in personal attacks or vendettas. This, in my opinion, is how controversy in psychotherapy should be confronted.

What precipitated my gathering eleven of my papers and putting them together in one book and asking two experts to discuss each article arose from a recent experience with the *Clinical Social Work Journal*, edited by Mary Gottesfeld, one of the contributors to this work. About a year ago, when I submitted a paper to Mrs. Gottesfeld called, "A Critique of the Newer Treatment Modalities," it was Mrs. Gottesfeld who suggested that she find four experts to critique the paper and then asked me to write "the final word." The paper on the treatment modalities is the lead article in this book. It is the only one followed by four discussants' remarks and concluded with my rejoinder. Although I was tempted to use the format utilized by *Clinical Social Work Journal*, I concluded that it would be much better for the reader to have "the final word." Consequently, with the exception of the first article, I have omitted rejoinders and hope that the reader will write his or her own rejoinders and submit them to the many journals that would enjoy receiving them.

Controversy will always be part of the very web of psychotherapy and it seems to me that all psychotherapists have a responsibility to themselves and to their clients and patients to consider and reconsider the controversial issues inherent in our professional work. In this book, I believe we have demonstrated that the material before psychotherapists, people and their situations, should not and need not create rivalries and dissension among helping professionals. All clinicians are faced daily with human beings beset by difficulties in living, and it is our joint task to help them cope more effectively with themselves and others. Contributions to clinical work have come from many individuals and "schools" and the theoretical positions to which contributors claim allegiance have very little relevance.

It is my hope that the issues presented in this book will provoke therapists to continually consider and reconsider what is most helpful to our clients and patients.

HERBERT S. STREAN
New Brunswick, N.J.
August 30, 1981

Chapter 1

A CRITIQUE OF SOME OF THE NEWER TREATMENT MODALITIES

During the past decade a number of treatment modalities have become very popular; many of them have been assimilated into social work practice and into social work theory (Turner, 1979). In contrast to the days when long-term one-to-one therapy was the modality of choice in social work, short-term treatment, task-oriented casework, and crisis intervention have assumed priority. Notions like transference, resistance, the unconscious—concepts from psychoanalysis and ego psychology—are being repudiated, while practices such as conditioning, reinforcement, reward and punishment are being heralded (Wodarski and Bagarozzi, 1979; Briar and Miller, 1971; Fischer, 1973). Many of the adherents of the newer treatments aver that they can achieve better results than the traditional therapies. Proponents of "primal scream" intimate that they, not Freud, have discovered "catharsis." Behaviorists, while touting their "conditioning," wish to ignore (among many other things) that human beings have wishes, anxieties, defenses, form transferences, and often fear change. Sensitivity and encounter movement enthusiasts talk and write as if "confrontations" are their discovery. "Multiple impact" therapists are convinced that instant character, like instant coffee, is a cure-all (Shapiro, 1976) and many system theorists believe that short-term tinkering with role-sets of fathers, mothers, and children can bring enduring happiness to families.

As increasing numbers of people are entering a vastly expanding arena of therapies and quasi-therapies, they are being subjected to ap-

From *Clinical Social Work Journal*, vol. 9, no. 3 (September 1981), pp. 3–16. Reprinted by permission of Human Sciences Press.

proaches to human problems that depart sharply from the better known means of helping people. Eschewing the saliency of the patient's history, wishes, defenses and terrors, these therapies often capitalize upon sensationalism and promise substantial results in brief periods of time. Significant change in these therapies is often predicated upon an intense emotionally charged experience for the client.

As Dr. Hans Strupp (1977) has pointed out, any massive assault on a person's defenses, as occurs in weekend encounter groups, marathons, primal therapy, Erhard training seminars and others, heightens the potential for arousal of uncontrolled powerful affects and the possibility of decompensation or other negative effects. Because of these hazards, Strupp raises the question as to whether one might expect that closer attention would have been paid by researchers and clinicians to the study of outcomes from these therapies. This has not been the case and the few reports available are self-serving testimonials gathered by the proponents of a particular approach rather than objective and dispassionate investigation.

Even within the province of the more traditional therapeutic approaches, there is a movement toward very brief interventions. Evaluations of results are focused on a narrow range of outcomes or changes in "target complaints" which fail to provide a complete assessment of the impact of these short-term therapies on the client's total life. Very often short-term symptomatic gains are achieved at the cost of sacrificing the client's long-term developmental potential. One tends to concur with the psychiatrist Dr. Robert Langs (1976) who points out that many deviations in technique are not undertaken primarily because of the patient's needs, but are rationalizations of the extensive counter-gratifications they offer the therapist.

There has been limited dialogue in the social work literature on the assets and liabilities of these newer forms of therapeutic intervention. In addition, there have been few examinations of whether these treatments are in consonance with social work values and its perspective on people-in-their-situations (Hollis, 1972; Strean, 1971). Finally, their implications for the growth and development of the social work profession have not been seriously debated.

In this article, I would like to examine some of the cultural forces in our contemporary social scene which contribute to the popularity of therapies like behavior modification, primal scream, short term therapy, and the encounter movement. I would also like to examine some of these therapies in terms of their therapeutic efficacy and ethical significance. Lastly, I would like to discuss the impact of these new therapies on contemporary social work practice.

THE CONTEMPORARY SOCIAL SCENE AND THE NEWER MODALITIES

In one of his last essays, *Civilization and Its Discontents* (1930), Freud forecast a rather gloomy picture for twentieth-century man and woman. Convinced that the human being is an egocentric species who is constantly seeking narcissistic satisfaction and becomes very angry if he does not receive his rightful due, Freud alleged that man's only salvation was strong libidinal ties with other human beings. Only if people could enjoy sustained relationships, particularly with leaders whom they love, would they be able to control some of their destructive wishes and destructive actions. Freud was pessimistic about the possibility of strong, capable, and respectable leaders arriving on the scene; consequently, he prognosticated a society where competition would be more prevalent than cooperation, and interpersonal relationships would be governed more by hatred than love—a form of society that Reuben Fine has called a hate culture (Fine, 1975a).

A contemporary of Freud's, the French sociologist Durkheim, advanced a thesis similar to Freud's. Durkheim (1897) hypothesized that when families attain a high degree of cohesion, when men and women are secure in their identities and feel close to and aware of their roots, the incidence of psychosis, suicide, and divorce is less; conversely, Durkheim contended that when roles are ill defined, people are mobile, and family structure is weak, social disorganization and anomie are much higher.

Just a superficial glance at current interpersonal relations reveals that Freud's and Durkheim's propositions are correct. In the last couple of decades, few if any of our national leaders have been loved unambivalently, and the pessimism and distrust toward them that has evolved from the Vietnam War and Watergate also seem to be present in familial and other relationships. Vance Packard has dubbed our society "A Nation of Strangers" (1972) and has demonstrated how rootlessness is destroying American society. The soaring divorce rate, unrest between parents and children, the drug culture, and the high rate of teen-age alcoholism and suicide are some of the manifestations of our discontented civilization and apathetic culture.

As people become more hedonistic and live for the moment, expressions of infantile omnipotence and magical thinking become more plentiful. "Use Ponds and you'll be engaged," or "Men, use this aftershave lotion and she'll be yours" are statements that cater to our deep hunger, ambitiousness, and craving for the magical solution that will lead us into the Garden of Eden. Many social commentators question whether the institution of marriage can endure (Hunt, 1969; Ziskin and Ziskin, 1973) as they observe one out of two marriages ending in divorce and many of those that remain intact are characterized by sado-masochistic orgies and one-upmanship fracases. Herbert Hendin, in his book *The Age of Sensation* (1975), has shown how people have almost completely forgotten about such notions as commitment, love, and tenderness and are concentrating instead on manipulating and controlling others to gratify themselves as much as possible.

When men and women want instant gratification; when control and manipulation become dominant means of relating; when people tend to attribute the source of most of their dissatisfactions and frustrations to their social orbits; in short, when human beings want what they want when they want it and insist others must give it to them, therapies that cater to these infantile, narcissistic, and omnipotent yearnings will be in vogue. Screaming at one's parents with sound and fury for the slings and arrows that have caused outrageous fortune becomes more appealing than investigating why one wants to remain an angry and deprived child. Being rewarded and punished by a therapist who is ascribed a great deal of power seems a lot easier than studying why one must hate rather than love, why one wants indulgence rather than autonomy, and why one prefers an authoritarian boss instead of a benign co-pilot in the venture of self-understanding.

In our society, emotional turbulence seems to block meaningful associations within democratic groups; therefore, individuals seek their identities in units which appear similar to totalitarian governments. How different are the emotional experiences in e.s.t.—where a leader tells his patients that they are a bunch of dopes who don't know how to live—from some of the interpersonal processes in dens of the Communist Party or the Hitler Youth?

When an individual feels lonely, uncertain, depressed, and alienated, he can easily become very enamored with a totalitarian therapist who demonstrates limited concern for his feelings and fantasies, as often occurs with a behavior-modifier. When sources of one's hatred and sadism are unknown, but feelings of depression and guilt are pervasive, a sado-masochistic ritual like e.s.t. can be enticing.

Short-term therapy, which is extremely popular today, is quite congruent with contemporary man's and woman's resistance to intensive exploration of their inner lives. The yearning of so many people for instant gratification without too much self-reflection can make therapies like "Quick Response," "Task Oriented Casework," or "Crisis Intervention" very attractive. In these short-term treatments, issues like personal history, the unconscious, resistances, transference, and counter-transference are frequently by-passed in favor of an unscientific action-oriented approach in the here-and-now.

In American society people have an urgent need for remedies that will reduce their feelings that they are in the midst of strangers (Packard, 1972). Therefore, sensitivity groups and encounter groups, in which they are hugged and fondled, will be more attractive than procedures which will help them better understand how their marital complaints are really unconscious wishes and their desires to be fed and held are in many ways fights against the reality principle. When lonely adults are yearning to be psychological children, they will resent their own children and not want to explore how they are recapitulating their infantile pasts in the present. Instead, they will find a social system tinkerer very inviting because he will not try to help them see how they are frightened and reluctant to be parents but instead will infantilize them by telling them how to behave.

So many Americans feel an inarticulate sense of loss, unrelatedness, and lack of connection. Because they do not want to introspect or take much responsibility for their plights, because they want soothing rather than confrontation, reward and punishment rather than interpretation, and manipulation rather than self-understanding, a host of treatments are competing with one-to-one dynamically oriented treatment. Most of the adherents of these newer treatments hate dynamically oriented therapy and all it stands for. They hate it for pointing out that certain "lifestyles" such as homosexuality are neurotically motivated; they hate it for demonstrating that behavioral change means very little unless therapist and client understand how the client's entire metapsychology contributes to it, and they hate dynamically oriented therapy for insisting that psychotherapy, without taking into consideration concepts like the unconscious, id wishes, defenses, superego, transference and counter-transference, and history is "hit or miss" treatment.

Behavior-Modification Therapy

One of today's most popular therapies is behavior-modification therapy. Although few of its adherents acknowledge it, the major premise in this therapy is Pavlov's (1927) classical conditioning paradigm. In Pavlov's experiment, a dog was simultaneously presented with meat paste and the sound of a tuning fork. After being rewarded and punished several times, the dog was able to learn to salivate when he heard only the sound of the tuning fork. This was and is conditioned learning.

Behavior-modification's major treatment procedures are rewarding and punishing. An enuretic child, for example, is punished for his enuresis by hearing a gong every time he begins to urinate while sleeping. Eventually the wish to urinate while sleeping is accompanied, in the child's mind, by the sound of a gong and he can then wake up in time and make it to the bathroom before "an accident" takes place. Similarly, a homosexual man can be punished with 400 electric shots in the left armpit every time he participates in homosexual sex. After a while "being shot" is not worth the pain and the man can give up his overt homosexual practices. Wolpe (1969), the behaviorist, terms this form of treatment "aversive conditioning," but upon close examination it is nothing else but the punishment routine of Pavlov.

Sometimes behaviorists try to emphasize the "rewarding" in their treatment and de-emphasize the "punishing." For example, several years ago there was an article in the *New York Times* describing how a male homosexual was rewarded with ice cream every time he could look at pictures of a vagina. Eventually, the vagina was experienced by him as something delicious! Similarly children, mental patients, and others have improved in their promptness and cleanliness by being rewarded with gold stars and tokens.

One of the major claims of the behaviorists is that they are quite capable of helping people overcome phobias and compulsions. Masters and Johnson (1970) and Helen Kaplan (1974) have become very popular among those who have sexual problems such as frigidity and impotence. Unresponsive to their clients' unconscious hatreds, oblivious to problems of unconscious bisexuality and dependency, by-passing issues like transference and countertransference, and ignorant of the fact that consistent complaints that a spouse has of his or her partner are usually disguised wishes of a sadistic or masochistic type, sex therapists try to teach people how to use their bodies more effectively. For example, when a man has a problem of premature ejaculation, his partner helps him control his ejaculation by grabbing his penis when he is about to ejaculate. Eventually, the thought of a crushed penis can help the man with his ejaculatory problems. Similarly, a frigid woman can be helped to overcome her inability to be orgastic when her partner manipulates her sexual organs.

Even if behavior modifiers can effect quick cures for sexual problems, enuresis, phobias, compulsions, and addictions like smoking, should we endorse their practices? Enuretone can stop enuresis and grabbing a man's penis can affect his sexual functioning—but, so is torture effective at times! Chomsky of M.I.T. once said in a lecture, "Under the threat of punishment, you can get a man to say that the world is flat even if he does not believe it." People can behave differently when rewarded and punished but may like themselves less.

Behaviorists constantly compare the human being to animals. Although humans can sometimes become almost as helpless as animals and be manipulated by gongs and buzzers, it is well know that only man can dream, report his dreams, and analyze them (Sharpe, 1978). Only a human being is able to empathize in a complex and profound manner with another human being. How capable are animals of having ethics, morals and deep compassion? Just as behaviorists do not discuss the ethics, morals, or compassion of animals when they compare them to human beings, they also seem to avoid these issues in their own work with people.

Perhaps a more important issue that the behaviorist avoids is the existence of internal motives. According to Skinner (1971), one of the foremost exponents of behaviorism, the human being is not actuated by purposes, is "beyond freedom and dignity," and may or may not have an unconscious mind. Reuben Fine (1975b) asked in his paper "The Bankruptcy of Behaviorism," "If man has no purposes, hopes, dreams or ideals, how do we account for an institution like the U.N.?" Fine also points out in this paper that behaviorism is most popular in totalitarian countries where psychoanalysis is often repudiated and that psychoanalysis is much more accepted in democratic societies.

Another dynamic of behaviorism which the behavior modifiers virtually ignore is the therapist–patient relationship. They wish to overlook that people are motivated to alter attitudes and behavior when they feel loved and understood and find it difficult to make substantial changes when they feel misunderstood or unloved. If transference and countertransference are dismissed, if the relationship component of therapy is set aside, how can we truly evaluate the interpersonal experience of therapy and its impact on the patient?

The behaviorist seems to be interested almost exclusively in symptom relief and this he can achieve with some of his patients. While he is quick to argue that symptom substitution does not take place in his therapy, even if this is correct, we still have to wonder about the maladaptive character defenses that can be reinforced under the aegis of rewarding and punishing. We also have to wonder about how much self-confidence the patient can really achieve if he has been infantilized by the praise and the withholding of a parental figure. We also have to wonder how much hunger for power is operant in the well-conditioned behaviorist.

Basically, the scientific statements of Skinner and the behaviorists are simply incorrect. Freedom and dignity *do* exist; man *is* actuated by purposes, aims, and goals. There is no valid comparison between the internal states postulated by modern dynamic psychologists and the inner states attributed to animals. Of the behaviorists' notion that introspection is not a valid scientific method, Bertrand Russell (1948) commented, "This view seems to me to be so absurd that if it were widely held I should ignore it."

One of the reasons that behaviorism has been attractive to some is that it is experienced as an exact science relating only to tangible stimuli and responses. Because behaviorism ignores the variables of human wishes, hopes, ambivalences, relationships, and superego injunctions, Fine refers to it as a pseudoscience and states:

> Clinicians are usually mixed up about the scientific status of their enterprise, mistakenly assuming that behavioristic experimentation is really the royal road to truth and knowledge, while theirs is just an ad hoc adaptation made inevitable by the great difficulties of experimentation and the pressing need for some practical answers. It is important to recognize that clinical research represents a perfectly valid scientific method while experimental is frequently mere pseudoscience. [Fine, 1975b, p. 446]

Short-Term Therapy

In consonance with the mores of our Future Shock society (Toffler, 1971), in which we all want a great deal and pronto, are therapies that reflect the type of modus vivendi we champion: "short term treatment," "crisis intervention," "quick response therapy," "brief treatment" and "time-limited treatment." Regardless of the label attached to these therapies, their advocates contend that people can be helped in a short period of time if both therapist and patient consciously relate to the problems the patient presents and conjointly muster their cognitive and other adaptive skills to tackle the presenting problem. Reactive depressions in adults, school phobias in children and certain situational problems such as homesickness and vocational distress have been reported to respond well to short-term treatment.

Brief treatment was initiated and became popular for many spurious reasons. As a response to the dearth of therapists at many mental health clinics and social agencies, short term therapy was viewed as a partial solution to the manpower problem.

Another factor contributing to the growth of short term therapy has been the biases of therapists. Short term treatment has often been viewed as the therapy of choice for lower socio-economic patients, poorly educated patients, and seriously disturbed patients (Hollingshead and Redlich, 1956). It should be noted that many psychoanalysts have contributed toward the acting out of this bias (Strean & Blatt, 1969) and over the years many of them have averred that long term intensive therapy is the treatment of choice for the healthy, articulate, introspective patient while brief treatment is for "the borderline" and other seriously disturbed patients (Tarachow and Stein, 1967).

Influenced by the psychoanalyst Franz Alexander (1948), who coined the term "the corrective emotional experience," many therapists in the 1940s and 1950s began to believe that if patients were provided with unique relationships, different from what they experienced with their parents when they were children, they could be appreciably helped and helped quickly. For example, it was suggested that if the adult patient had an authoritarian father, the therapist should behave democratically and permissively with him. According to Alexander and his followers, the patient would then be relieved of his self-hatred and other problems much faster than through classical Freudian analysis.

Stimulating the popularity of brief treatment are research reports which suggest that patients and therapists have found this form of therapy much more beneficial than long term treatment (Wolberg, 1965; Phillips and Weiner, 1967; Masserman, 1965). Basing their decisions on research results, many clinics and agencies have stopped providing long term treatment altogether and have substituted short term therapy.

All of the aforementioned factors that have aided and abetted the rise of brief treatment do not justify the therapy's existence. A dearth of therapists calls for more therapists, not less therapy for more patients.

To use a medical analogy, if one hundred patients had tuberculosis and there were only a few physicians available to treat them, is it professionally responsible to give all the patients aspirins and then send them home?

Because individuals do not speak English in an erudite manner or because they do not share middle class therapists' values, is it humane to provide them with less treatment than their middle-class confreres receive? Furthermore, if people have weak egos and fragile defenses, is the answer to their problems always less treatment? Seriously disturbed people need intensive treatment for long periods of time; when they do not receive the therapeutic time they need, it is often because their therapists resist them. One means that therapists sometimes use to handle their contempt toward clients is assigning diagnostic labels to them, e.g. "borderline," "pseudo-neurotic schizophrenic," "hard to reach," "prognosis guarded," etc.

Although it is true that some of our very disturbed clients fear involving themselves in an intimate therapeutic relationship, it is one thing to respect their resistances and not insist on long-term treatment; however, it is often nothing but the therapist's counterresistance operating when he tells a very disturbed individual that the treatment of choice for him is a brief therapeutic encounter.

Using Alexander's "corrective emotional experience" is not only a therapeutic short cut but may also be viewed as a therapeutic blunder. If a client has had an authoritarian father and is still influenced by the image of his father, what the client really needs is to experience the parental introject in the transference relationship with the therapist and learn why he wishes to sustain a relationship with an authoritarian father. It is naive to believe that the therapist's enactment of a role that is different from the client's introject is going to rid the client of the introject. Frequently, short-term therapists do not realize that if people are negatively influenced in the present by past experiences with parental figures, they still wish to be so influenced. For effective treatment to take place, the client should experience the therapist in the many ways he perceived key figures of the past. To stop a client from wanting to hate us, feel ambivalent toward us, or fall in love with us by offering short-term treatment and a corrective emotional experience, is reminiscent of the parent who gives a child an ice cream cone when the child needs to have a long talk with the parent about many complex issues.

Virtually all of the research reports on brief treatment should be questioned because of their lack of scientific accuracy. To rely on the self-reports of patients and therapists that are gathered from questionnaires or from one interview is really short-term research! Clinicians have recognized for some time that there are a myriad of variables in operation when an individual responds to questions either in an interview or on a questionnaire—transferential factors, defenses, superego admonitions, id wishes, etc. The only way that one can really study the effects of therapy is to observe the client over time and watch his fluctuating transference responses, his shifting defenses, his voices from the superego, etc. This type of research takes much time and effort but is mandatory in studying the effects of any treatment.

Short-term treatment rarely helps an individual become happier nor can it appreciably reduce neurotic suffering. It can help some people cope better with a situational distress and it can be supportive of those individuals who are too frightened to commit themselves to long term treatment, but need somebody on whom they can rely if an emergency arises. However, brief treatment has never increased a patient's maturity, substantially enriched his ego strengths, or profoundly affected his capacity for pleasure.

Short-term therapists often utilize learning theory to undergird their therapeutic efforts. Yet, anybody who has been involved in a learning situation knows that learning is never a completely smooth process. Every learner moves forward and backward, has impasses with the teacher, and can get stuck at crucial times. Both therapist and patient must allow these processes to take place for therapeutic learning to be effective.

Family Therapy

When the child guidance movement began, only the child was treated. The mother, after presenting the child's problems and history at intake was relegated to the waiting room and did not participate in the treatment any further. It became apparent that mothers, albeit unwillingly and unconsciously, frequently had to sabotage their youngsters' therapy because changes in their children threatened their own emotional status quo. Consequently, in the 1940s, child therapists and social workers began to point out that "mothers are clients, too," and saw mothers in treatment.

In the 1940s, an important paper was published called, "The Father Gets Worse: A Child Guidance Problem" (Burgum, 1942). Therapists began to realize that fathers were also affected by changes in their children and in their wives. However, there was difficulty in involving fathers in treatment; many of them viewed the child guidance clinic as part of the women's world and stayed away from it and occasionally therapists felt uncomfortable working with fathers (Strean, 1962).

In the late 1950s, Nathan Ackerman (1958) introduced family therapy. He believed that the existence of problems in a child always implied that there was a disturbance in the entire family network. If the child was to be helped, Ackerman contended, all of the family members had to confront how each of them contributed toward making the child a scapegoat. As the entire family became the unit of diagnosis and the unit of treatment, the therapy became focused on interpersonal problems rather than intrapersonal; on the here and now, rather than on the past; on family defenses rather than on individual pathology; on reality rather than on fantasy and on action rather than understanding.

Family therapists began to seriously question psychoanalytic theory and became enamored with the systems approach. The marital subsystem, the parent–child subsystem, and the sibling subsystem were examined to see how each affected the family homeostasis (Pollak, 1956). "Double-bind" messages (Bateson, 1956) "pseudo-mutuality" (Wynne, 1958) and other forms of dysfunctional behavior became important issues as therapist and family examined the discomplementarity of roles in the family system.

System theory and family dynamics can be valuable aids for any therapist. I found them very helpful in my research on "A Family Therapist Looks at Little Hans" (Strean, 1967). In that study I was able to demonstrate that Hans's phobia of horses was not only a manifestation of his oedipal conflicts, but his symptom was exacerbated by conflicts between the parents, conflicts between each of the parents and himself, and conflicts between Hans and his sister. I concluded that it was much more than a coincidence that Little Hans's parents divorced as soon as he was cured of his phobia, i.e. the symptom had held the family together.

Family therapists in their desire to help family units have frequently overlooked some important and crucial dynamics of therapy. Concentrating on the here and now, they can ignore how parents recapitulate their own idiosyncratic pasts with their children and how they unconsciously experience their youngsters as siblings, parents, and projected parts of themselves. When the past is overlooked and unconscious wishes and defenses are given limited consideration, it is really impossible to be experts on the dynamics of day to day behavior.

What is perhaps the most questionable feature of some current family therapy is the manipulation of family roles. I recently participated in a panel where a distinguished family therapist told of her ordering a father when and how to have sexual intercourse with his wife, when and how to give the children allowances, and when and how to watch T.V. On my asking the family therapist why she was so busy giving instructions to the father, she pointed out that the father was too passive a man and she wanted "to make him more assertive." When I suggested that perhaps she was helping the father become very passive with her, she said that was "irrelevant."

When transference and countertransference factors are overlooked and orders are given instead, when resistances are by-passed and history is neglected, when people are treated as part of a role or system network and their loves, hates, anxieties, defenses, dreams and other unconscious variables are not seriously examined, role tinkering ensues and sound psychotherapy goes underground.

The Encounter and Sensitivity Movements

In the United States today, only 16.3 percent of our population lives in a setting consisting of father, mother and children (Howard, 1978). Many natural families are broken up, extended family members are frequently unreachable, and because we are a mobile population, social groups are constantly being disbanded. It was recently reported that over forty million Americans change residences each year (Packard, 1972).

Catering to our social hunger are encounter and sensitivity groups. These groups take such forms as twenty-four hour marathons, EST lectures, primal screams, exercises in handholding and other types of sexual foreplay. Proponents of these groups want people to relax more and enjoy more emotional intimacy (Kovel, 1976).

In order to resolve barriers and reduce emotional distance between himself and his peers, the client is usually persuaded to take some action in the group setting. He might be encouraged to hand-wrestle so that he can overcome his fear of assertiveness; he might be seduced into holding hands so that he can resolve some of his resistances to tenderness; or he might be directed to "tell somebody off" so that he can feel more confident about being aggressive.

In these groups where activity is crucial, incidents from one's past might be uncovered, but persistent historical themes, subtle defensive maneuvers, neurotic transferences, and rigid fixations are frequently by-passed. The client, because he is so often viewed as deprived, is fed and stimulated. Although sexual stimulation can make him feel better, his sexual and other interpersonal problems can never be worked through because his *infantile* sexual fantasies are rarely, if ever, addressed.

Encounter and sensitivity group specialists often fail to recognize that the source of most people's sexual and interpersonal troubles lies in their unconscious *childish* fantasy world. Handholding cannot help an individual too much when his unconscious wish is to devour his mother. Falling and being picked up cannot resolve masochistic wishes to be raped and maimed. Hugging a member of the opposite sex cannot resolve homosexual anxieties and oedipal conflicts.

All of the therapies that we have reviewed emphasize behavioral change and deemphasize introspection. Feelings are less important than action. The unconscious is often demeaned while the conscious mind is alleged to be all important. These therapies pay insufficient heed to resistances and defenses but all too often seek to manipulate people to behave differently. Transference and countertransference are almost forgotten and *infantile* sexuality often means next to nothing. Clients are not helped to embark on a discovery of self-understanding. Rather, they are usually gratified and encouraged to regress without understanding the anxieties that propel their regression. Non-analytic therapists seem to disagree with Freud's conclusion in his *Introductory Lectures* (1916) in which he said, "We are forced to the inescapable hypothesis that there are purposes in people which can become operative without their knowing about them" (Freud, 1916, p. 84). They also seem to reject his advice to all patients:

> Turn your eyes inward, look into your own depths, learn first to know yourself! Then you will understand why you were bound to fall ill, and perhaps you will avoid falling ill in the future. [Freud, 1917, p. 24]

THE NEW THERAPIES AND SOCIAL WORK

As we review the therapeutic scene in social work today, it reminds us of the conditions prevailing in the political and social scenes. There appears to be a kind of "anomie" in both the therapeutic scene and in the social and political scenes—an absence of organization and aim-orientedness. In direct services in social work, we tend to see the emergence of therapeutic interventions determined by fashion, created very often by people whose work is insufficiently based on clinical studies but who nonetheless propose therapies insufficiently measured against criteria of usefulness. Although we have much clinical evidence in social work that treatment is hit or miss without taking the client's history into consideration, we see in social work practice much instant treatment carried out with the mistaken belief that one can reduce conflict by focusing on the here and now and by forgetting history.

Social workers who live in the Age of Sensation—which favors instant gratification over the reality principle, narcissism over interpersonal cooperation, and ventilation over introspection—have at times been too seduced by the encounter movement, the marathons, and the sensitivity movements. These so-called therapies all too often promote a type of aggressive foreplay—stimulating, exciting, but regressive and rarely ego-building.

We social workers sometimes get overly influenced by our hate culture and can forget our mission with married couples and families. Instead of using our knowledge of the unconscious and defenses to help a wife or husband who blasts the marital partner, we are too often tempted to join the client in his or her attacks, under the guise of enhancing assertiveness and freedom. When a husband or wife complains about the partner's sadism, stupidity, or lack of sexuality, we always have to ask, "Why does the client unconsciously want it that way? What protection does it offer the client when he or she experiences the spouse as a punitive superego, a half-dead mammal, or a ninny?" In family therapy we always must ferret out why a particular member of a family is used as a scapegoat. What's in it for the goat and what's in it for the family members who are abusing him or her?

If one looks at the profession of social work one would have to characterize a good deal of current practice as regressive and fragmentary. In the days of Mary Richmond, although most help was limited to manipulating the client's environment and attempting to influence the client's "significant others," the friendly visitor was a disciplined professional who, though rigid and moralistic, had a clear focus in his diagnostic and interventive efforts (Richmond, 1922).

When the friendly visitor learned that all clients did not respond positively to environmental manipulation and advice, psychoanalysis helped the social worker understand that even though people may consciously want to change, they have unconscious wishes to preserve the status quo and can derive neurotic gratification from their suffering (Hamilton, 1958).

Although the metapsychology of Freud was and is helpful to social workers, his theory of treatment was misused and abused by many of them. It took social workers some time to realize that interpretations of defenses and unconscious wishes have to be done judiciously. Of more importance, techniques like free association and dream analysis, social workers slowly and painfully realized, are more applicable to middle-class clients with observing egos and full stomachs.

The Depression and the war years helped social workers once again appreciate the fact that people lived in situations and that all of the self-understanding in the world cannot rectify a dilapidated house, a decrepit neighborhood, or a chaotic welfare system. Social workers by the 1950s were actively talking about the person-situation constellation; they recognized that we cannot help a client unless we appreciate how and why his situation influences him and vice-versa (Hamilton, 1951).

I believe that the person-in-situation focus with its strong emphasis on study, diagnosis, and treatment, so widely adhered to in the 1950s, is what makes social work unique and what social workers should stress more today. Instead, practitioners have not taken sufficient pride in their understanding and skill in working with inner man and his environment, but have been unduly influenced by manipulative techniques which do not focus very much on person–situation interaction. All too often the social worker of the 1980s is too intimidated by the knowledge explosion and feels that his practice must be viewed in the language of system theory, role theory, organizational theory, and communication theory. To surround social work practice with a flock of theories that are not always applicable to the person-in-his-situation is not even a constructive intellectual exercise! The social worker of the 1980s always must ask of the new theoretical perspectives: What is pertinent to practice? How will the concept help clients?

As new modalities confront social workers such as task-oriented casework, crisis intervention, and brief family therapy, they are too often experienced as panaceas and used indiscriminately. Insufficiently asked by social workers are the following questions: What is the level of psychosocial functioning of the individual and/or family members that makes a particular modality the intervention of choice? What are the defensive patterns of the client or client system that makes one form of intervention threatening while another one is more palatable? How does the client experience the worker transferentially as he enacts the broker role, the crisis intervenor, short-term therapist, or advocate? Does the particular modality induce regression or progression, and what will be the most therapeutic now? In sum, there seems to be in current social work practice an absence of careful selection of modalities and an absence of a careful assessment of their usefulness for specific person–situation constellations.

Just as our Age of Sensation has induced much regressive behavior, more social workers seem to be attracted to regressive therapies. More frequently in the social work literature one notes the endorsement of therapeutic interventions which reduce the human being to an aggregate of stimuli and responses, devoid of hopes, dreams, fantasies, values, hurts, joys, and no unconscious mind. In our current era, the social work practitioner all too often overlooks the uniqueness of the person as he pigeonholes people into roles and subsystems and loses sight of the unifying genetic and experiential bases and the dynamic interaction of its parts. In many quarters social work's traditional commitment to problem-solving is whittled down from the person with the problem to just the problem.

As practitioners have become enamored of superficial interventions, as panaceas become popular like gurus are to young people, we have been witnessing more and more of what I have referred to as "The Flight from the Client" (Strean, 1978). In current social work we have a reward and punishment system which demeans practice. If a practitioner does good work with clients, he is promoted by removing him from clients and making him a supervisor. In effect, the more ability the worker has, the more he'll be removed to the periphery of practice. The same phenomenon exists in our schools of social work where those who are nearest to practice and to clients, i.e., the field work instructors, have the least status. A social work educator, like a practitioner, is also rewarded by being removed from practice. If he does well as a field work instructor, he'll be transferred to the classroom and if he does well in the classroom, he'll become a sequence chairman or a dean and be further removed.

In conclusion, social work has a value base which sees the human being as one who has freedom and dignity, an internal life that consists of hopes, wishes, guilts, and anxieties but who is capable of loving, working, and rational thinking. As we attempt to help our clients we should not be seduced by the dictates of our hate culture and our age of sensation, but instead should use our tried and true knowledge of people and their situations, our respect for their internal states and affects, and our skills in listening, assessing and humanely intervening in an individualized person–situation constellation.

REFERENCES

Ackerman, N. *The Psychodynamics of Family Life*, New York: Basic Books, 1958.

Alexander, F. *Fundamentals of Psychoanalysis,* New York: Norton, 1948.

Bateson, G. "Toward a Theory of Schizophrenia," *Behavioral Science,* Vol. 1, 1956.

Briar, S., and H. Miller. *Problems and Issues in Social Casework,* New York: Columbia University Press, 1971.

Burgum, M. "The Father Gets Worse: A Child Guidance Problem," *American Journal of Orthopsychiatry,* Vol. 12, 1942.

Durkheim, E. *Suicide: A Study in Sociology,* Glencoe, Ill.: (1897).

Fine, R. (a) *Psychoanalytic Psychology,* New York: Jason Aronson, 1975.

―――. (b) "The Bankruptcy of Behaviorism," *The Psychoanalytic Review,* Vol. 62, No. 3, 1975, pp. 437–452.

―――. *The Healing of the Mind,* New York: David McKay, 1971.

Fischer, J. "Is Casework Effective?" *Social Casework,* Vol. 18, 1973, pp. 5–22.

Freud, S. "Analysis Terminable and Interminable," Vol. 23. London: Hogarth Press, 1937.

―――. "Civilization and Its Discontents," Vol. 21. London: Hogarth Press, 1930.

―――. "A Difficulty in the Path of Psychoanalysis," Vol. 17. London: Hogarth Press, 1917.

―――. "Introductory Lectures on Psychoanalysis," Vol. 15, London, Hogarth Press, 1916.

Grossbard, H. Book Review of *Personality Theory and Social Work Practice,* H. Strean, ed., in *Social Work,* Vol. 21, No. 4, 1976.

Hamilton G. "A Theory of Personality: Freud's Contribution to Social Work," in H. Parad, ed., *Ego Psychology and Dynamic Casework,* New York: FSAA, 1958.

―――. *Theory and Practice of Social Casework,* New York: Columbia University Press, 1951.

Health, D. "Not Just Intellectual Growth," *Contemporary Psychology,* Vol. 14, No. 5, 1969.

Hendin, H. *The Age of Sensation,* New York: Norton, 1975.

Hollingshead, A., and F. Redlich. *Social Class and Mental Illness*, New York: Random House, 1956.

Hollis, F. *Social Casework: A Psychosocial Therapy*, 2nd ed. New York: Random House, 1972.

Howard, J. *Families*, New York: Simon and Schuster, 1978.

Hunt, M. *The Affair*, New York: The New American Library, 1969.

Kaplan, H. *The New Sex Therapy*, New York: Brunner/Mazel, 1974.

Kovel, J. *A Complete Guide to Therapy*, New York: Pantheon Books, 1976.

Masserman, J. "Short-Term Therapy" in *Short Term Therapy*, L. Wolberg, ed. New York: Grune and Stratton, 1965.

Masters, W., and V. Johnson. *Human Sexual Adequacy*, Boston: Little and Brown, 1970.

Nisbet, R. *Community and Power*, London: Oxford University Press, 1962.

Packard, V. *A Nation of Strangers*, New York: David McKay, 1972.

Pavlov, I. *Conditioned Reflexes*, London: Oxford University Press, 1927.

Phillips, E., and J. Weiner. *Short Term Psychotherapy*, New York: Basic Books, 1967.

Pollak, O. *Integrating Sociological and Psychoanalytic Concepts*, New York: Russell Sage Foundation, 1956.

Richmond, M. *What Is Social Casework?* New York: Russell Sage Foundation, 1922.

Shapiro, S. *A Moment of Insight*, New York: International Universities Press, 1976.

Sharpe, E. *Dream Analysis*, New York: Brunner-Mazel, 1978.

Skinner, B. F. *Beyond Freedom and Dignity*, New York: Alfred A. Knopf, 1971.

Strean, H. "A Means of Involving Fathers in Family Treatment: Guidance Groups for Fathers," *American Journal of Orthopsychiatry*, Vol. 32, No. 4, 1962, pp. 714–727. Also in *New Approaches in Child Guidance*, H. Strean, ed. Metuchen, N.J.: Scarecrow Press, 1970.

————. "A Family Therapist Looks at 'Little Hans'," *Family Process*, Vol. 6,

No. 2, 1967, pp. 227–234. Also in *New Approaches in Child Guidance*, H. Strean, ed. Metuchen, N.J.: Scarecrow Press, 1970.

———. *Social Casework: Theories in Action*, Metuchen, N.J.: Scarecrow Press, 1971.

———. *Clinical Social Work*, New York: The Free Press, 1978.

———, and A. Blatt. "Long or Short Term Therapy: Some Selected Issues," *Journal of Contemporary Psychotherapy*, Vol. 1, No. 2, Winter 1969, pp. 115–122.

Strupp, H.; S. Hadley; and B. Gomes Schwartz. *Psychotherapy for Better or Worse*, New York: Jason Aronson, 1977.

Tarachow, S., and A. Stein, "Psychoanalytic Psychotherapy," in *Psychoanalytic Techniques*, B. Wolman, ed. New York: Basic Books, 1963.

Turner, F. *Social Work Treatment*, New York: Free Press, 1979.

Wodarski, J., and D. Bagarozzi. "A Review of the Empirical Status of Traditional Modes of Interpersonal Helping," *Clinical Social Work*, Vol. 7, No. 4, 1979, pp. 231–255.

Wolberg, L. *Short Term Psychotherapy*, New York: Grune and Stratton, 1965.

Wolpe, J. *The Practice of Behavior Therapy*. New York: Pergamon Press, 1969.

Wynne, L. "Pseudo-Mutuality in the Family Relations of Schizophrenics," *Psychiatry*, Vol. 21, 1958.

Ziskin, J., and M. Ziskin. *The Extramarital Arrangement*, London: Abelard-Schuman, 1973.

DISCUSSANT: MARGARET BONNEFIL

To paraphrase an old saying: With a friend like Herbert Strean psychodynamic therapy doesn't need any enemies. One may be charitable and assume that he feels the pendulum has swung too far away from humanistic values, careful diagnosis and attention to the intrapsychic aspects of human problems and that he is simply making an

emotional appeal for a return to those values and practices. Unfortunately, his paper makes a poor case for this point of view. It is simplistic and poorly researched. At times, it exhibits the very dehumanizing tendencies it decries. I refer, particularly, to his remark regarding homosexual and other, presumably deviant, lifestyles and to his implication that patients who do not choose long-term treatment are "very disturbed."

The most glaring flaw in this paper is the peculiar mythology that lumps one to one, long-term psychodynamic therapy together with traditional values, humanism, and even democracy, while all those new (devilish?) therapies are linked with totalitarianism, self-indulgence, narcissism, infantile character traits, the "hate" culture, and all that is wrong with social work practice and the larger society.

The logical flaws, the confusion of belief with fact and the almost religious dogmatism must all confirm the uneasiness of those who have been troubled by the sometimes dehumanizing, authoritarian and paternalistic aspects of psychoanalytic therapy. To those of us who feel the critics have "thrown the baby out with the bath," Dr. Strean's paper may prove embarrassing. To identify one's own point of view with virtue and others with the opposite is dogmatic and smacks of the very totalitarianism Dr. Strean denounces. The lack of care in his analysis is inconsistent with his own plea for careful diagnosis.

I was particularly interested in the section on short-term therapy. If Dr. Strean's purpose in asserting that there is no value in any treatment relationship other than a long-term one is to remind us of the value of long-term therapy, he fails to do so simply because this is so obviously untrue. In fact, if one cared to argue on his terms one could just as well say that brief therapy, with its emphasis on strengths, adaptation, independence and its very availability is more humane and democratic than a medical model which may focus on pathology, "foster dependence," involve long waiting lists in agencies, and inflexibly fit the patient to the model.

He dismisses brief therapy as having developed for "spurious reasons" and seems ignorant of its development, in both social work and psychoanalysis, as an outgrowth of, among other things, expanded knowledge regarding the interaction between life events, such as bereavements, and intrapsychic functions, an area of considerable intere to social workers. One of the special contributions of social work h been its insight into the interplay between psychological and soc forces. This understanding has often been used in brief treatmen'

social workers, particularly in helping clients cope with stressful life events.

With regard to the role of psychoanalysis in the development of brief therapy, we might do well to remember that some of Freud's early cases were very brief. The case of Little Hans which Dr. Strean himself cites in his discussion of family therapy also happens to have been brief treatment as were "Dora" and Freud's cure of Mahler's impotence in one four-hour session in 1908 (Marmor, 1979).

Psychoanalysis lengthened as analysts became more passive but there were analysts who were interested in shortening it such as Ferenczi and Rank and, finally, Alexander and French. I felt that Dr. Strean's presentation of their work was distorted. He seems to confuse activity on the part of the therapist and focality with superficiality. In his recent paper entitled, "Short-Term Dynamic Psychotherapy," Dr. Judd Marmor states, "The first and most important principle that evolved from [Alexander's] studies, that of flexibility, seems obvious today. . . . Alexander insisted that in psychotherapy as in all medical therapy the physician should adapt his technique to the needs of the patient. 'Only the nature of the individual case,' he said, 'can determine what technique is best suited to bring about the curative process. . . . The therapist must understand not only the patient's current psychodynamics but also the genetic development of the difficulties.' [Marmor, 1979]."

Dr. Strean overlooks the more recent work of psychoanalysts Peter Sifneos, Habib Davanloo, and David Malan. Their work is characterized by active interpretations of the relationship of genetic material to both current relationships and to the transference—a technique which is neither easy nor superficial but one which demands great diagnostic and therapeutic skill and one with which they report considerable success. I would refer Dr. Strean especially to Dr. Malan's books on the work at Tavistock over the past 20 years. Also, he did not mention the current study by Mardi Horowitz and others at Langly Porter on brief treatment with the recently bereaved.

Dr. Strean included Crisis Intervention in his general denunciations early in the paper but did not present any discussion of it in the section on brief therapy. May one assume ignorance of the work of Eric Lindemann on mourning and the considerable and thoughtful literature on the subject developed over the past 40 years by Lindemann, Gerald Caplan and others, many of them social workers?

I found no reference to the role of short-term therapy in helping people deal with stressful life events and, therefore, to its importance in preventive mental health—an incredible omission for a social worker!

Dr. Strean seems to feel that social and professional changes, particularly new knowledge and treatment approaches, challenge older values and assumptions. No doubt they do, but I suspect this is as much a matter of style as of substance. He has reacted to the challenge by rejecting without understanding and this can serve nothing, least of all his own heartfelt plea on behalf of traditional values.

REFERENCES

Alexander, Franz, T. French, et al. *Psychoanalytic Therapy*, New York: Ronald Press, 1946.

Caplan, Gerald. *An Approach to Community Mental Health*. New York: Grune and Stratton, 1961.

DavanIoo, Habib. *Basic Principles and Techniques of Short-Term Dynamic Psychotherapy*. New York: Spectrum, 1978.

Horowitz, Mardi. *Stress Response Syndromes*. New York: Aronson, 1976.

Lindemann, Eric. "Symptomatology and Management of Acute Grief," *American Journal of Psychiatry*, 1944, 101, 141–148.

Malan, David. *The Frontier of Brief Psychotherapy*. New York: Plenum, 1976.

Marmor, Judd. "Short-Term Dynamic Psychotherapy," *The American Journal of Psychiatry*, February 1979, 136:2, 149–155.

Sifneos, Peter. *Short-Term Dynamic Psychotherapy Evaluation and Technique*. New York: Plenum, 1971.

Wilson, Robert. *The Short Contact in Casework*, Vol. 1. New York: National Association for Travelers Aid and Transient Service, 1937.

DISCUSSANT: DAVID EDWARDS

Strean criticizes encounter and sensitivity groups for their indulgence in displays of infantile omnipotence to the exclusion of analytic introspection. This distinction is inherent in the difference between therapy and growth groups. I understand growth to mean the resolution of infantile omnipotence in persons who do not present clinical symptoms of disturbance. This means that there is a different contract between the leader and the members of encounter (as compared to therapy) groups. And, I would advise participants in all kinds of groups to adhere to contracts clearly stated in advance. Groups that devote themselves to fishing for feelings and problems and rendering committee judgments are counter productive.

Strean well summarizes the needs which encounter groups fill:

1. establishment of social support networks to supplement the fragmented nuclear family.
2. provision of opportunities for healthy social intimacy.
3. provision of a safe arena to explore narcissistic needs.

His complaint is that encounter groups exploit their members' pathology instead of providing treatment. I am ready to admit that the encounter movement is guilty of many excesses. There are probably 100,000 encounter groups in the U.S. that do little good for most of their members and positive damage to a few. And, with fifty million television sets in the country, I am baffled as to why someone would want to pay for being entertained at e.s.t. meetings, but I know several professional colleagues who have had very positive experience with e.s.t.

Encounter group practice is holistic in method and is based on the principle that the provision of opportunity for authentic self expression can promote personal growth and obviate pathology rather than reinforcing it. Professional encounter group leaders trained in group dynamics do not contract to do therapy with group members. The founders of the National Training Laboratories, Lewin, Bradford, Benne and Lippitt, were social psychologists, not therapists. Their objective was to teach effective methods of social interaction in an experiential setting with an emphasis on cognitive learning. Holistic techniques such as nonverbal communication, bioenergetics, psychodrama, guided fantasy, autogenic meditation, and massage may be used by leaders trained in these techniques to remove blocks to cognitive awareness. In the use of these techniques, encounter groups share common ground with psychotherapy methods and, indeed, may activate psychopathology that cannot be dealt with under the encounter group contract. In these cases the individual should be referred for psychotherapy. Ethical encounter group leaders do not claim to provide all things for all people. What they do agree to provide is a model of social interaction that maximizes personal potential and fulfills human needs for intimacy and interpersonal understanding.

I do not think that lack of emphasis on introspection, defenses, and transference is necessarily a defect in any group—therapy or encounter. Strean is obliged to practice in the way in which he can be most effective but this does not mean that other approaches do not liberate pathology equally well. In fact, recent books by Grunberger (1979) and Kohut (1971, 1977) make a good case for bypassing defensive resistance in treating narcissistic personality disorder.

In the 330 years since the death of Descartes, who said, "I think, therefore, I exist," Western culture has come to disastrously overemphasize the value and necessity of introspective self examination. The characteristics of encounter and therapy groups that threaten Dr. Strean's professional equilibrium are a well merited, albeit intemperate, reaction to Cartesian dualism which psychoanalytic psychology seeks to defend; and I suggest to social workers that they do not exhaust themselves in masochistic efforts to man the barricades. I have led two therapy groups a week for the last ten years and I find it very refreshing to be in encounter groups where I do not have to work with therapeutic agendas.

I highly recommend Turner's book *Social Work Treatment* (1979) and Corsini's book *Current Psychotherapies* (1979) for their excellent presentation of therapy methods. One of the best books to date on group therapy, *Changing Lives Through Redecision Therapy* (1979), is co-authored by Mary Goulding, a social worker. I believe that well trained practitioners in any of these systems can effectively and ethically serve their clients and satisfy their own needs for narcissistic gratification.

The transference relationship is the basis of therapeutic change. Therapeutic change arises from experience rather than interpretation. The transforming experience of therapy is the client's recognition that she or he has encountered an intimate and intense relationship of mutual caring with a fellow human being that can be concluded with a sense of strength and enrichment. For the isolated, self reproachful client, and even for normally healthy individuals, this is not an experience that happens every day.

REFERENCES

Corsini, R. *Current Psychotherapies*. Itasca, Ill.: F. E. Peacock, 1979.

Goulding, M., and Goulding, R. *Changing Lives Through Redicision Therapy*. New York: Brunner/Mazel, 1979.

Grunberger, B. *Narcissism, Psychoanalytic Essays*. New York: International Universities Press, 1979.

Kohut, H. *The Analysis of the Self*. New York: International Universities Press, 1971.

_____. *The Restoration of the Self*. New York: International Universities Press, 1977.

Turner, F. *Social Work Treatment*. New York: The Free Press, 1979.

DISCUSSANT: ARTHUR L. LEADER

Dr. Strean is highly critical of those innovations in social work that are anti-psychodynamic. These include brief therapies, crisis intervention, task oriented treatment, behavior modification, family therapy, sex therapy, and the encounter movement. Although some of his criticisms, which I share, are justified, I believe that he has weakened his position by such a wholesale condemnation, failing to differentiate the concepts themselves from some of the existing bad practices or a fringe development from the mainstream operation and lumping a diverse group of innovations together.

Bad practices are always easy to locate, even in long-term one-to-one therapy, apparently Dr. Strean's favorite model. In focusing on the excesses or bad practices of innovations, Dr. Strean gives the impression that the innovations he attacks are sweeping the field and blotting out psychoanalytic thinking and psychodynamic practice. Although I, too, regret the reduced interest in the latter, in my opinion and experience including some familiarity with the professional literature my impression is that Dr. Strean has gone overboard. It is unfair to lump all cited innovations together and imply that within each one there is not a variety of schools of thought and practices. Family therapy, even with the proliferation of different models, for one, cannot be placed in the same category with the one-shot encounter phenomenon.

I, too, regret those practices which disregard or minimize diagnosis, meaning of behavior and feelings. And although they do indeed seem to be increasing, the therapies mentioned are not all of one stripe. In my experience, for example, with Quick-Response, which originated in this agency, with family therapy that had an early start in this agency with Nathan Ackerman and with crisis intervention, too, there has been a consistent psychodynamic base. Quick-Response continues as a very useful model—a facilitating introduction of the client to the agency; helping clarify problem, precipitant, family inter-relationships, purpose and goal quickly; working actively and intensively within a time limit; and, if indicated, advising client to go on for additional work (yes, long-term one-to-one when appropriate).

Dr. Strean's understanding of short term treatment as being opposed to exploring inner lives or having appeal because of the "yearning for instant gratification" results in a short changing of the depth, intensity, and effectiveness of this model—though not applicable to all people for all occasions. There is a rich variety of dynamic brief therapies and they are well described in the literature.

Some of the ways in which the innovations are applied are superficial, undynamic, mechanistic, and manipulative. This is true, for example, of some of the developments in family therapy. But here as well as with the other innovations, much of the work is "integrative" or dynamic. In the same way, in contrast to the existence of a very small encounter movement, there is a large practice of dynamic group therapy.

With the exception of the encounter movement, all of the modalities that are mentioned by Dr. Strean have been and can be used dynamically in special situations or as a part of or in combination with some traditional forms of treatment. One need not force a uni-dimensional conceptual template on all clients and all situations. Sex therapy may be used collaboratively and productively in conjunction with dynamic marital therapy. At certain points tasks may judiciously and selectively be assigned within more traditional therapies based upon diagnosis, purpose, and goal.

In his focusing on his preferred model of the one-to-one long term therapy model, Dr. Strean has also not shown cognizance of the theoretic findings and clinical applications of systems and communication theories. They are dynamic and useful especially in family therapy. Changes in communications and in behavior can lead to changes in emotional states as well as vice versa. A change in role that reduces conflict or any benefit from symptom relief in and of itself is valid and may be all that some individuals, couples, or families are ready for or capable of. Yet these changes might precede or be combined with a variety of approaches and modalities, discriminately, thoughtfully, and flexibly applied. In the same way medication is at times a facilitating adjunct to many forms of psychotherapy.

Not everyone can benefit from long term therapy for many reasons. I believe that the brief therapies and some forms of family therapy represent a sincere effort to help a greater number of people and a wider segment of the population more quickly and effectively. For example, although not everyone will agree with or feel comfortable in adopting Munuchin's "structural" approach, there is no question that he has been unusually effective in his work with families with anoretic or other psychosomatic members. Though I personally am unwilling to apply a paradoxical approach, finding it too manipulative, I don't think the final word is in with respect to what produces change in people.

What I object to in the emergence of innovations is the tendency to apply them wholesale and indiscriminately, to inflate them while minimizing and putting down theories and practitioners with different orientations, and to attract zealots who do not have a broad enough base in training and/or experience out of which to make a reasoned independent decision with regard to one's ideology. Structure, technique, task assignment and manipulation have their appeal especially when taught by highly charismatic leaders. And the followers are not always able to use them in the same way. Also, I'm not always clear which is more therapeutic—the method itself or the charisma personality, and style of the therapist, though of course this is applicable to some extent to any therapist.

In contrast to the growth of some anti-dynamic developments, there is at the same time a number of efforts in the therapeutic field that are expanding in new dynamic directions trying to understand clinical phenomena in holistic or ecological terms. In fact, the rapid growth of family therapy and communication theory represented an attempt to broaden the base of understanding individuals beyond their intrapsychic life to the subtle reciprocal interactional forces within the family and the social environment. There is still much catching up to do in this area.

My own view of the newer modalities is to try to keep an open mind that neither adopts wholesale nor rejects them totally out of hand. They have many excellent features that can be regarded as useful additions to professional armamentarium. For me they are not replacements or substitutes for the basic core of psychodynamic theory and practice, but they can be used selectively and purposefully by fully trained personnel. Despite my own psychodynamic orientation, I happen to believe that not every patient or family lends itself or is willing to work on its unconscious forces and can therefore benefit from a variety of approaches.

In summary, though Dr. Strean's criticisms are valid, I wish that he was more clearly able to differentiate only those innovations that are anti-dynamic from a large number that are dynamic, useful, and different from each other within each category; that he was able to separate a valid concept from a bad practice; and that he did not lump all innovations together, since they do represent considerable diversity. I wish, too, that he would have balanced his views by some reference to those developments that are attempting to comprehend the person-in-situation in a dynamic, integrated, interactional framework.

DISCUSSANT: JOHN S. WODARSKI

Introduction

Over the past few years I have acquired the label of behavior modification addict. I would like to take this opportunity to offer my criteria for choosing such a practice stand, criteria which stem from the values and ethics expounded by the social work profession. We are obliged in our Code of Ethics to choose knowledge that is empirically based. The National Association of Social Worker's *Code of Ethics* (1979), and the National Federation of Societies for Clinical Social Work, Inc., *Ethical Standards of Clinical Social Workers* (1970) state various guidelines that provide moral support for the use of the newer treatment modalities which include behavior modification techniques.
NASW's *Code* reads:

> I hold myself responsible for the quality and extent of the service I perform.

> I practice social work within the recognized knowledge and competence of the profession.

> I accept responsibility to help protect the community against unethical practice by any individuals or organizations engaged in social welfare activities.

NFSCSW *Standards* read:

> The clinical social worker carries responsibility to maintain and improve social work service; constantly to examine, use and increase the knowledge upon which practice and social policy are based and to develop further the philosophy and skills of the profession.
>
> The clinical social worker must not encourage (nor, within his power, even allow) a client to have exaggerated ideas as to the efficacy of services rendered. Claims made to clients about the efficacy of his services must not go beyond those which the clinical social worker would be willing to subject to professional scrutiny through publishing his results and his claims in a professional journal.

In response to Professor Strean's article, which incidentally contains many misconceptions regarding those who practice from a social behavioral perspective, I would like to address the following distortions. Behavioral therapists are deeply concerned about feelings—we are not totalitarian. We plan treatment plans with our clients and we practice from a scientific base. We consider that the client and the therapist are equal in the therapeutic endeavor. We maintain that if the client does not change, the therapeutic approach should be changed. We do not "hate" dynamic therapy—we question its ethics and effectiveness. Our "hunger" is not for power, but for accountability. As to "[b]ehavioralists constantly compare the human being to animals" (p. 7), we do no such thing. As is the case with most of the hard sciences, animal studies have provided preliminary evidence on which to build far more complex human studies. Where would medical practice be today without the information provided to us through laboratory research conducted on animals?

Professor Strean presents an extremely narrow view of behavior modification. Such concepts as punishment and conditioning are totally misrepresented as they appear in the current literature. Reference is made only to the Pavlovian respondent type of conditioning, the historical paradigm used by behavior modification theorists of the 1920s. Very few references are made to Skinner. Moreover, new developments in behavior modification such as Bandura's Self Efficacy Theory (Bandura, 1977), Mahoney's emphasis on self-control and cognitive conditioning procedures (Mahoney, 1977; Williams and Long, 1975), and Wodarski's Social System's Analysis (Wodarski, 1977) are not cited. Over thirty theories of learning are now available to account for the phenomena dealt with by social workers. If one is to critique new approaches, the critique should be based upon the latest literature in the field. For instance, the Professor is inaccurate in stating that behavioralists ignore the relationship, clients' wishes, anxieties, or defenses. We also recognize the client's resistance to change (Jahn & Lichstein, 1980; Kazdin & Hersen, 1980; and Kazdin & Wilson, 1978). His comments only reveal a naivete about behavior modification. Ironically, Alexander, whom the professor cites, once posited that psychoanalytical therapy could be best explained in a social learning framework (Alexander, 1964).

Assumptions Regarding Theory, Techniques, and People

Strean's article is replete with value assumptions regarding the right way to practice. Concepts such as id, ego, and superego are portrayed as accepted truths. Criteria are never explicated for the choice of these concepts as the "right" foundation for practice.

On page 12, we are offered a naive answer for the complexity of the divorce process in Little Hans's example. How do we rule out all other possible factors influencing a divorce? On page 14, the basis for the encounter group movement is questioned; however, the classic references evaluating the encounter movement are not cited (Bednor and Kaul, 1978; Lieberman, Yalom, & Miles, 1973). Statements are made such as, "What is destroying America is rootlessness," while selected literature is cited to support them. Ignored by Strean are the world economic situation, mobility and life complexity, and their effects on society. Other assumptions, such as "marital complaints are really unconscious wishes" and "homosexuality is neurotically motivated," are highly biased and unsubstantiated. Human behavior is a complex phenomenon that requires much talent to address the issues. Simplistic answers to phenomena will not advance the credibility of social work practice.

Structure and Therapy

Substantial research has shown that structure and goal-setting, characteristic of short term therapy, facilitate behavioral change (Butcher & Koss, 1978; Feldman and Wodarski, 1975). Professor Strean seems to believe that long-term therapy is necessary. In what cases is it necessary?

How does one make the decision that someone should receive long-term versus short-term therapy? What are the ethics involved in positing that long-term therapy should be utilized with the majority of clients served by social work practitioners (Briar, 1968; Briar & Miller, 1971)? We are told that we can "study the effects of therapy only through observing the client over time" (p. 15). Behavior modifiers *systematically* observe and record data to note effects of therapy and to justify its continuance or discontinuance.

Professor Strean posits that task-oriented casework is unscientific when the best integration of research and practice has occurred in task-oriented casework. Where is the professor's reading of the literature? Task-oriented casework is the approach that social work has built, one that has originated out of social work practice and that is well integrated with research findings (Reid & Epstein, 1972; Reid, 1978).

Professor Strean's essay is not a critique! It is an emotional statement. It is a relatively simple matter to write how one feels about a phenomenon. A critique, however, involves presenting both sides of the story and then choosing the strongest rationale on which to base your arguments. Questions have to be asked: What are the outcome variables for the theories to which Professor Strean refers and the therapies that are subsequently based on them? Why argue about symptom substitution when no data exist to prove that such a phenomenon occurs? In fact, the studies that have been conducted provide data to the contrary (Paul, 1978; Cahoon, 1968).

The Real Issue

The real issue is do we base social work practice upon data or upon a philosophy of life. A profession does not accept a philosophy of life without questioning it. Why are psychiatric authorities always right and anyone who disagrees with them wrong? I agree with Professor Strean that new therapies should be evaluated. All therapies should be subjected to the same stringent, empirical criteria. He chooses to ignore, however, the accumulated literature on evaluative endeavors (Lieberman, Yalom, & Miles, 1973). This essay is not a scholarly analysis— reasons chosen to support the professor's view points are referenced poorly or not at all. Likewise, reasons for others repudiating the professor's viewpoint are not addressed. Classic references rebutting the traditional theories are omitted, e.g. Bandura (1969), Bergin & Lambert (1978), Kazdin & Wilson (1978), and Segal (1972). Where is the evidence in support of the effectiveness of the traditional therapies expounded by Professor Strean?

Traditional theories based on Freud and others that are derived from the ego-psychoanalytical framework are losing ground among professionals. They are not now and *were never appropriate* for adoption by the profession for the majority of its clientele. Kuhn (1962 & 1970) discusses how traditional paradigms are shaken. According to him we are in the first and second phases of shaking the traditional social work paradigm. First, new approaches are being posited, and second, an attack on these new approaches is being waged. However, along with the attack is an evaluation of the relevancy of the new versus the old approaches. As this evaluation occurs, and depending on the data available, the old paradigms will fade or will be incorporated into the new paradigms, or they will remain the major theory thrust. This is a situation that I find extremely exciting. Why should we endorse traditional paradigms forever when data indicate that for the majority of the clients they are not relevant (Briar 1968, Briar and Miller 1971)? Why base our practice on Freud's philosophy of life, which is gloomy, by which people are beset by conflicts, uncontrolled impulses, and so forth. I much prefer a social learning viewpoint toward life which takes a positive view of people, by which people are constantly learning and constantly changing their personalities. Such an approach gives us hope that changes can take place in our clients (Wodarski & Bagarozzi, 1979). I base my choice of theoretical paradigms on the basis of data and will change as new data develop. Can the Professor claim likewise?

Finally, Strean discusses our tried and true knowledge of people. The critical question remains: Is the knowledge accurate and can it do the job in helping people change. While we await data to substantiate the claims of traditional modes of interpersonal helping, data concerning the effectiveness of behavioral approaches are accumulating at impressive rates. The challenge is clear. Collect the data, publish your results and subject them to scientific scrutiny. Then, and only then, can we compare the effectiveness of traditional therapies with the "newer treatment modalities."

REFERENCES

Alexander, I. "The dynamics of psychotherapy in light of learning theory," *American Journal of Psychiatry*, 1963, *120*, 441–449.

Bandura, A. _Principles of Behavior Modification_. New York: Holt, Rinehart and Winston, 1969.

―――. "Self-efficacy: toward a unifying theory of behavioral change," _Psychological Review_, 1977, _84_, 191–215.

Bednor, R. L., and Kaul, T. J. "Experimental group research: current perspectives," in Garfield, S., and Bergin, A. (eds.), _Handbook of Psychotherapy and Behavior Change: an empirical analysis_ (second edition). New York: John Wiley and Sons, 1978.

Bergin, A. E., and Lambert, M. J. "The evaluation of therapeutic outcomes," in Garfield, S., and Bergin, A. (eds.), _Handbook of Psychotherapy and Behavior Change: an empirical analysis_ (second edition). New York: John Wiley and Sons, 1978.

Briar, S. "The casework predicament," _Social Work_, 1968, _13_, 5–11.

―――, and Miller, J. _Problems and Issues in Social Casework_. New York: Columbia University Press, 1971.

Butcher, J. N., and Koss, M. P. "Research on brief and crises-oriented psychotherapies," in Garfield, S., and Bergin, A. (eds.), _Handbook of Psychotherapy and Behavior Change: an empirical analysis_ (second edition), New York: John Wiley and Sons, 1978.

Cahoon, D. D. "Symptom substitution and the behavior therapies: a reappraisal," _Psychological Bulletin_, 1968, _69_, 149–156.

Jahn, D. L., and Lichstein, K. L. "The resistive client: a neglected phenomenon in behavior therapy," _Behavior Modification_, 1980, _4_, 303–320.

Kazdin, A. E., and Hersen, M. "The current status of behavior therapy." _Behavior Modification_, 1980, _4_, 283–302.

―――, and Wilson, C. T. _Evaluation of Behavior Therapy: issues, evidence, and research strategies_. Cambridge, Mass.: Ballinger, 1978.

Kuhn, T. S. _The Structure of Scientific Revolutions_. Chicago: University of Chicago Press, 1962.

―――. _The Structure of Scientific Revolutions_ (second edition). Chicago: University of Chicago Press, 1970.

Lieberman, M. A.; Yalom, I. D.; and Miles, M. B. _Encounter Groups: first facts_. New York: Basic Books, 1973.

Mahoney, M. M. "Reflections on the cognitive-learning trend in psychotherapy," _American Psychologist_, 1977, _32_, 5–13.

National Association of Social Workers. *Code of Ethics.* Washington, D.C.: N.A.S.W., 1979.

National Federation of Societies for Clinical Social Work, Inc. *Ethical Standards of Clinical Social Workers.* Madison, Wisc.: N.I.S.C.S.W., 1970.

Paul, G. L. "Strategy in outcome research in psychotherapy," *Journal of Consulting Psychology,* 1967, *31*, 109–118.

Reid, W. J. *The Task-Centered System.* New York: Columbia University Press, 1978.

———, and Epstein, L. *Task-Centered Casework.* New York: Columbia University Press, 1972.

Segal, S. P. "Research on the outcome of social work therapeutic interventions: a review of the literature," *Journal of Health and Social Behavior,* 1972, *13*, 3–17.

Williams, R. L., and Long, J. D. *Toward a Self-Managed Life Style* (second edition). Boston: Houghton Mifflin Company, 1979.

Wodarski, J. S. "The application of behavior modification technology to the alleviation of selected social problems," *Journal of Sociology and Social Welfare,* 1977, *4*, 1055–1073.

———, and Bagarozzi, D. A. "A review of the empirical status of traditional modes of interpersonal helping: implications for social work practice," *Clinical Social Work Journal,* 1979, *7*, 231–255.

RESPONSE TO DISCUSSANTS

I am extremely grateful to have the unique opportunity to present my views on an important issue in social work—the newer modalities—and have experts in these modalities critique my discussion. Just as I did not expect these experts in short term therapy (Ms. Bonnefil), encounter and sensitivity groups (Mr. Edwards), family therapy (Mr. Leader), and behavior modification (Dr. Wodarski) to heartily endorse my views, I am sure they do not anticipate that I will heartily endorse theirs! In responding to their criticisms, I would like to clarify what I did and did not say, and try to ascertain what all clinical social workers can derive from this total discussion.

Yes, my perspective is a psychoanalytic view of the human being. I strongly believe that the meaning of the client's behavior cannot be fully grasped by a clinician unless he or she has an understanding of the client's unconscious wishes, defenses, history, and psychic structure of id, ego, and superego. I further contend that unless the therapist is fully aware of how he or she is unconsciously experienced by the client (the transference), treatment is hit or miss. I also aver that all clinicians should not only be in touch with the unconscious meaning of their clients' behavior, activity and productions, but should also know themselves very well. Although a couple of the discussants would like to believe otherwise, psychoanalytically oriented psychotherapy has been subjected to rigorous evaluation on numerous occasions (Fenichel, 1930; Jones, 1936; Knight, 1941; Feldman, 1968; Fisher, 1978; Sarnoff, 1971; Fine, 1980), and has been shown to be an extremely effective therapy when in the hands of those who know what they are doing. It is equally true that some social workers and other clinicians, have injudiciously utilized its notions and achieved poor results. In my book *Psychoanalytic Theory and Social Work Practice* I pointed out that one cannot really expect an economically and socially impoverished client whose ego functions are tenuous to "free associate." It is also close to preposterous to ask a rebellious juvenile delinquent who is referred for help involuntarily and who is full of mistrust to immediately confide in the social worker.

No, I do not advocate long-term one-to-one treatment for everybody! What I do advocate is that before we decide on any form of therapeutic intervention, we should *take sufficient time* to get to know how the client experiences himself, the worker, and the agency; see how his significant others experience him and his problems; ascertain how his history is being recapitulated in the present, and bring together other dynamic data which will help us make a comprehensive diagnostic assessment. The client's own motivation and resistances to help will in many ways also determine if the treatment will be long or short, family treatment, crisis intervention, etc.

In another volume, *Clinical Social Work*, I pointed out that based on a full diagnosis, short-term treatment or family therapy might very well be the treatment of choice. For example, there are certain clients who are so frightened of a relationship that to impose long-term treatments on them would be disastrous. Similarly, there are certain symbiotic families that would only respond positively to one form of treatment—namely, family therapy—and anything else would threaten them much too much. What I have said in my paper is that all too often the client must adapt to a form of therapy that is imposed on him by the worker and agency and is not sufficiently related to his unique maturational needs, conflicts, and ego capacities. I believe that all clinicians should keep an open mind as to what client will do best with what form of therapeutic intervention at which time.

I contend that any clinician who is responsible, ethical, scientific, and humanistic would have to take the position that people who experience chronic character problems, constant stress in interpersonal relationships, intrapsychic conflicts, and who cannot cope with their environments very well often need a long-term relationship with a sensitive, empathic therapist and that anything else would be to ignore who the client is. I further contend that the modal client in social work practice is a very troubled person.

Yes, I believe that in trying to understand people and plan treatment, it is helpful to assess their judgment, reasoning, interpersonal relationships, defenses, etc. This is what many clinicians mean by the ego and its functions. I believe many of our clients are tormented by guilt, have a low self-esteem and cannot enjoy pleasure because they have a punitive conscience. This is what clinicians mean by a superego. A crucial dimension of the client's life is his sexual life. I believe that many clinicians fail to help clients get in touch with their sexual wishes and sexual fears, particularly as they emerge in the client-worker relationship. I have seen many clients achieve much more pleasure from living, loving, working, and playing when their id wishes are voiced and genuinely accepted by an understanding therapist. In contrast to Skinner and some of the behavior modifiers who endorse a practice that is "Beyond Dignity and Freedom," I believe that when a client has time to pour his heart out and is not rushed or reinforced, but understood and loved, treatment can work to his or her advantage. Yes, I believe this is providing the client with freedom and dignity.

No, I do not believe it is possible to achieve real and lasting growth in self-esteem, a decline in the oppression of the superego or a building of the ego's coping mechanisms through short-term work. People and their problems are too complex to expect much change in them after a few sessions. To expect much from ourselves or our clients from a half-dozen treatment sessions is unrealistic. This does not mean that I am saying that short-term work should be abolished. It can be helpful to clients who want it either because their psychological and social needs require it (e.g. people who fear intimacy, clients who want help for just a specific issue, adaptive people) or because they abhor any other kind of treatment. No, I did not say that "patients who do not choose long-term treatment are 'very disturbed'." There are very disturbed people in long-term therapy and mature clients in short-term treatment.

Many of psychoanalysis's findings can be very threatening to clients and clinicians and obviously are to some of the discussants. In appraising any form of behavior or "life style" we must always differentiate between a client's civil rights and his or her intrapsychic conflicts. A homosexual man or woman should never be deprived of his civil rights or "life-style," but to disregard the evidence that the homosexual man or woman has strong fears of intimacy, has much unconscious hostility, feels very vulnerable, and has suffered interpersonally is not giving these clients the understanding and therapeutic respect they deserve. It also negates the findings of solid research studies like those of Socarides (1978) and Bieber (1962). Similarly, if one observes clients over time one will inevitably note, providing he or she is an unbiased therapist, that every chronic marital complaint is an unconscious wish. Yes, show me the man who constantly says "my wife is always cold and frigid" and I'll show you the man who is afraid of a close and sustained relationship with a woman. Yes, show me the woman who says "my husband is unassertive" and I'll show you the woman who fears an assertive man. Furthermore, show me the therapist who maintains a neutral attitude toward the marital conflict and I'll show you how the chronic marital complaints always emerge in the transference relationship with the therapist. Finally, show me the therapist who believes in these aforementioned concepts, and I'll show you some successful treatment results.

Yes, I do endorse "the psychoanalytic ideal" as formulated by Dr. Reuben Fine which states that the goal of therapy should be to help people love rather than hate, have sexual gratification, express their emotions yet be guided by reason, have a role in the family, have a sense of identity, be constructive, be able to work, be creative, have a role in the social order, be able to communicate, and be free of symptoms. This is far from a gloomy philosophy as one of the discussants erroneously states, nor does it imply that those who do not endorse it are "devils," as another discussant mistakenly opines.

Psychoanalysis does not propound that introspection is the only way to self-actualization. It does contend that in order to mature, a client needs love and understanding in a disciplined therapeutic relationship which relates to his complex metapsychology. It highly values the client's internal life—his fantasies, wishes, dreams, defenses, hopes, etc.—which behaviorism essentially rejects. Behaviorism, when pushed to its conclusion, leads to an inherent logical contradiction. If we confine ourselves to purely objective data, we cannot explain them. And if we try to explain them we get away from pure objectivity. The behavioristic position rests upon essential misconceptions of scientific theory and scientific method. The crucial role of inner psychological data cannot be denied. To put the emphasis of our work on the client's tasks without a full appraisal of his id wishes, ego functions, and superego mandates is to psychologically neglect him. That is why I believe that sex therapy or any therapy which ignores the client's feelings, anxieties, etc. is short-sighted.

In reviewing the discussants' remarks, I would like to again state that I am not knocking all of family therapy and short-term treatment nor comparing all of family therapy with one-shot encounter phenomena. Rather, I am arguing for an individualized assessment of our clients and a therapy which views the client as a complex bio-psycho-social organism living in a complex, difficult society. I do believe that many, perhaps most of our clients, in order to really mature, need one-to-one long term treatment.

I am hopeful that Ms. Bonnefil, Mr. Edwards, Mr. Leader, Dr. Wodarski and I can agree that the material before social workers, people and their situations should not and need not create rivalries and dissension among us. Reasonable people can differ. Can we all agree that all social workers are faced daily with human beings beset by difficulties in living, and it is our joint task to help them cope more effectively with themselves and their environments? Can we also agree that contributions to social work practice have come from many individuals, and that perhaps all of us have something positive to offer clinical social work?

REFERENCES

Bieber, I. *Homosexuality*. New York: Basic Books, 1962.

Feldman, F. "Results of Psychoanalysis," *Journal of the American Psychoanalytic Association*, Vol. 16, 1968.

Fenichel, O. *Zehn Jahre Berliner, Psychoanalytisches Institute*. Berlin: Berlin Psychoanalytic Institute, 1930.

Fine, R. *The History of Psychoanalysis*. New York: Columbia University Press, 1979.

Fisher, S. *The Scientific Evaluation of Freud's Theories and Therapy*. New York: Basic Books, 1978.

Jones, *Decennial Report of the London Clinic of Psychoanalysis*. London: London Clinic of Psychoanalysis, 1936.

Knight, R. "Borderline States," *Bulletin of the Menninger Clinic*, Vol. 17, 1953.

Sarnoff, I. *Testing Freudian Concepts*. New York: Springer Publishing Company, 1971.

Socarides, C. *Homosexuality*. New York: Jason Aronson, 1978.

Strean, H. *Clinical Social Work*. New York: Free Press, 1978.

_____. *Psychoanalytic Theory and Social Work Practice*. New York: Free Press, 1979.

Chapter 2

EXTRA-ANALYTIC CONTACTS: THEORETICAL AND CLINICAL CONSIDERATIONS

Most psychoanalysts subscribe to the notion that preserving the analyst's anonymity is a worthy aim, if not an essential ground rule of psychoanalytic treatment. Freud never abandoned the model of the abstinent, anonymous surgeon who is an opaque mirror for his analysand (Freud, 1912, 1915, 1918), but as Lipton (1977, 1979) has recently demonstrated, he seemed to define technique more narrowly than is the case today and he regularly established and maintained a personal relationship with his patients which he took for granted and tended to exclude from the analysis.

Just as there appears to be some ambivalence in Freud's attitude concerning the analyst's anonymity and abstinence, there is also a lack of unanimity among analysts on how much the practitioner can or should be a cool, detached, surgeon who consistently behaves as a blank screen. There are those writers who advise the analyst to sacrifice conspicuous participation in and out of the consultation room, to refrain from involving himself even in worthy social and political causes, and to maintain his private person at all times (Sharpe, 1930; Greenacre, 1954; Paul, 1960; Langs, 1976). While recognizing that the principles of abstinence and anonymity are indispensable and distinctive positions of the analyst, other writers have contended that these principles are always subject to modification (Fenichel, 1945; Menninger, 1958; Stone, 1961; Greenson and Wexler, 1969; Lampl-de-Groot, 1976).

If a conflict does exist between safeguarding the analyst's anonymity as opposed to his emerging as a "real" person, it can become most appar-

Reprinted by permission from *The Psychoanalytic Quarterly*, vol. 50, no. 2 (April 1981), pp. 238–259.

ent when analyst and patient meet outside the consultation room. If the two parties are face to face at a professional meeting, in the theatre, at the supermarket, or on the street, unconscious transference and countertransference fantasies can be activated and unresolved infantile conflicts of both parties can come to the fore.

One of the possible sources of tension in the extra-analytic contact is that both patient and analyst may wish to gratify exhibitionistic and voyeuristic wishes but concomitantly feel obliged to defend against their expression (Allen, 1974; Tarnower, 1966). A corollary of this is that both parties may also become frightened if they feel that the image they would like the other to maintain of them has a chance of being punctured. It is difficult, if not impossible, for an analyst to sustain his surgeonlike countenance while his patient observes him laughing or crying at a play, asserting a strong position at a political rally, or disagreeing with a colleague at a professional conference. Similarly, a patient can experience a narcissistic blow if his self-image of favorite child, perfect lover, or skilled combatant is threatened as his analyst observes him reacting to a play, participating at a political rally, or debating at a professional meeting.

Because treasured unconscious transference and countertransference positions risk being altered; because regressive wishes can be stimulated; and because new and different behaviors are often prescribed when the analysand is not on the couch with the analyst behind him, the extra-analytic contact can assume a phobic and neurotic quality for either patient and/or analyst. Particularly if patient and analyst meet in the presence of others, both can fear that the confidentiality of their sessions is in danger of being violated. And even if the parties go unobserved by others, both patient and analyst can become unduly concerned about the injunction to avoid acting-out. Finally, in many extra-analytic contacts, the parties are often caught unprepared, a situation that usually induces some anxiety.

The extra-analytic contact has the potential of releasing hidden anxiety provoking transference and countertransference fantasies and affects, such as primal scene conflicts, oedipal and homosexual desires, sadistic and masochistic urges and oral incorporative yearnings; this may be why few analysts have reported on their extra-analytic contacts with patients. In any event, the dynamic meaning of this experience for the patient (and analyst) has been relatively unexplored and has tended to be shrouded in secrecy.

One of the few papers written on the extra-analytic contact is by

Tarnower (1966). Tarnower pointed out that extra-analytic experiences can modify or influence transference fantasies, but he also discussed the phobic wish of some analysts and patients to avoid such contacts. He suggested that extra-analytic meetings can provide important material for the analysis and that analysands generally respond intensely to them. While the analyst may justify his wish to avoid this type of contact in an effort not to contaminate the transference, this avoidance, Tarnower states, may serve defensive purposes for him. Because extra-analytic contacts may gratify a variety of transference and countertransference wishes, the author concludes that these contacts must *always* be subjected to analytic exploration.

In a paper, "A Psychoanalyst's Anonymity: Fiddler Behind the Couch," Katz (1978) writes of his experiences with patients after they observed him play the leading role of Tevye in the Topeka Civic Theatre's production of *Fiddler on the Roof.* His patients' associations were generously peppered with curiosity, secret yearnings to look, earnest wishes that the analyst would do the patient proud by sparkling, or grim hopes that he would fail. Whatever and however intense his patients' responses were, Katz concluded that they fell into the familiar categories of transference and resistance phenomena and could be managed without employing special techniques. Katz became more convinced after this experience that the patient perceives, evaluates, records accurately, or distorts the analyst in line with his built-in biases and colorations and reacts to extra-analytic contacts in much the same way he does to any other interpersonal phenomena.

Weiss (1975) has referred to extra-analytic contacts as falling under the general category of "special events." These "special events" that reveal the analyst as a "real person" tend to always evoke, according to the author, strong transference affects.

Greenson (1967) points out that whatever the source, whether picked up in the consultation room or from an extra-analytic contact, knowledge about the analyst must become subject matter for analysis because it usually is the vehicle for unconscious fantasy.

Greenacre (1959) has indicated that because of the potentially disruptive effects on the analysis and the unfolding of the patient's transference reactions, extra-analytic contacts are best avoided. Yet, Greenacre does not point out how to consistently avoid them.

Langs (1976) has stated that the extra-analytic contact always modifies the patient's transference constellation, offers neurotic gratifications, reinforces resistances, and undermines basic therapeutic work.

Like Greenacre (1959) Langs feels that the extra-analytic contact should be carefully avoided and has also suggested that even after treatment is completed, contact between analyst and patient should not take place.

Whether or not an analyst carefully avoids extra-analytic contacts and/or tries to prohibit his patients from meeting him or seeing him outside the consultation room, the extra-analytic contact is a fact of therapeutic life for many analysts and patients. Even in large communities, patients can meet their analysts at the theater, at the restaurant, at the concert hall, at the swimming pool, or at the supermarket. In smaller communities they drive by each other's homes, meet in office buildings, at P.T.A. meetings, at social gatherings, in the park or on the street. Mental health professionals in large and small communities meet their analysts as teachers in the classroom, in the audience of a lecture, on the podium at scientific meetings or in journals and textbooks.

Inasmuch as the extra-analytic contact is a clinical reality for many analysts and analysands, it is incumbent on both parties not to try to avoid or stimulate such contacts, but to analyze their dynamic meaning to the patient when they do occur. If the extra-analytic contact is viewed as an interpersonal experience that is not to be encouraged nor discouraged but to be thoroughly analyzed, it can then be utilized in the analysis as an event that can promote understanding of transference and countertransference phenomena, clarify resistances, and serve as a barometer of analytic progress.

When analytic neutrality is truly valued as an important dimension of treatment, the responsible analyst will not prohibit nor permit a specific action of the patient; rather, he will analyze it when it occurs. Consequently, his orientation toward the extra-analytic contact will be similar to his stance on other interpersonal events that transpire between analyst and patient, e.g., cancelled appointments, late or early payment of fees, telephone calls, referrals of patients, etc. He will attempt to help the patient freely associate to these events so that fantasies, dreams, history, and other dimensions of the patient's psychic life will be revealed and increased self-understanding and self-mastery will evolve.

CATEGORIES OF EXTRA-ANALYTIC CONTACTS

The term "extra-analytic contact" has been utilized very generally and somewhat loosely in the literature. In order to deepen our dynamic understanding of this important interpersonal event, it appears useful to differentiate between various types of extra-analytic contacts.

1. Extra-Analytic Contacts Actively Brought about by the Patient

During the course of an analysis many patients do become aware of the fact that the analyst will be giving a lecture in the community, will appear on a professional panel, will be present at a social gathering or political rally, and then bring this information into analytic sessions. Some of these analysands have actively and consciously sought the opportunity to become involved with the analyst outside the consultation room. When they begin to consider that their hopes may be realistically gratified, they can demonstrate a wide variety of affects, e.g. sexual excitement because oral, anal, homosexual, or phallic-oedipal wishes are being stirred up toward the analyst; acute embarrassment and dread of punishment for seeking the gratification of exhibitionistic, voyeuristic and other forbidden wishes, and contempt toward the analyst and triumph over him as he is thought to be corruptible for abdicating his role of abstinent surgeon.

On the patient's directly or tentatively informing the analyst that he would like to be present when the analyst lectures, participates on a panel or is a guest at a party, the analysand's concern, at first, is usually whether he will receive the analyst's permission or prohibition. Like virtually all requests that are brought into an analysis, the analysand's request for permission to attend e.g., a lecture by the analyst, is neither gratified nor frustrated but is analyzed. Most of those patients who bring their wish for a specific extra-analytic contact directly to the analysis are usually able to associate freely to the fantasies, dreams, anxieties, and memories that are conjured up by the imminent extra-analytic contact.

Some analysands react with guilt and shame when they begin to recognize that their desire for extra-analytic contact is an expression of incestuous, homosexual, or oral incorporative fantasies; they can then become immobilized and give up the idea of the extra-analytic contact. However, as with any phobic reaction, it is important for analyst and patient to continue to expose the infantile sexual and aggressive fantasies that are stimulating the anxiety connected with the encounter.

Although few patients experience the idea of an extra-analytic contact without some conflict, many are able to do the anticipatory forework and eventually "act out" their wish to be with the analyst at a lecture, committee meeting, or discussion group. Without the analyst's approbation or disapproval, they nonetheless participate in the extra-analytic contact and then return to the analytic situation and further explore their transference reactions, fantasies, dreams and memories that were provoked by the encounter.

While working with the patient's associations to the desired, extra-analytic contact (and after it has taken place), the analyst is obliged to analyze his own feelings about being observed and observing and to assess the overall dynamic meaning that the event has for him. If the idea of the extra-analytic contact sparks exhibitionistic, voyeuristic, or other sexual and aggressive fantasies in the analyst, of which he is consciously unaware, he may unwittingly and subtly encourage or discourage extra-analytic contacts, rather than stay with the patient's productions and neutrally analyze them so that the analysand can make his own independent, autonomous decision.

Despite the fact that patients in analysis are asked to abide by the fundamental rule and report everything that is on their minds, some analysands find the injunction very difficult to cope with. Consequently, there are analysands who actively arrange for an extra-analytic contact, but do not bring their desire for the contact into the analysis. Anxious or guilty about voyeuristic or exhibitionistic wishes, desirous of embarrassing or humiliating the analyst because of unresolved competitive fantasies, or eager to sadistically expose and shock the analyst, a patient can arrange for the analyst to proceed to a podium, a party, or a meeting and without any prior knowledge, see his patient right in front of or beside him.

When the analyst meets his patients and is unprepared for it, the analyst has to first face how he feels within himself and towards the patient when he is uninformed about activities of the patient that involve him. The analyst may also have to cope with a blow to his own narcissism when he has to acknowledge that he was not able to detect a wish for extra-analytic contact in the productions of the patient heretofore. Furthermore, the analyst may also have to confront counter-resistances in himself that prevented him from perceiving wishes of the patient for an extra-analytic contact. A candidate in analytic training who was exposed to this type of arrangement found himself impulsively exclaiming to the patient when she turned up at a small committee meeting that he was attending, "How did you know I hate surprise parties?"

When the patient has not informed the analyst of the extra-analytic contact prior to its taking place, the patient is usually defending against strong primal scene, incestuous, homosexual, or some other sexual and aggressive fantasies that he feels are forbidden. Obviously, the analyst's role in this situation is to help the analysand feel safe enough to explore and express the unacceptable wishes that were motivating him to create "the surprise party" in the first place.

As has already been suggested, analysands almost always respond intensely to the extra-analytic contact. Consequently, the analyst, after the contact, must always be in a state of readiness to help the analysand deal with intensified and/or modified transference fantasies, reactivation of childhood memories, and new and different resistances to the analytic situation. In addition, he must be sensitive to modified countertransference feelings and the reactivation of childhood memories in himself.

2. *Extra-Analytic Contacts That Are "Accidental" for Both Parties*

From a psychoanalytic perspective, there are few pure "accidents" (Freud, 1901). Just as unplanned pregnancies or car collisions may be unconsciously arranged, it can be more than mere coincidence when analyst and analysand "bump into each other" at the theater, restaurant, park, social gathering or professional meeting. If these types of "accidents" occur repetitively (particularly with the same patient), it is incumbent on the analyst to first explore his own wishes for contact with the patient away from his office, and then to ascertain if he and the patient are unconsciously colluding in a mutual and complementary fantasy, e.g., a wish for merger, incest, homosexual contact, avoidance of formal analysis, etc.

In contrast to the dynamic event described above in category 1, in "accidental" extra-analytic contacts both parties are caught unprepared. Reactions on the part of both analysands and analysts to being caught unprepared can range all the way from joy and ecstasy to rage and depression. For many patients (and for analysts, as well) the accidental meeting can be experienced as a long-awaited blissful reunion with a dead parent, a fantasied lover, or a much prized ego-ideal. Patients who project their own omnipotent fantasies on to the analyst and then resent him for his "god like," "inhuman," or "imperious" qualities can welcome, at least initially, accidentally seeing the analyst cheering at a football game, laughing or crying at a play, or sleeping at a concert. As one patient commented after accidentally seeing her analyst at a restaurant, "You eat, too? I didn't think perfect gods ate hamburgers!" How much the analyst needs to be experienced as the unseen omnipotent god will, of course, influence his response to being caught unprepared.

Frequently patients (and analysts) can resent the accidental contact, experiencing it as an intrusion, rape or engulfment. Patients (and analysts) have reported reactions similar to the following: "I was caught with my pants down"; "I don't want you in my bedroom"; or "My life isn't my own." When analysts or patients have strong defenses against intimacy and therefore want distance, the accidental extra-analytic contact catches them off-guard and they can then feel very vulnerable. Said one patient after accidentally meeting his analyst at a library, "I wanted an evening by myself. Do you have to come along and pry into my thoughts, some more?" On accidentally meeting her female analyst in a ladies' room of a movie theater, another analysand remarked, "You have to follow me everywhere, don't you? I can't even go to the bathroom without you checking up on me!" An analyst, on accidentally meeting a patient while on vacation, reported: "I was so irritated. I go on vacation to *get away* from patients."

For some patients, an accidental contact occurring early in the analysis can be quite disruptive to the treatment. When the patient has many unresolved infantile wishes and conflicts that have not reached conscious awareness, and which need to be strongly defended—e.g. homosexual yearnings, wishes for symbiotic merger, oral cravings, etc., the extra-analytic contact may be experienced as an alluring, stimulating, but frightening event. Consequently, the analysand may try to leave the analytic situation because he is so threatened by being entrapped by the omnipotent, omniscient analyst. Stated one patient after meeting her analyst accidentally on the subway, "I thought I had enough armor to ward you off, but you persist in trying to invade me. I may be paranoid, but I think you are a rapist."

If the therapeutic alliance has not been well established—which is frequently the case early in an analysis—the "accidental" extra-analytic contact can interfere with the utilization of the analyst as a fantasy figure because the patient may wish to relate to him exclusively as the friend or colleague that he appeared to be at the swimming pool party or restaurant.

Particularly when the accidental contact that occurs early in treatment involves a triad, can the triadic arrangement be utilized to express anxiety about unresolved oedipal fantasies or unresolved sibling rivalries. One woman patient was so angry and felt so rejected and humiliated on observing her analyst with his wife because he appeared so "happily married," that she suppressed oedipal fantasies and tried to cope with depressed feelings on her own—i.e. she did not want to share her depressed feelings with her analyst. A male analysand who had been in treatment three months and who had strong but unresolved sibling rivalry problems, on seeing his analyst with his two sons became so rageful and so frightened of his rage, that he could hardly talk in his analytic sessions for a couple of weeks.

In general, the "accidental encounter" with its dyadic or triadic shape and content, particularly when it occurs early in the analytic work, seems to pose larger problems of containment and analytic working through than the planned encounters described in category 1. Without the benefit of forework, the encounter can puncture habitual modes of defense and activate intense affect, something akin to a classical traumatic reaction.

3. Extra-Analytic Contacts That Are about to Happen When the Analyst Has Foreknowledge but the Patient Does Not

In this category are those extra-analytic contacts where the patient speaks of a party or gathering that he plans to attend, as will the analyst, but the patient does not know he will meet the analyst at the function.

Some analysts can and will respond to this kind of situation by avoiding the extra-analytic contact. On hearing that the patient will be at the party or meeting that he is planning to attend, the analyst will just decline to go.

What frequently poses a dilemma for the analyst when he plans to attend the function where his patient will also be present, but which the patient has no knowledge of, is whether to alert the patient so that anticipatory work can be done—or, remain mum and work with the event after it has occurred.

It should be recognized at the outset that similar to "accidental" extra-analytic contacts (category 2), it cannot always be assumed in category 3 contacts that the patient truly does not know that he will meet the analyst at the function to which he is referring. The very fact that he mentions the anticipated event to his analyst suggests some potential transference significance. A male patient when told by his female analyst that she would be attending the same alumni reunion that the patient reported that he was planning to attend, went on in the same session that his analyst told him her plans, to report a dream in which he was dancing with a woman at a college campus whose first name and surname had the same initials as his analyst.

Although there have not been any reports in the psychoanalytic literature of situations where the analyst has enacted the "surgeon-like role" and remained mum about his plan to be present at an event where the patient also plans to be, reports from therapists and analysts on this issue tend to suggest that this stance can be detrimental to the therapy. Although each patient will react idiosyncratically, most patients feel betrayed by the analyst when he does not inform them in advance that he will be present at an event that the patient has discussed in his sessions. Stated one patient vehemently, "You know damn well that our analytic relationship is something unique and special. To see you away from the office is tough enough. But, not to warn me is like a hit over the head. You remind me of my mother who always hit me when I least suspected it."

When therapists and analysts have not prepared the patient for the extra-analytic contact that the analyst knows will take place, most patients have also reported feeling entrapped by a stronger, more powerful human being, i.e. an omnipotent, sadistic parental figure, and several have wanted to abandon treatment altogether. It would appear that when the patient speaks of a party or gathering that the analyst is also planning to attend, the analyst should inform the analysand of his intentions so that anticipatory work can be done. Then, the analytic situation becomes very much similar to that described in category 1.

During the last ten years I have had the opportunity to analyze with several patients the dynamic meaning that their extra-analytic contacts with me had for them. As I began to appreciate how much these contacts clarified transference, countertransference, and resistance phenomena and provided, as well, an index of therapeutic progress, I started to record brief summaries of these encounters when they did occur. Not only did I note the patient's reactions to these extra-analytic contacts but I also recorded some of my own thoughts and countertransference reactions immediately after the meetings. Consequently, I could then compare my own impressions with the patient's associations and interpretations and get a view of the complementarity of the patient and me at work. The following is a case illustration.

CASE ILLUSTRATION

Jane is a single, thirty-year-old teacher of emotionally disturbed children. She sought treatment because she suffered from severe bouts of depression, psychosomatic ailments, lack of work satisfaction, and poor interpersonal relationships, particularly with men.

Significant in Jane's history was the fact that her mother died when the patient was three years old. Jane viewed her own life as enjoyable prior to her mother's death. She reflected, "Daddy and I were like lovers and buddies and I was in heaven! Mother was sick most of the time and I don't really remember her very much." Jane's mother died a few months after she gave birth to Jane's brother. After her mother's death Jane was described by her father and other relatives as "paralyzed, depressed, and green" for many years.

After a short period of resisting taking the couch because she feared being overwhelmed by strong oral and symbiotic cravings, Jane moved eagerly into a four-times-a-week analysis. During the first eighteen months of treatment, Jane became aware of feelings of guilt because she experienced herself as an oedipal victor and also uncovered strong yearnings to be close to her mother. While analyzing her wishes to merge symbiotically with her mother, Jane brought out a desire to attend a lecture that I was giving for social workers and psychologists. "It [the lecture] is in a little over a week and I'll need a 'yes' or 'no' answer because we won't have time to analyze all my motives by then!" Jane declared. When I remained silent, Jane expressed indignation and irritation that I would not make the decision for her.

In a latter session prior to her first extra-analytic contact, when I interpreted Jane's wish for permission or prohibition from me, Jane began to feel considerable anguish about her fantasies toward me. With much hesitation and reluctance she brought out that the prospect of the extra-analytic contact was stimulating wishes to eat various parts of my body—arms, legs, penis, etc. While Jane associated to some of her cannibalistic fantasies toward me, she cried, felt nauseous, and was very uncomfortable—feeling very "disgusted" with herself.

The cannibalistic fantasies that became stimulated by the idea of seeing me in a face-to-face encounter made Jane feel so guilty and shameful that she began to wonder whether she should in fact attend the lecture. She began to experience herself as an "odd-ball" and pointed out: "Everybody there will know I'm a hungry and peculiar baby who wants to gobble you up." Although Jane continued to have her misgivings about attending the lecture, the extra-analytic contact, with its hope of blissful merger with me, filled her with more excitement than guilt. Yet, her ambivalence and teasing continued. She pointed out at the session before the lecture, "I'm going, I think. You haven't stopped me like some analysts do—but then again, you haven't approved of the idea, either. I'll take my chances about how much I'll be improper and look peculiar."

At the lecture I noticed that Jane was animatedly taking notes. Part of my recording after the lecture stated: "Jane was eager to get everything that she heard on paper. She seemed to value what I said and I feel that she experienced the lecture as if she were at her mother's breast, taking in everything she could." With regard to my own reactions, I recorded, "I enjoyed seeing Jane and I really got to feel how pleasureful it must be for a mother to feed an infant. For me, the lecture gratified my countertransference wish to be the mother that Jane yearns for."

At the analytic session immediately following the lecture, Jane came in excitedly. She quickly spoke of her reactions to the lecture: "You became a real person for me, rather than some distant figure. I saw you smile, clean your glasses, and a whole lot of stuff that I never get to see. . . . It was great—but I was too stimulated. I had fantasies of sucking in each and every one of your words. I wrote down everything you said so I could go over it again and again. At the lecture, and later when I went over your work, I had fantasies of first sucking in your words, then eating up your tongue; and then later your whole head, and then your body. . . . I remember at one point in the lecture feeling that your penis was like a big breast that was covering me snugly."

Later in the same session Jane associated to her taking notes at the lecture. She pointed out that she wanted to "hold on to every one of your words and never let them go away" and then later brought out that "if I didn't busy myself writing, I was afraid that I might come up to the podium, grab you and devastate you . . . I was and still am so scared of my crazy appetite."

Toward the end of the session Jane reported a dream: "I found my mother in a kitchen of a building but as I looked at her, I wanted to hug her but was scared to do so." Jane had several associations to the dream. The building appeared very similar to the one where the lecture was. Just as she felt very conflicted about hugging and eventually devouring me, so did she feel very frightened about her wishes to incorporate her mother. Said Jane, "I was so scared of gobbling you up in the dream—I guess—if I let myself go, I'd rip my mother apart." Near the end of the session while Jane was associating to her wishes and fears of devouring me, she mentioned that yesterday (at the lecture) "you seemed so near yet so far—oh, just like I made my mother in the dream!... But if I don't keep you far away, God knows what I'll do to you."

While Jane was working on her wish and fear to devour me, she referred again to the lecture and thanked me for feeding her for over an hour. While she did not have any associations to this fantasy during the session, in a later one, approximately a week later, she was able to recognize that thanking me was her way of getting my permission "to feed on you." "What I'd really like to do though" said Jane, "is to be a superwoman and tear you limb from limb."

In subsequent sessions after her first extra-analytic contact, Jane's excitement slowly moved to depression. She referred to the extra-analytic contact as my "holding out a carrot" and that the whole situation "was a tease." She admonished me for not stopping her from going to the lecture and reflected, "All you did was make me think I could have a close relationship with a good parent and then you let me down." Her depression eventually turned to strong rage. In the transference, she experienced me as the mother "who promises but doesn't deliver and may as well be dead."

As Jane's treatment continued, she moved back and forth between her wish for merger with mother, her hatred at her mother for dying, and her oedipal competition and guilt. By the third year of her treatment she was dealing with phallic issues and her competition with father, brother, and me (whom she was experiencing as father and brother in the transference). During the third year of treatment, Jane became aware of a panel discussion in which I would be participating and stated that she was planning to attend. In contrast to her initial reactions to her first extra-analytic experience, Jane did not become preoccupied with receiving my approbation or disapproval but did have a dream in which she was chairman of a panel discussion and made me a young boy who flubbed his lines.

In Jane's associations to her dream, she brought out that she would like to feel like a boss to me "instead of always feeling bossed around" by me. "I'd like to have you feel uncertain of yourself and be weak, like I often feel when I'm with you," exclaimed Jane. She likened me to her father who always seemed so extraordinarily confident of himself. "You are smug and cocky just like he is," Jane stated angrily. She then had a fantasy of putting a rusty meat-hook up my anus and castrating me by yanking off my penis and then "chewing it up savagely." This was followed by another fantasy about both of us being soldiers and her shooting me with two dozen bullets.

At the second extra-analytic contact, I thought I saw Jane in the audience, frowning, but I was not sure. After the panel discussion, I wrote, "Jane has been associating to her phallic wishes and phallic competition. The transference has been essentially negative. She experiences me as the father that she would like to castrate and then hostilely incorporate his penis. I suspect that she will report negative feelings about my participation in this panel. . . . I felt somewhat vulnerable as I thought about Jane hearing me talk and had associations to my younger sister with whom I competed. I have to observe more carefully my own wishes to compete with Jane and whatever sense of threat I feel when with her."

Following the second extra-analytic contact, Jane entered her analytic session in a rage. She bellowed, "You are a big exhibitionist! A twenty-foot prick is what you are—always showing off! Why don't you keep quiet for a while? You take up too much room! You make too much noise! Your voice is too booming!" Later in the same session, Jane reported a dream in which she and I were boxers in a ring and she had me knocked down for a count of 9. Among her associations to the dream was one in which she likened me to the boy who was the valedictorian in her senior class of high school and whose academic average was .005 higher than hers. Stated Jane, "I wanted to beat the shit out of him in the same way I want to beat the shit out of you. You are both cocky big-heads who get all the laurels . . . I hated my brother for the same reason and my father, too. . . . and all men who think because they got something dangling between their legs, they're somebody." When Jane associated to her knocking me down for a count of 9, she thought of her wish to hurt me, make me suffer, and fight some more. "If I knock you out, the fight is over. I want you to suffer and suffer and suffer while I beat you and beat you and beat you," she averred.

Jane's dream and her further associations to the second extra-analytic contact—which were replete with competitive and hostile associations to father, brother, male colleagues and male friends in the past and present—eventually led to increased understanding of her internalized battle with father and brother. For several weeks after the second extra-analytic contact she discussed her depreciation of her own vagina, her penis envy, and her overidealization of the man (particularly father, brother, and me) whom she wished to castrate.

Toward the end of Jane's third year of treatment she began to focus more directly on oedipal issues and had fantasies and memories of running off with father and having a baby with him. These rather classical oedipal fantasies also were recapitulated in her transference relationship with me. Around this time Jane mentioned that she had heard from a colleague in an organization of which she was a member that I would be addressing that organization the following week. Jane told me that she felt very differently about seeing me extra-analytically than she did prior to the last encounter. She fantasied walking off with me after the lecture and going to a hotel. Furthermore, she had a wish to exhibit our affair to the audience and "beat them all to the punch." She was further able to talk about how she was repeating with me her fairly strong conviction that she really did murder her mother and capture father. In the session preceding the lecture she slipped and said, "I'm looking forward to marrying you . . . I mean meeting you . . . at the conference."

At the third extra-analytic contact, I did not see Jane in the audience but knew she was there. I wrote: "Lately Jane has been talking about oedipal issues. She is freer to express and analyze her sexual fantasies toward her father and toward me. She is looking at her competition with mother with less trepidation. Perhaps this extra-analytic contact will provoke more sexual fantasies toward father and me." With regard to my own countertransference feelings I wrote, "When I was giving my paper, a couple of times I was really reading to Jane and felt like a lover reading poetry and trying to seduce his woman. The extra-analytic contact really brings my unconscious and pre-conscious libidinal wishes toward Jane to the surface!"

In the session that followed the lecture, Jane reported that she spent much of her time and energy at the presentation looking for and looking at my wife. As she associated to her interest in my wife, she recalled memories of looking for her mother after her mother died. Jane also had several fantasies of merging with my wife and for the next five sessions came to her appointments dressed in green—the color of my wife's attire at the meeting. In a dream, two sessions after the extra-analytic contact, Jane was in a cave looking for a woman with whom she could have oral sex.

In Jane's associations to her dream, she thought the woman in the dream was my wife and she went on to describe how she, Jane, wanted to take my place with my wife. She likened my wife's appearance—height, facial features, etc.—to her mother's appearance, and had several fantasies of having mutual masturbation and cunnilingus with my wife. In the cave, Jane associated to a house, then a stomach, and then a whole body. She had wishes to merge with my wife and went back and forth between being a man with my wife, a little girl with her, or a mother herself, while my wife was her younger daughter.

Jane's associations to the dream seemed to have a negative-oedipal and homosexual theme and helped me to recognize some of my own counterresistance problems at this particular stage of the analysis. In many ways, I was resisting confronting Jane's wish to take my place with my wife. I diminished, in my mind, her desire to compete with me by overemphasizing and concentrating too much on her oedipal fantasies toward me.

During Jane's fourth year of treatment, she went deeper into her oedipal fantasies and also dealt with many homosexual fantasies toward her mother and my wife. Occasionally she would use the oedipal position to defend against the inverted oedipal position and vice versa. As she analyzed these fantasies in depth, her external life changed. She became a supervisor on her job, dated men with regularity, and felt much less depressed. In this period Jane and I had an "accidental" extra-analytic contact (category 2). We met in the theater and Jane was with a male companion and I was with my wife. Jane and I extended smiles and "Hi's" and Jane commented that the play was "very moving." I recorded: "Jane has been intensely involved with many oedipal issues, particularly incest and murder. My hunch is that this extra-analytic contact will intensify some of these wishes. . . . When I saw Jane with a man at the theater, I felt like a proud papa attending the wedding of his daughter. I also felt some narcissistic satisfaction in realizing how much Jane has progressed in her treatment."

At Jane's session following the encounter described above, she reported a dream in which my wife and Jane's male companion got killed in a car accident, and she and I arranged a liaison with the expectation that we would be married. Jane's associations exposed a wish to wipe out my wife and be my wife. She also voiced a lot of resentment toward her male companion for not being a perfect lover and omnipotent human being like me, as she was currently fantasizing. She then recalled some memories from her early childhood when she did acrobatics and gymnastics with her father and was sexually stimulated by him. At those times she would fantasy being father's "queen" and wish mother had died. Jane then spent several sessions having fantasies of first wiping her mother out, then having sex with father, feeling guilty about it, and then merging with mother. After feeling too engulfed by mother, she would repeat the same sequence of fantasies—killing mother, having sex with father, etc.

About three weeks after Jane's last extra-analytic contact she began to recall resenting her parents' sexual relationship. She had fantasies of getting in between them in bed and shoving her mother on to the floor. She realized that she briefly fantasied doing this to my wife when she saw her at the theatre with me. The parallel between Jane's reactions of seeing my wife and me in the theatre with her childhood reactions to her parents' sexual relationship was apparent.

During Jane's fifth and sixth years of treatment she continued to work on many pre-oedipal and oedipal themes. She had consistent fantasies of being in mother's body and was ambivalent about staying in or breaking out of the body and killing mother. In addition, oedipal fantasies similar to those noted above and competitive, phallic fantasies where she would wrestle and castrate father, brother, or me were expressed. In Jane's seventh year of treatment, she attended a panel discussion on which a supervisor of hers and I appeared. I recorded, "Jane is much more individuated and is enjoying her work and love relationships. She is relaxed much of the time. That's the way she seemed today. Maybe she'll respond to the lecture with less infantile transference fantasies. . . . I experienced Jane as a colleague—an equal of mine. Most of the time I forgot she was in analysis with me. I think she is getting ready (and so am I) for termination."

After the above meeting, Jane mentioned in her next session that she was struck by the fact that she saw me and her supervisor as "real people who were competent but not gigantic, imperfect but far from ineffective, sexual but not Superman or Batwoman."

DISCUSSION

In reviewing the sequence of Jane's reactions to her extra-analytic contacts, it would appear that she perceived, evaluated, and distorted the analyst in line with her current transference position and unique constellation of resistances. Although all of Jane's extra-analytic meetings provided material for the analysis and although each extra-analytic contact induced an intense response on her part—evoking a dream after each contact except the last one—the extra-analytic contact did not appear to be a "parameter" which contaminated the transference. As we have observed from our presentation of Jane's associations to her extra-analytic contacts with me, the encounters seemed to serve as day residues for the dreams that she presented immediately after seeing me outside the consultation room.

That Jane's unconscious transference fantasy governed the manner in which she organized her perceptions of the extra-analytic contacts is best illustrated by briefly reviewing what was transpiring in her analysis prior to the extra-analytic contacts and what dreams and other associations emerged after these encounters.

Jane's first extra-analytic contact came at a time when she was working on her symbiotic yearnings for her mother. Before the first extra-analytic contact, she was experiencing me in the transference as the mother with whom she wanted to merge and who would feed her and nurture her. Concomitantly, she voiced considerable ambivalence toward me, feeling very frightened of her wishes to devour and destroy me. The first extra-analytic contact highlighted her conflicts around devouring me and served as a day residue for her ambivalent dream immediately after she attended my lecture. In the dream she made me her mother and utilized the lecture-hall as a kitchen, but could not hug me or have too much to do with me, lest she would eat me up. From Jane's associations and dream we learned that the fantasy of being attached to her mother was a dominant motive in bringing Jane to the lecture so that she could be more closely attached to me and fed by me.

During the third year of treatment when Jane was working on her phallic wishes, competition, and penis envy, she utilized the extra-analytic contact to try and compete with me and weaken me. Her associations to her dream of being chairman of a panel discussion while I was a floundering boy and to the one where she was a boxer who had me knocked down for the count of 9, revealed her current transference fantasy of wanting to weaken and castrate me while she would be the strong, phallic "boss."

All of Jane's subsequent extra-analytic contacts seemed to highlight her current transference position and unique set of resistances. When Jane was working on oedipal themes in the analysis, her extra-analytic contact stimulated associations of marrying me and destroying my wife. When her oedipal conflicts created anxiety and Jane was regressing to a negative-oedipal position (an issue which I resisted facing for a while) she utilized her extra-analytic contact to confront homosexual fantasies toward my wife. Finally, as Jane became increasingly able to love and to work more maturely, she experienced me quite realistically in her last extra-analytic contact.

Although we have discussed three types of extra-analytic contacts—with Jane there were two, categories 1 and 2—my finding with Jane and with other patients is that regardless of the type of extra-analytic contact, the patient seems to respond to it in terms of his or her current transference fantasies and current set of resistances.

It is often asked whether the extra-analytic contact is valuable to an analysis or does it create hazards? Is it a necessary evil? Or, is it merely grist for the analytic mill? Is there some unique experience for the patient when there is an extra-analytic contact?

My own experiences with extra-analytic contacts and my discussions with analysts and therapists on the subject have prompted me to formulate a few tentative answers to the above questions which only future research can confirm or refute.

Whether an extra-analytic contact is viewed as valuable or hazardous depends to a large extent on how the analyst feels about seeing his patient and being seen by the patient outside of the consultation room. If he is anxious about treasured transference and countertransference positions being altered; if he is worried that regressive wishes in the patient or in himself will not be able to be contained; if he is uncomfortable in departing from his anonymous, unseen role behind the couch—then, he will in all probability find many reasons to prescribe as to why the extra-analytic contact should be avoided.

As my experience with Jane has depicted, the extra-analytic contact usually highlights and intensifies the current transference position. One of its values, therefore, is to aid analyst and patient in further understanding how the patient is experiencing the analyst. A corollary of this is that the analyst has the opportunity of increasing his understanding of his current countertransference position. As I recorded my reactions to the extra-analytic contacts with Jane and reviewed her reactions to me (in and out of the sessions) the extra-analytic contacts had the distinct value of enriching understanding of the transference for both patient and analyst and understanding of the countertransference by the analyst.

Although the patient tends to develop a more experientially poignant mode after an extra-analytic contact and certain genetic and dynamic issues become highlighted, the encounter can be potentially hazardous to the smooth flow of an analysis. At times the extra-analytic contact can serve to lessen the possibility of the analyst being a fantasy object. Jane, after her first extra-analytic contact said, "You became a real person to me!" The extra-analytic contact, particularly if it occurs early in treatment, can stimulate the possibility that infantile fantasies will actually be gratified. Then, the patient may have to deal with more frustration than he or she can bear. Jane, it will be recalled after one of her contacts, said to me, "You are holding out a carrot. . . . You are a tease."

As has been suggested in the earlier part of this paper, the extra-analytic contact is a fact of therapeutic life for many analysts and patients. While it has values and potential hazards, like other departures from routine—e.g., cancellations by the analyst, vacations of the analyst, hearing realistic gossip about the analyst, the analyst raising his fees—the best means of utilizing extra-analytic contacts constructively is by subjecting them to analytic exploration. As Greenson (1967) and other analysts have reiterated (Tarnower, 1966; Weiss, 1975; Katz, 1978), whatever the source, whether picked up in the consultation room or from an extra-analytic contact, knowledge about the analyst must become subject matter for analysis because it usually is the vehicle for unconscious fantasy.

In sum, the extra-analytic contact has the value of highlighting transference and countertransference themes. It also has the potential hazard of diminishing the strength of the analyst's role as fantasied object. Another potential hazard is that it can force the patient to deal with more frustration and teasing than he can bear. Like any other interpersonal event between analyst and patient, it is always imperative for the analyst to help the patient intensively explore his associations to meeting the analyst outside the consultation room and utilize all extra-analytic contacts as grist for the analytic mill.

SUMMARY

The conflict between safeguarding the analyst's anonymity as opposed to the advisability of his being a "real person" becomes most apparent when analyst and patient meet outside the consultation room. The encounter can stimulate many secret wishes which create anxiety in both parties: voyeuristic and exhibitionistic fantasies, primal scene conflicts, oedipal and homosexual desires, sadistic and masochistic urges, and oral incorporative yearnings.

It is important for the analyst to maintain his neutrality in working with the patient's wishes and fears regarding extra-analytic contacts. He should neither encourage nor discourage the encounters; rather, he should analyze their meaning to the patient when they occur.

A case illustration was presented to demonstrate how an analysis of the patient's associations to the extra-analytic contact can clarify transference, countertransference and resistance phenomena and serve as an index of therapeutic progress.

Though the extra-analytic contact serves to intensify and highlight certain transference and countertransference themes, it can create excessive stimulation and anxiety for the patient, diminish the analyst's role as a fantasy object, and disrupt the resolution of the patient's transference neurosis.

REFERENCES

Allen, D. *The Fear of Looking: Scopophilic-Exhibitionistic Conflicts*. Charlottesville, Va.: University Press of Virginia, 1974.

Berman, L. "Countertransference and Attitudes of the Analyst in the Therapeutic Process," *Psychiatry*, Vol. 12, 1949, pp. 159–166.

Doolittle, H. *Tribute to Freud*. New York: McGraw-Hill, 1956.

Fenichel, O. *The Psychoanalytic Theory of Neurosis*. New York: Norton and Co., 1945.

Ferenczi, S. "Introjection and Transference," (1909), in *Sex and Psychoanalysis*, ed. S. Ferenczi. New York: Robert Bruner, 1950.

Fine, R. *The Healing of the Mind*. New York: David McKay, 1971.

———. *The History of Psychoanalysis*. New York: Columbia University Press, 1979.

Freud, S. "The Psychopathology of Everyday Life," *Standard Edition*, Vol. 6. London: Hogarth Press, 1901.

———. "The Future Prospects for Psychoanalytic Therapy," *Standard Edition*. London: Hogarth Press, 1910.

———. "Recommendations to Physicians Practising Psychoanalysis," *Standard Edition*, Vol. 12. London: Hogarth Press, 1912.

———. "Observations on Transference-Lo-e," *Standard Edition*, Vol. 12. London: Hogarth Press, 1915.

———. "Lines of Advances in Psychoanalytic Therapy," *Standard Edition*, Vol. 17. London: Hogarth Press, 1919.

————. "An Outline of Psychoanalysis," *Standard Edition*, Vol. 23. London: Hogarth Press, 1940.

Greenacre, P. "The Role of Transference: Practical Considerations in Relation to Psychoanalytic Therapy," *Journal of the American Psychoanalytic Association*, Vol. 2, 1954, pp. 671–684.

————. "Certain Technical Problems in the Transference Relationship," *Journal of the American Psychoanalytic Association*, Vol. 7, 1959, pp. 484–502.

Greenson, R. *The Technique and Practice of Psychoanalysis*. New York: International Universities, 1967.

————, and M. Wexler. "The Non-Transference Relationship in the Psychoanalytic Situation," *International Journal of Psychoanalysis*, Vol. 50, 1969, pp. 27–39.

Kardiner, A. *My Analysis with Freud*. New York: Norton and Co., 1977.

Katz, J. "A Psychoanalyst's Anonymity: Fiddler Behind the Couch," *Bulletin of the Menninger Clinic*, Vol. 42, No. 6, 1978, pp. 520–524.

Lampl-de-Groot, J. "Personal Experience with Psychoanalytic Technique and Theory During the Last Half Century," *Psychoanalytic Study of the Child*, Vol. 31, ed., R. Eisler. New Haven: Yale University Press, 1976.

Langs, R. *The Therapeutic Interaction*, Vols. I & II. New York: Jason Aronson, 1976.

Lipton, S. D. "The Advantages of Freud's Technique as Shown in His Analysis of the Rat Man," *International Journal of Psychoanalysis*, Vol. 58, 1977, pp. 255–273.

————. "An Addendum to 'The Advantages of Freud's Technique as Shown in His Analysis of the Rat Man,'" *International Journal of Psychoanalysis*, Vol. 60, 1979, pp. 215–216.

Menninger, K. *Theory of Psychoanalytic Technique*. New York: Basic Books, 1958.

Paul, L. "A Note on the Private Aspect and Professional Aspect of the Psychoanalyst," *Bulletin of the Philadelphia Psychoanalytic Association*, Vol. 9, 1960, pp. 96–101.

Roazen, P. *Freud and His Followers*. New York: Alfred A. Knopf, 1975.

Sharpe, E. "The Technique of Psychoanalysis," *International Journal of Psychoanalysis*, Vol. 11, 1930, pp. 251–263.

Stone, L. *The Psychoanalytic Situation.* New York: International Universities Press, 1961.

Tarnower, W. "Extra-Analytic Contacts Between the Psychoanalyst and the Patient," *Psychoanalytic Quarterly*, Vol. 35, 1966, pp. 399–413.

Weiss, S. A. "The Effect on the Transference of 'Special Events' Occurring During Psychoanalysis," *International Journal of Psychoanalysis*, Vol. 56, 1975, pp. 69–77.

Wortis, J. *Fragments of an Analysis with Freud.* New York: Simon and Schuster, 1954.

DISCUSSANT: REUBEN FINE

In this excellent little paper, Dr. Strean calls attention to a little-discussed phenomenon: contact between analyst and patient outside the analytic hour. It may be accidental (which he properly questions, but accidents do happen) or planned. From Freud on, the mainstream tradition has been to avoid any contact at all, but it has remained silent about the situations where such contact is harmless, or may even be helpful.

There are, in fact, established situations where extra-analytic contact may not only not be avoided, but even encouraged by the analyst. Two such arrangements which have received some attention are the student in an analytic institute and group therapy.

Some institutes take an extremely rigid attitude; e.g. one forbids any entry into classes until the student has had one or more years of analysis. Others do not care, and admit the student at once, evidently in agreement with Strean's position that it is better to analyze the transference complications than to maintain a taboo. Anna Freud has rightly pointed out that the treatment of a candidate in an analytic institute violates all the basic canons of analysis, yet it goes on all the time. Again the vital element is, as Strean points out, the airing of all transference reactions.

In group therapy, handled in an analytic manner as by Alexander Wolf and his colleagues, the analyst actually forces the patient to engage in an extra-analytic contact. From the very beginning Wolf insisted that the transferences should be analyzed, not avoided. Others, however, violate this approach, with results that are often wild and unpredictable.

The history of psychoanalysis is characterized by extreme positions on this issue. On the current scene, Robert Langs wishes to isolate the "frame" from any kind of contact, even questioning the validity of contact after the analysis (but how can this really be avoided?). Greenacre once recommended that analysts should refrain from engaging in any political cause or action because the ensuing transference reactions would interfere with the analytic process. Stone, however, has recently stigmatized such extremes as caricatures of the classical position, which stem from some of Freud's followers rather than from Freud himself.

At the other extreme are those who feel that the distance posture is too artificial, and that the analyst should actively share his reactions with the patient. Tauber once reported that when a female patient advised him that she was leaving analysis to go to another city he began to cry. Singer wrote a paper in which he told how he had used his patients as "auxiliary therapists" to relieve him of the burdensome feelings that overcame him upon his wife's death. Recently I saw one of these patients in consultation; she stated that Singer's sharing of his feelings in this way cast a tremendous weight on her shoulders, which she bitterly resented but could not mention to him.

Thus, as with infants, there are the two poles of frustration and indulgence, with the mainstream tradition in the middle (though lending itself to frustration), while revisionists have generally tried various forms of indulgence. Ferenczi is well known for his experiments, but others have gone much further since. Strean rightly sticks to the mainstream position, but avoids the excesses mentioned above.

I am in agreement with his general stance, but I would like to see him enlarge it somewhat. The patient he uses as an example was particularly receptive to the extra-analytic contacts, and could handle the transference reactions appropriately. Others may have more emotional reactions. In one case of mine, I met a patient on the street accidentally, and she expected me to buy her a cup of coffee. When this did not materialize, she flew into a rage that lasted several weeks. On the other hand, with a patient whose main defense was a narcissistic indifference to close contacts, a chance encounter on the street produced no reaction whatsoever, nor could it even be analyzed.

Another variation arises when the analyst is also a writer, and the patient deliberately seeks out his writings, and reacts to them. In view of Dr. Strean's productivity this must happen to him with some frequency. It would be interesting to see how patients handle his written pronouncements. In my experience, the distortions that ensue pose an even greater transference problem.

Then again there are the artists, musicians, painters and sculptors who invite their analyst to a showing of their works, or bring them in for analytic approval or comment. Writers may do the same. This, too, poses a transference problem, since the patient would like the analyst to be an authority on his work of art, while the analyst cannot possibly function in that capacity.

A pseudo–extra-analytic contact takes place with the waiting-room romance: two patients who are attracted to one another, each one seeing the other as a replacement for the analyst. Some analysts try to forestall any complications by placing a taboo on any contact with other patients, but as with so many taboos this one is also unenforceable. Nor need the analyst do more than what Strean does in his cases, simply handle the transference reactions. In one case, a young man waited downstairs for the young woman who followed him, and they had one date. After that, the attraction vanished. The transference was glaringly obvious.

Then, too, there is the question of contact with those who are close to the analyst, sometimes his family members. In the analysis of Helene Deutsch, Freud went so far as to accept milk from her husband Felix during the harsh years of World War I; in view of Helene Deutsch's extraordinary accomplishments, this "contamination" of the transference can hardly be said to have had harmful consequences.

In one instance, an analyst in a very orthodox situation where she deliberately avoided any kind of contact with her analyst, even refusing to go to meetings where she might be present, nevertheless was involved in a society where her analyst's husband and she were leading figures. It need come as no great surprise that the analyst–patient and the husband were fighting constantly, and that eventually they both left the society, unable to work with one another at a professional level.

In short, Dr. Strean's splendid paper opens all kinds of new possibilities for our scrutiny, and he could easily write another, considering the various contingencies (and others) mentioned above.

As far as the polarity of frustration–indulgence is concerned, I am fully in accord that it is the analysis of the transference and its vicissitudes that is decisive, not any arbitrary rule. Psychoanalysis is an interaction of two people and is hard to fit into a preformed mold. The analogy with the change in attitude toward the mother–child relationship strikes one immediately. In the current literature the perennial problem of frustration–indulgence has been replaced by a careful study of the innumerable interactions that go on between mother and child.

At some point in technique we try to trace the transference back to its infantile roots. If the child's basic experience is one of interaction, then necessarily that will also be the keynote for the analysis of the transference.

DISCUSSANT: MARTIN GREENE

Dr. Strean has written about a fascinating topic. Extra-analytic contacts appear to be frequent occurrences. As Strean notes, they are common in analytic institutes where students are bound to meet their analysts. Yet this is another of those topics, like the home office and third party payments, which are rarely written about, perhaps because they involve matters in which analysts have important personal and economic stakes. Thus, in helping to bring the topic out of the dark, Strean makes an important contribution and provides an opportunity for an open dialogue. In addition, he develops a comprehensive overview of the types of extra-analytic contacts: those brought about by the patient, those that are "accidental" for both parties, and those that are anticipated by the analyst but not by the patient.

He wisely cites the dangers that are inherent in such contacts, including the contamination of the transference and the provision of infantile forms of gratification. Of course, while he does not mention it, these dangers are as applicable to the therapist as they are to the patient. Despite his recognition of such dangers, Strean is quick to brush them aside. After citing Freud as the prime example of the analyst who disregarded his own rule of anonymity, he proceeds to set about proving his thesis that extra-analytic contacts are of considerable value, intensifying the current transference position, aiding the analyst's understanding of how the patient is experiencing him, and providing an opportunity to intensify and gain a better understanding of his countertransference.

Strean clearly represents the view that all is grist for the mill; so long as it is analyzed, most anything goes. True, it is a deviation from neutrality to prohibit such contacts, but if one is to respect neutrality as a principle that is basic to the analytic position, how is it possible to disregard the anonymity that is of a similar degree of significance and so closely allied to neutrality (Dorpat, 1977, pp. 43–46)?

In proof of his thesis, Strean presents a discussion of thirty-year-old

Jane, a "teacher of emotionally disturbed children," seen four times per week for eight years. These eight years are summarized in a condensed form that provides about one page per year. The discussion focuses on the patient's and his own reactions to four contacts that the patient initiated by first discussing and then attending lectures given by Strean and one unplanned meeting at a movie in the presence of the patient's male companion and Strean's wife. In addition, and I think it is most important to note, the patient's "supervisor" was in the audience at one meeting, and another "supervisor" also participated in a panel discussion with Strean at the final extra-analytic meeting. Moreover, at one meeting the patient recognized Strean's wife. Altogether, one is given the impression that patient and analyst are involved in a rather close, intimate network where even a modicum of anonymity would be impossible, perhaps reinforcing Strean's need to prove his thesis.

Prior to discussing the content of his analysis of Jane, I would like to comment on two technical issues that I believe play a major role in determining the style in which Strean works, how he listens to, and how he understands the clinical material. The first seems rather evident. He doesn't put much stock in the significance of what Langs (1975a) and others have to say about the "frame": those rules and procedures—including neutrality, anonymity, confidentiality, set fees and hours—which together with the analyst's human qualities, such as empathy and compassion, are basic to psychoanalytic technique and the psychoanalytic method. Any of these, from Strean's perspective, may be disregarded so long as it is analyzed. But there is an alternative view that these ingredients cannot be so easily disregarded since together they distinguish the analytic space from all other situations, foster the ideal therapeutic environment, provide the secure therapeutic hold that makes it possible for the patient to express and work through his pathology, and actually determine the nature of the communicative field established (Langs, 1978).

Since all is grist for the mill, disregarding analytic methodology (from Strean's perspective) is of no consequence since it can further the work if properly analyzed. This notion suggests a misunderstanding of the very foundation of psychoanalytic work, the nature of unconscious processes. And that is the second issue I wish to discuss. The material that Strean reports, both the patient's and his own, consists entirely, except for some dream material, of conscious fantasies, mistakingly viewed as manifestations of the unconscious. For example, after the first contact the patient reports, "I had fantasies of sucking in each and every one of your words." Or later, Strean notes, "She had fantasies of merging with my wife. . . . [or] Jane then spent several sessions having fantasies of first wiping her mother out and then having sex with father. . . ." It is important to note that there is a distinction between unconscious fantasy and the sort of conscious fantasies that provide the content from which Strean makes most of his interpretations. The unconscious is expressed through symbols, and as Jones has stated (1916, p. 116), "In most uses of the word [in psychoanalysis], a symbol is a manifest expression of an idea that is more or less hidden, secret, or kept in reserve. Most typically of all, the person employing the symbol is not even conscious of what it actually represents." The unconscious is only known indirectly, metaphorically, through its derivatives in the form of condensations, displacements and symbolization since the content is dynamically repressed (Arlow, 1979). It is a common error to equate conscious or at best preconscious reports with unconscious material. Strean seems to accept manifest reports as if they were latent material, which they are not. Or he transforms conscious fantasies into genetic equivalents (the wish to suck on Strean equals the wish to suck on mother), assuming that the unconscious element is the transference displacement from the past expressed in an obvious and linear manner. But transference always alludes to unconscious fantasy constellations, found in disguised and derivative compromise formations (Langs, 1981, p. 453). And moreover, both conscious and unconscious fantasies must be distinguished from conscious and unconscious perceptions based upon the patient's adaptive responses to the realities and actualities that the analyst introduces.

Strean emphasizes that the patient's associations following each extra-analytic contact represents an intensification of the transference theme that had already emerged spontaneously in the prior sessions. I would like to present an alternative hypothesis. Strean notes his reflections before, during, and after each extra-analytic contact, and views his associations as responses stimulated by the patient's material. I would like to posit that the reverse could be equally true, that the patient's associations represent her attempts to adapt to the countertransference problems Strean has been having and that are further intensified through the mutual acting-out inherent in the extra-analytic contacts, particularly those planned in advance. Thus, what Strean views as the current transference position, assumed to emerge spontaneously within the analysis, could in fact represent the patient's conscious and unconscious responses to current and actual stimuli introduced by Strean, and unconsciously communicated to the patient as a consequence of Strean's difficulties in managing his countertransference, most cogently expressed in his failure to interpret and, through his interpretations, to curtail the destructive consequences of the gratifications inherent in the extra-analytic meetings.

At the first meeting, a lecture that Strean gave, believing that Jane was struggling with her symbiotic yearnings for her dead mother, Strean comments to himself, "I enjoyed seeing Jane, and I really got to feel how pleasureful it must be for a mother to feed an infant. For me, the lecture gratified my countertransference wish to be the mother that Jane yearns for." With such gratification to be gained, is it any wonder that Strean failed to either see or interpret the mutual acting out inherent in the contact? Following manifest comments on the benefits of having seen him as a "real person," the patient expresses conscious fantasies of sucking him in, wanting to have gone up on the stage and devoured him, but of being over-stimulated, and, "I was and still am, so scared of my crazy appetite." But is the problem really her "crazy appetite"? As an alternative explanation, Jane has truly been over-stimulated by her analyst who had, even prior to the extra-analytic contact, communicated his need to be the feeding mother. In turn, she has introjected Strean's attitude and wish for indulgence.

Following the second extra-analytic contact, which is believed to stimulate Jane's phallic-competitive strivings, there emerges, in what is presented as the unfolding of a natural and orderly psychosexual developmental sequence, an intensification of oedipal themes, with a rampant expression of conscious sexual fantasies believed to be representative of her current transference position. The intensification of sexual themes is not surprising given Strean's reflections during the third extra-analytic contact, another lecture. "When I was giving my paper, a couple of times I was really reading to Jane and I felt like a lover reading poetry and trying to seduce his woman." While it is courageous to share such private thoughts, isn't it possible that Jane had already unconsciously perceived that her analyst wished to be her lover, thus stimulating fantasies of sex with Strean and of cunnilingus and mutual masturbation with Strean's wife, whom Jane had recognized at the lecture? Did her erotic fantasies and wish to replace Strean's wife arise spontaneously as a manifestation of her transference position, or had she both introjected Strean's romanticism and succumbed to his wishes?

At the final lecture, at which Jane's "supervisor" participated in a panel discussion, Strean was pleased to see how Jane had matured, and comments, "I experienced Jane as a colleague—an equal of mine. Most of the time I forgot she was in analysis with me. I think she is getting ready (and so am I) for termination." This comment reveals something crucial about Strean's basic attitude. Therapy never ends; instead it is transformed into a peer relationship. Thus neither patient nor analyst will ever have to experience the pain of real separation and loss since both know that they will have ample opportunity for further extra-analytic contacts. And along the same line, there is a sixth extra-analytic contact that has not as yet been mentioned. From what we know of Jane it is easy to surmise that she will read this paper. Having been memorialized in print, her special relationship with her analyst will continue to be gratified and can only serve to perpetuate her unresolved symbiotic state.

The alternative hypothesis I have proposed is that the extra-analytic contacts have served not to intensify current transference positions, but rather to create them. In essence, the patient's symbiotic, phallic-competitive, and oedipal material represents her unconscious responses—not displacements from the past, but actual perceptions and attempts to cope with the real, current stimuli her analyst is introducing through the unconscious acting-out of his own fantasies. Though it is true that an awareness of one's countertransference is essential to the handling of the transference since both are intertwined, my argument is that Strean ignores what he activates in the patient while only emphasizing what the patient activates in him. Since countertransference is an unconscious process, it is liable to be expressed by the analyst indirectly and without his awareness. As Racker (1953, p. 324) notes, "The realization of our relative unconsciousness as regards our own neurotic processes of countertransference should constitute a reason for doubly observing the fulfillment of the rule of abstinence with respect to acting out not only on the part of the patient but also on the part of the analyst. A cure is to be achieved—as Freud repeatedly stressed—only by overcoming the resistances . . ." and I would add, not by joining them. Since countertransference is largely unconscious and liable to be expressed without the analyst being aware of it, and this is not to disregard its positive uses, it is essential to maintain the safeguards that are provided by a rigorous adherence to the basic rules and procedures that Freud discovered, including abstinence, anonymity, and confidentiality. It is primarily through framework deviations that patient and analyst join in misalliances (Langs, 1975b) that serve to seal off and exclude the most primitive and disturbing fears and conflicts of both participants.

When the unconscious, interactional motives of such misalliances are interpreted and understood, providing the potential for constructive introjects, the conflicts motivating them may be resolved, not gratified and left to fester and to erupt again at some later date.

While responding to Strean's view that extra-analytic contacts serve to intensify the orderly, sequential unfolding of transference positions, I have presented an alternative that emphasizes the part that the analyst plays in creating such themes. In actuality the truth lies somewhere in between: In psychoanalysis and psychoanalytic psychotherapy, all is not so neat and orderly. Both patient and analyst influence each other, contributing to the spiraling interactions that are the very essence of the analytic process.

REFERENCES

Arlow, J. "Metaphor in the psychoanalytic situation," *Psychoanalytic Quarterly*, 48, 1979, 363–385.

Dorpat, T. L. "On neutrality," *International Journal of Psychoanalytic Psychotherapy*, 6, 1977, 39–64.

Jones, E. "The theory of symbolism," 1916, in Jones, E. *Papers on Psychoanalysis.* Baltimore: Williams and Wilkins, 1948.

Langs, R. (a) "The therapeutic relationship and deviations in technique," *International Journal of Psychoanalytic Psychotherapy*, 4, 1975, 106–141.

———. (b) "Therapeutic misalliances," *International Journal of Psychoanalytic Psychotherapy*, 4, 1975, 77–105.

———. "Some communicative properties of the bipersonal field," *International Journal of Psychoanalytic Psychotherapy*, 7, 1978, 89–161.

———. "The clinical referents of transference and countertransference," in Langs, R. *Interactions.* New York: Jason Aronson, 1981.

Racker, A. "A contribution to the problem of countertransference," *International Journal of Psycho-Analysis*, 34, 1953, 313–324.

Chapter 3

THE UNANALYZED "POSITIVE TRANSFERENCE" AND THE NEED FOR REANALYSIS

In one of his last writings, "Analysis Terminable & Interminable," Freud[6] enumerated some of the conditions for termination of psychoanalysis: the patient has to have lost all symptoms, inhibitions, and anxieties; repressions have to be undone, and the blank spots caused by infantile amnesia have to be filled out; the childhood history has to be reconstructed and, most important, as a means to these ends, the transference has to be resolved.

Freud, in explicating the conditions for termination, was rather pessimistic about the possibility of helping analytic patients achieve sustained happiness. He enumerated a number of elements that frustrate therapeutic efforts such as the intensity of instincts, ego weakness, the stickiness of the libido, and an unwillingness to give up once cathected objects. He also called attention to the human being's propensity to feel that the "grass is always greener on the other side" in that many men analysands cling to the fantasy for a long time that a woman's life might be better, and many women patients find it difficult to renounce their wish for a penis. Indeed, Freud was so pessimistic about the outcome of analysis that one of his statements about the results of analysis is not too frequently quoted by contemporary analysts, namely, that the aim of analysis is to substitute neurotic suffering with common misery. He even went so far as to aver that psychoanalysis does no more for the neurotic than the normal person accomplishes alone.[6]

Despite Freud's pessimism, he emphasized that the conditions for failure of analysis should be studied more thoroughly. In a paper "On

Reprinted by permission from *The Psychoanalytic Review*, vol. 66, no. 4 (December 1979), pp. 493–506.

the Termination of Analysis," written in 1950, A. Reich[17] stated that Freud's call for studying the conditions of failure had not been heeded to any great extent; in a panel sponsored by the American Psychoanalytic Association in 1963 entitled "Analysis Terminable & Interminable—Twenty-Five Years Later,"[15] several of the participants held convictions similar to the ones Reich held thirteen years before.

One of Freud's brilliant and creative discoveries is the notion of transference: "a universal phenomenon of the human mind, it decides the success of all medical influence, and in fact dominates the whole of each person's relations to his human environment."[7] As Fine has so aptly stated, by understanding the unfolding transference in psychoanalysis, a variety of different types of therapeutic phenomena can be more readily and better understood.[4]

Inasmuch as most psychoanalysts would concur with the notions that every patient has transference reactions, that most patients form a "transference neurosis," and that profound therapeutic changes occur through an analysis of the transference, it would seem to follow that an effective means of accounting for our failures would be to discover those dimensions of the therapeutic situation that maintain a more or less consistent or static transference state.

Some consideration has been given in the literature to some of the variables that seem to maintain a consistent negative transference. In 1923 in "The Ego and the Id," Freud elaborated on "the negative therapeutic reaction."[9] Here Freud noted that many patients who could verbalize all of the explanations and interpretations offered to them still came back over and over again with the same symptoms. He reasoned that there must be some inner force that prevented the utilization of the insights gained, and this force is the superego. Because the strength of the superego is directly related to the strength of the patient's hostility, many authors have been able to corroborate that the negative therapeutic reaction is in many ways a direct product of the negative transference and that if attempts are made to analyze the negative transference (i.e., the patient's efforts to defeat, spite, and render the analyst impotent), then therapeutic progress and emotional maturation can transpire.[4, 13, 20, 21]

In my efforts to evaluate therapeutic progress or lack of it in my own work and in the work of others, I have been extremely impressed with the transference as a powerful tool that seems to clarify many baffling and mysterious phenomena. Two phenomena (one of which I will elaborate in more detail here) that were not completely understood by me for a long time became much more comprehensible with a more thorough understanding of the nuances and vicissitudes of transference productions: (1) the phenomenon of the patient who spends many years in treatment and never gets better until he or she leaves the analyst and then feels quite well after separation, and (2) the phenomenon of the patient who spends many years in treatment, always reports progress, and feels quite well, only to feel miserable soon after leaving the analysis.

Interestingly, the literature has many more case reports of the first situation (i.e., the patient who spends many years in treatment getting nowhere only to report progress and growth after separation). Eissler, in "Notes on the Psychoanalytic Concept of Cure,"[3] reports a case of a woman suffering from erythrophobia (fear of blushing) who for three years fought Eissler on every point; every interpretation was met with denial, and the analyst, as far as the patient was concerned, could not do anything right. Much to Eissler's surprise, eight years later, he received a letter from the patient thanking him for all he had done and telling him that she had received everything she wanted from analysis. Sternbach and Nagelberg have reported on a case in which all attempts to help a woman with her chronic marital problems did not get anywhere until the therapist gave up trying. Suddenly, the patient had better sex than ever before and achieved a state of loving harmony with her spouse that seemed better than that of Romeo and Juliet.[20] Similarly Kesten, in "Learning Through Spite,"[12] reported on a young boy who, despite his high IQ, could not read. He successfully defeated several therapists, and it was only when Kesten gave up trying to help the patient that the boy began to read. These case illustrations demonstrate that when the patient gains some gratification in defeating the therapist and/or begins to feel and experience his or her wishes for a battle with the therapist, certain intractable resistances become partially or fully resolved.

Psychoanalysts are perhaps less reluctant to report on situations that involve patients who seem to get nowhere and then finally do show some gains from the therapy than they are when they have patients who seem to be progressing, but end up nowhere. Perhaps, too, patients who experience an interminable or lengthy honeymoon with their analysts and reexperience their symptomology after the prolonged honeymoon is over, do not go back to the original analyst. Consequently, the phenomenon is not sufficiently observed by one analyst and can only be reported by the second analyst.

I have tentatively concluded from my examination of the few cases reported in the literature that patients who after doing well in analysis experienced a return of the repressed in the form of symptoms, conflicting interpersonal problems, etc., because their seeming idealized positive transferences were negative fantasies that went unanalyzed. In "Incompleteness in 'Successful' Psychoanalyses: A Follow-Up Study"[14] it was reasonably clear that underneath the positive oedipal transference in one case and underneath the positive homosexual transference in another were negative fantasies toward the analyst that went unanalyzed. Similarly, in an article by Schlessinger and Robbins, who conducted follow-up interviews on a successfully analyzed case, the woman patient's flare-up of symptoms could be attributed to a latent transference attitude of disdain.[19] Paralleling the patient who has a negative therapeutic reaction and gets better only after he or she leaves the analyst because positive feelings and fantasies toward the analyst induced anxiety and therefore had to be defended, it is my contention that the patient who forms a seemingly overt love and beloved transference that consistently maintains itself until after the analysis, when there is a flare-up of symptomology, is defending against negative fantasies and negative feelings toward the analyst.

Most if not all patients have, in Arlow and Brenner's words, "a hate-love polarity" that reflects a fusion of libido and aggression.[1] Hate can frequently defend against love and love can defend against hate. Both defensive operations form part of almost every transference and are transference resistances that must be consistently analyzed.

Before we consider some case illustrations of the unanalyzed "positive transference," let us discuss some definitions of it and present some of the reasons why the positive transference is not always so easy to analyze fully. Psychoanalysts usually use the term "positive transference" with two meanings in mind: (1) confidence in the analyst, which leads to what Greenson has called "the therapeutic alliance,"[11] and (2) the erotic portion of the transference which, if not analyzed and genetically reduced to the infantile neurosis, represents a resistance standing in the way of analysis.

Starting with Freud and for many years afterwards, psychoanalysts tended to maintain the view that the whole analysis should take place within a positive transference. Certainly in none of Freud's case illustrations, with the possible exception of Little Hans,[5] where Freud was the supervisor and not the analyst, does one see a full-fledged analysis of the negative aspects of the transference. An examination of case illustrations of some of the other pioneers of psychoanalysis will also reveal this gap. In A. Reich's article "On the Termination of Analysis"[17] referred to earlier, she states:

> Even after the transference has been well analyzed and its important infantile sexual elements have been overcome, even after the neurotic symptoms have been given up, the relationship to the analyst is still not a completely mature one. We have to state that the transference is not completely resolved. The analyst is still an overimportant person for the patient and is still the object of fantasy expectations.

Most analysts have observed what Reich[18] further reports.

> In nearly all cases which I have analyzed, there remained a wish to be loved by the analyst, to keep in contact with him and to build a friendship.

Very often these wishes to be loved, to have continued contact, and to build a friendship with the analyst are gratified rather than analyzed, particularly in those analyses where the parties are training analysts and analysts in training. Yet further analysis of these wishes usually proves them to be derivatives of an early relationship with the parents, mostly oral in nature but acceptable to the ego.[17, 22]

Because the analyst is unknown and unseen, he or she becomes the recipient of the patient's fantasies; the lack of reality surrounding the analyst makes it virtually impossible to see him or her with foibles and limitations. It should therefore not surprise us that this unique figure who listens and gives help can be endowed with special power, special intelligence, and special wisdom. It is easy to ascribe to this figure the omnipotence that the child had attributed to the parents.

Complicating the patient's wish to view the analyst as omnipotent can, of course, be the analyst's wish to be viewed in the same way. Even analysts would rather be loved than hated, and this wish can frequently be rationalized because patients do grow within the framework of a positive transference and positive relationship. I will never forget the first meeting of a psychoanalytic society that I attended after graduating from its training institute. One of the leading members proudly proclaimed at a panel discussion, "In twenty-five years of practicing psychoanalysis, I have rarely had the 'negative transference.'" He obviously did not want to see it.

Although I will deal later with the dynamics of the patient who tends to maintain a fairly constant positive transference throughout the analysis and then reexperiences his or her pathology after termination, I would like first to discuss a couple of case illustrations. Where I have particularly noticed this type of patient are in two types of situations with which I have been intimately connected for many years. The first situation where the unanalyzed positive transference is quite ubiquitous is among social work therapists and their patients; the second is in the so-called training analyses. I tend to think that the nature of much social work therapy, with its emphasis on "giving," "support," and the misuse of the "corrective emotional experience," intensifies the possibilities for the appearance and maintenance of the unanalyzed positive transference. I also believe that the social context of the typical training institute tends to provide enormous fuel for the analyst to be endowed with superordinate powers and for the student in analysis to be experienced as a beloved child.[22] Although these are special situations that make the unanalyzed positive transference more of a possibility, exaggerated examples often do provide good material for research and learning.

CASE ILLUSTRATION NO. 1

Marilyn came for reanalysis after a two-year respite from her previous analytic therapy at a mental health clinic which lasted for five years. When Marilyn was twenty-three years of age and entered her first therapy, she was suffering from migraine headaches, depression, frigidity, intense sado-masochistic battles with men, frequent promiscuity, stuttering and limited job satisfaction. A high school graduate, she seemed much brighter than her limited formal education would imply. Although physically very attractive, she described herself as feeling unappealing, stupid, and not very engaging.

At the time of her reanalysis, Marilyn had just become separated from her second husband. She described both of her husbands as bright, dominating, successful businessmen with whom she was passionately in love at first but grew to resent because of their domination and sadism. She compared her husbands to her father with whom she had a very close relationship and with many erotic overtones. From the ages of four through twelve Marilyn was awakened nightly by father, brought to the bathroom to urinate where she was wiped by him always. Mother was a quiet person who seemed very much in the background.

When Marilyn sought reanalysis she was in a state of active self-hate, depression and surprise. She had a "wonderfully warm analyst who was good looking, patient, kind, and supportive." Because the analyst was the finest man she had ever met and she was convinced of his competence, she found it hard to explain that within three months after termination of the therapy all of her symptoms that she began treatment with had returned.

As Marilyn described her first analysis, it became quite clear that a constant, mildly erotic positive transference maintained itself throughout her five years of treatment. The analyst's interpretations, as much as could be gathered, centered around Marilyn's fear of her aggression towards men because she was intimidated by her father. Although none of the fear of the aggression emerged in the transference in the first analysis, Marilyn was helped to assert herself more with men and she was able to separate from her husband without too much conflict.

During her first treatment her depression had lifted, her stuttering had diminished, her self-esteem had been strengthened, and she went on to a better job. Although her frigidity remained, analyst and patient felt that termination was in order.

As mentioned, Marilyn's symptoms and interpersonal problems returned a few months after termination of her first therapy. Although she tried to do it alone, the need for more analysis began to be felt quite keenly by her after a while. She did not want to go back to her first analyst because "something must have gone wrong."

Within two months after she began her reanalysis, Marilyn became involved in a rather stormy negative transference with her male analyst. When her questions about the analyst's life were turned back to her and her own fantasies requested, when her pleas for advice about how to handle boy friends were frustrated and her own thoughts were sought, Marilyn brought out many hostile and sadistic fantasies towards the analyst. She wanted to take an axe and hit him over the head, saw off his legs and castrate him. She contrasted her second analyst with her first, "He never let me feel empty or vulnerable. He was always there. You feel so separate and never part of me."

Following fantasies and dreams of castrating the analyst, Marilyn's transference became erotic and quite positive. However, when she was able to fantasize an affair with the analyst during the sixth month of analysis, three times a week, the sexual encounters in her fantasies and dreams took place in jungles. The analyst would be chasing her and attempting to subdue her, rape her and then beat her up unmercifully. The patient was to pay a price for a crime and the crime was that at four years old she had stolen her father's penis. This penis was of enormous size—it extended from the bottom of her toes through her mouth. Because Marilyn had part of the analyst's penis in her mouth, she was able to understand for the first time in her life why she stammered and stuttered and further analysis of her incorporated phallic wishes resolved her frigidity.

DISCUSSION

The analysis of Marilyn clearly demonstrates that behind her un-analyzed positive transference were strong phallic and aggressive fantasies, oral incorporative wishes, and penis envy. Because her first analyst "supported" her, answered her questions and gave advice, she felt attached to him symbiotically as if his penis were always part of her. In her reanalysis, when her requests and demands were subjected to investigation, the ensuing frustration released her phallic aggression, her wish to castrate, and her penis envy. Furthermore, when her expressions of erotic wishes were not met with reassurance, as in her first treatment, but were analyzed and her fantasies exposed, after she led the analyst on a chase, she could finally experience a fantasy that had been with her most of her life: she had stolen her father's phallus.

Although there are many dimensions of Marilyn's first and second analyses that have not been discussed, we have enough information to demonstrate how the positive transference was used defensively in the first analysis to protect the patient from expressing and the analyst from hearing Marilyn's sadism, phallic fantasies, and wishes to castrate the analyst.

From the case of Marilyn we learn that an attitude of too much friendliness and support by the analyst which, of course, maintains a positive transference, can deprive the patient of the possibility to dissent. It seems quite clear that a protective and supportive approach, so frequently advocated by so many therapists, turns the analyst into a gratifying parent. The result is that the patient is forced to idealize the analyst. This offers both patient and analyst a passive form of narcissistic joy, but the negative fantasies go underground only to reappear after separation and termination in the form of symptomology.[13, 20]

When the patient is psychologically required to suppress and disguise aggressive reactions to frustration, the resistance against feeling and expressing the hateful parts of the love-hate polarity is, of course, maintained, and the unanalyzed positive transference leads to what is really a negative therapeutic reaction after the termination of analysis. However, when the patient is helped to discharge aggressive fantasies, the ego and superego are freed of their excessive destructiveness and the creative energy of the personality is made available for healthier productivity.[13]

The case of Marilyn, drawn from a social work setting where support, help, and overfeeding are too common, may be compared to the analysis and reanalysis of a student analyst. Before discussing the second case, a few comments are in order on some of the problems that are not infrequent in training analyses.

In an article entitled "Psychological Aspects of Psychoanalytic Training,"[22] I suggested that some of the problems that transpired between Freud and his students (e.g., Jung, Rank, and Adler) are frequently recapitulated in current training analyses.

Every training analyst would probably agree with Freud's statement:

> Whoever is familiar with the nature of neurosis will not be astonished to hear that even a man who is very well able to carry out analysis upon others can behave like any other mortal and be capable of producing violent resistances as soon as he himself becomes the object of analytic investigation.[8]

Yet Freud found it very difficult to tolerate too much dissent, and his wish to be considered the omnipotent God by his psychoanalytic children certainly seems evident. This tendency, which Rado has called a "parentifying spirit,"[16] seems to slip into our psychoanalytic educational systems, where the training analyst becomes a very important person, often the one who decides when the patient (the student analyst) can take courses and begin doing psychoanalytic treatment. I have sometimes wondered how often those training analysts, who are members of institutes where they administer part of their patient's education, give their permission for the student to move ahead when the patient is in the throes of negative transference. Furthermore, even if that were the case, what would happen to that negative transference if the patient received that wonderful gift from the training analyst—the permission to move ahead into a position that is similar to the analyst's.

In the article "On Psychoanalytic Education," Bernfield remarked, "The teachers grow into excessively important personages and most of the students are strongly tempted to ingratiate themselves with them and convince everyone in authority of their powers of compliance."[2]

Unlike most patients, the analyst in training often has contact with the analyst in the classroom and elsewhere. The numerous facts that the student knows about the analyst often compound resistances and may not be fully analyzed. Finally, one has to be aware of the student's frequent attempts to identify with the analyst and with his or her special ideas and interests, behavior, and particular analytic technique. These flattering identifications cannot be accepted at face value, because they always cover some other, deeper analytic content that must be analyzed.[12] About twenty years ago, when I was a student in analytic training, I attended a party given by the training institute. By looking around the room and observing the students' speech patterns and movements, and reflecting on their values, I was able to guess in nine out of ten cases who was in analysis with whom! I am sure this same experiment could be conducted by many others with similar results.

Let us now look at a case of a student in analytic training who required reanalysis.

CASE ILLUSTRATION NO. 2

Jack was a thirty-seven year old man who came for reanalysis one year after he completed a "successful" training analysis. Problems he had worked on and apparently had resolved had reappeared plus new conflicts arose at the time he came for reanalysis. He was unable to cope with the rather severe aggression of his teenage son and daughter, was in constant arguments with colleagues, was very depressed, occasionally impotent and was becoming more and more unsuccessful with his patients. What appeared to trigger his seeking out analysis a second time was that he was finding it increasingly difficult to cope with his female patients' erotic transference fantasies.

Regarding Jack's history, when he was three years of age, his mother died and his father placed him in an orphanage in the South never to see him again. He had virtually no real memories of either parent but described the personnel at the various orphanages and institutions that he attended as punitive, sadistic, and rejecting. Although he was a good student he was often teased and scapegoated by peers. Occasionally an aunt and uncle visited him but the contact was minimal.

Jack participated in a lot of group sex at the institutions, both homosexual and heterosexual. Although he usually felt like an odd ball and was frequently depressed, he graduated college, medical school and completed his psychiatric residency with flying colors.

Jack described his first analyst as "the father I never had. He was warm, kind, loving and encouraging." He spent a lot of time in the first analysis mourning his mother and father and damning the people at the orphanages and institutions. This relieved him of his depression, raised his self-esteem, and he began to feel quite positively about his marriage, family life and work. As far as could be determined the conflicts that evolved during his childhood and teen age years, though discussed quite thoroughly in his analysis, were not relived in the transference. His analyst was consistently experienced as the warm and tender father and mother.

When Jack started his reanalysis he focused on his inability to cope with his women patients' erotic fantasies. He singled out one patient whom he contrasted very sharply with his wife. The patient was admiring, tender, and loving in contrast to his wife who was experienced as cold and rejecting. Jack didn't know what to do with his sexual excitement and narcissistic joy and asked the analyst what to do. When his helplessness was called to his attention, he responded with intense depression which masked his resentment. He began to have masochistic fantasies involving the analyst who scorned the patient for being incompetent. When the patient asked and even begged for reassurance and wanted to be told that he was competent as a professional, the analyst suggested that he explore his doubts.

This brought to the fore the negative transference. Jack began to experience the analyst as the rejecting figures from his past who didn't care. He cried and yelled at the analyst for being a tormentor. Then he acted out with this woman patient by kissing her and told the analyst to arrange to throw him out of the training institute and the profession. When his strong masochistic wishes and wishes for punishment were brought to his attention, Jack was able to recall masturbatory fantasies where he was beaten and maimed. "Maybe after that, some father figure would love me," he reported.

Further analysis of Jack's masochistic fantasies stimulated homosexual fantasies towards the analyst. Slowly Jack began to recognize his strong identification with his female patients and was able to realize that what they wanted from him he wanted from his analyst.

As Jack's negative transference was further analyzed, as his masochism and homosexual fantasies were discharged, he became more confident in his work, in his marriage, and in his family life.

DISCUSSION

Although Jack, like Marilyn, is still in treatment, we can learn from both of them that their positive transferences in their first analyses served as powerful resistances. Gratified and reinforced by their first analysts, the negative fantasies and infantile wishes went underground during their first analyses, only to reappear after termination in the form of neuroses and character problems.

Although we might refer to Marilyn and Jack's responses to their first analyses as "positive therapeutic reactions," I do not see too much difference between these patients and those who respond with the so-called negative therapeutic reaction. Jack, Marilyn, and the patients with negative therapeutic reactions are all masochistic patients with corrupt and punitive superegos. All have strong resistances against the expression of aggressive fantasies, and usually all of them have strong narcissistic and omnipotent fantasies. I suspect that the major difference in the course of the therapy between those who are given the label negative therapeutic reaction and those who seem to react positively in therapy and negatively later is that in the latter the analyst gratifies, supports, and encourages. The aggression gets more repressed, and the more conscious positive feelings toward the analyst carry the therapy. Jack and Marilyn's first therapeutic relationships might be compared to those that an angry child has with intimidated parents. Each time the child complains or asks for indulgence, the parents capitulate. The aggression that the child feels is never verbalized, because he or she gets all the indulgence needed. However, if the parent is not available or does not gratify the child, we can see temper tantrums and other forms of maladaptive behavior. When Jack's and Marilyn's therapists were unavailable (i.e., when the patients could no longer be indulged), their aggression mounted and their unresolved infantile conflicts came out in the form of symptomology.

Just as the negative therapeutic reaction can be resolved by working with the resistances against aggression and sadism, so was this true of Jack and Marilyn. I would suggest this whether the patient idealizes the analyst and seems to get better only to have the symptoms reappear later or whether we see a more frank negative therapeutic reaction; in both there is a denial of destructive impulses, a strong wish for a blissful symbiotic state with the parents, and a hope that the omnipotent parent will rescue the patient.

In summary, the positive and negative transferences are always in operation in all analyses. If we reinforce or neglect either the positive or negative transference, the patient tends to continue the regression and may use objects in his or her life outside the analysis to act out unanalyzed fantasies and not mature. Ambivalence toward the analyst is always there and must always be subjected to a comprehensive analysis.

As Freud said in "The History of the Psychoanalytic Movement,"[10] any attempt to shy away from self-examination and a comprehensive analysis of the patient's total metapsychology signifies abandonment of psychoanalysis and defection from it. His conclusion in that article is also worth repeating.

> Men are strong as long as they represent a strong idea; they become powerless when they oppose it. I can only conclude with the wish that fate may grant an untroubled ascension to all who have been discommoded by their sojourn in the underworld of psychoanalysis. May it be vouchsafed to the others to carry their work in the depths peacefully to an end.

REFERENCES

1. Arlow, J., and C. Brenner. *Psychoanalytic Concepts and the Structural Theory.* New York: International Universities Press, 1964.

2. Bernfeld, S. "On Psychoanalytic Education," *Psychoanalytic Quarterly,* Vol. 31, 1962, pp. 453–482.

3. Eissler, K. "Notes on the Psychoanalytic Concept of Cure," *Psychoanalytic Study of the Child,* Vol. 18. New York: International Universities Press, 1963, pp. 424–463.

4. Fine, R. *The Healing of the Mind.* New York: David McKay, 1971.

5. Freud, S. "Analysis of a Phobia in a Five Year Old Boy" (1909), *Standard Edition,* Vol. 10. London: Hogarth Press, 1955.

6. ———. "Analysis. Terminable and Interminable" (1937), *Standard Edition,* Vol. 23. London: Hogarth Press, 1964.

7. ———. "An Autobiographical Study" (1925), *Standard Edition,* Vol. 20. London: Hogarth Press, 1959.

8. ———. "On Beginning the Treatment, Further Recommendations on the Technique of Psychoanalysis" (1913), *Standard Edition,* Vol. 12. London: Hogarth Press.

9. ———. "The Ego and the Id" (1923), *Standard Edition,* Vol. 19. London: Hogarth Press, 1961.

10. ———. "On the History of the Psychoanalytic Movement" (1914), *Standard Edition,* Vol. 14. London: Hogarth Press, 1959.

11. Greenson, R. "The Working Alliance and the Transference Neurosis," *Psychoanalytic Quarterly,* Vol. 34, 1965, pp. 155–181.

12. Kesten, J. "Learning Through Spite," In H. Strean (ed.), *New Approaches in Child Guidance.* Metuchen, N.J.: Scarecrow Press, 1970.

13. Nagelberg, L. "The Meaning of Help in Psychotherapy," *The Psychoanalytic Review,* Vol. 46, No. 4, 1959, pp. 50–63.

14. Oremland, J.; K. Blacker; and H. Norman. "Incompleteness in 'Successful' Psychoanalyses: A Follow-Up Study," *Journal of the American Psychoanalytic Association,* Vol. 23, 1975, pp. 819–844.

15. Pfeffer, A. "Analysis Terminable & Interminable—Twenty Five Years

Later," *Journal of the American Psychoanalytic Association*, Vol. 11, No. 1, 1963, pp. 131–142.

16. Rado, S. "Adaptational Development of Psychoanalytic Therapy," *Psychoanalysis of Behavior*. New York: Grune & Stratton, 1956.

17. Reich, A. "On the Termination of Analysis" (1950), *Psychoanalytic Contributions*. New York: International Universities Press, 1973.

18. ———. "Special Types of Resistance in Training Analysis" (1965), *Psychoanalytic Contributions*. New York: International Universities Press, 1973.

19. Schlessinger, N., and F. Robbins. "The Psychoanalytic Process: Recurrent Patterns of Conflict and Changes in Ego Functions," *Journal of the American Psychoanalytic Association*, Vol. 23, No. 4, 1975, pp. 761–782.

20. Sternbach, O., and L. Nagelberg. "On the Patient-Therapist Relationship in Some Untreatable Cases," In H. Strean (ed.), *New Approaches in Child Guidance*. Metuchen, N.J.: Scarecrow Press, 1970.

21. Strean, H. *The Experience of Psychotherapy*. Metuchen, N.J.: Scarecrow Press, 1973.

22. ———. "Some Psychological Aspects of Psychoanalytic Training," *The Psychoanalytic Review*, Vol. 52, No. 4, 1965, pp. 41–50; also in H. Strean (ed.), *Crucial Aspects of Psychotherapy*. Metuchen, N.J.: Scarecrow Press, 1976.

DISCUSSANT: JUDITH R. FELTON

I.

A review of the literature indicates that termination criteria are formulated in terms of improvement of symptomatology, the judgment and intuition of the analyst, ego functions and relations with others, delay of gratification and increased frustration tolerance, and increased capacity of success and pleasure in work and love.[1] Although object constancy, improved self esteem and self concept, and capacity for pleasure in one's leisure time (i.e. play) are mentioned less frequently, they are implied because they usually accompany the other criteria.

Discussions with colleagues reveal a variety of methods for handling the termination phase. Some analysts prefer experimental interruptions to "test the waters." Others prefer a weaning procedure. Still others continue the fundamental rule through the last hour.

Further, based on the length of their patients' analyses, another group appears to avoid termination. In these instances, it is possible that a countertransference—the analyst's personal need for the analysand, and/or the analyst's own unhealthy narcissism—is precluding an appropriate termination. Alternately, inappropriately long analyses may be the result of confusing the specific goals of treatment with longterm life goals.[2] Regardless of unconscious or intended methods employed for termination, what is significant is that countertransference criteria do play a role in this phase.

No less significant in the area of termination criteria is the analyst who (as exemplified by Dr. Strean's plea for a more thorough and balanced approach to the analysis of both the positive and negative transferences) uses the state of the transference as a primary indicator for termination. Unfortunately, there are inherent problems with the transference as an indicator for termination. First, it is difficult to appraise important unfulfilled wishes which may persist through and beyond termination. Second, one truly knows the transference reverberations only after the event of termination has actually occurred.[3] In addition, most analysts would agree that one can work only with those conflicts which are active in the person's life at the time of the analysis, and that transference resolution usually continues in the post-analytic period. Thus, some conflicts will not be manifested in transference developments.

Yet despite these rather general limitations in the concept itself, Dr. Strean's paper is instructive and very important. He has presented a useful and highly specific reminder for a thorough analysis of the transference. This is rarely mentioned in the literature.

II.

The question of the position in the life phase is raised by the case presentation of Jack. It is not clear how much time elapsed between the analysand's first analysis and his reanalysis. It is also not clear whether, given Jack's level of professional training and his probable lack of experience (both in life and in terms of the type of psychiatric practice maintained), he could have manifested the negative transference issues in his first analysis. Dr. Strean's implication that the first analyst may have ignored the negative transference may be true. But it may also be true that the conflicts active in Jack's life were of a nature that required a continuing analysis before the transference could reveal the later scenario of analyst as tormentor, and Jack as victim and lover.

A relevant example from my own practice is Sharon B., who at the time of her first analysis was a highly intelligent woman of twenty-three, unmarried and pre-orgasmic. During her first analysis, which lasted five years, she was able to work through her work inhibitions, interpersonal difficulties with her father and young stepmother, childhood neuroses related to the untimely death of her narcissistic and depriving mother, an eating disorder, and her sexual dysfunction. After an interim of five years, Sharon B. returned to me for another analysis at the age of thirty-three.

While at the time of her first analysis Ms. B. had met all of the important criteria for termination, we had not been able to work through her competitive strivings and lesbian wishes toward me beyond a moderate point. Such conflicts were not manifested in an intense way until the second analysis. And, unless this author had been of the school of analysts who believe in provoking and manipulating the transference, there was no way at that time there could have been a resolution of the deeper hostilities.

One might disagree that the analysand should not have been terminated but kept in treatment for another five years. However, such a decision would seem to be more reflective of a countertransference indicator and reminiscent of therapy as a "substitute for living," rather than as an "aid to living." Later, after the patient became a columnist for a prestigious international publication in her field and had also married, there were life phase developments which made it possible for a deeper and more thorough analysis of the heretofore insufficiently analyzed positive transference.

In Dr. Strean's case example, the fact that Jack sought another analyst, rather than his former analyst, may well be evidence that the first analyst was too much the "Good Parent" instead of an empathic, neutral analyst. However, it would be interesting and helpful to know if in fact the patient sought his second analyst because of other factors, such as financial considerations, relocation, or unavailability of the analyst. Further, is it always a sign of a lack in the analyst or the patient when she or he chooses a different analyst for reanalysis? It may instead be a sign of health and positive change.

III.

The third aspect of this discussion centers on definition clarity and narcissism. Although Dr. Strean tends to freely interchange the wish to love and be loved with the wish for omnipotence, a differentiation leads to increased clarity.

In my experience, when the patient continues to overidealize her or his analyst, the inevitable consequence is envy and self devaluation. Historically, there has been the expectation that at termination the analysand would show emotional and interpersonal freedom in relation to the analyst, and no longer be uncomfortable in front of the analyst.[4]

It follows then, that when the patient continues the need to idealize the analyst in the search for an omnipotent parent—or the need for the projective identification of her or his own pathological narcissism onto the figure of the analyst—she or he continues to be self hating and not fully competent to find pleasure in work, love, and play. This corroborates Dr. Strean's position and is really the heart of the matter.

Dr. Strean could not be more correct when he states that the wish to love and be loved should not be overemphasized to preclude the wish to hate and be hated. But in addition to these drive psychology issues, we also need to examine theories in the area of ego psychology, developmental arrests, the psychology of the self, and the pathology of narcissism.

With this body of knowledge one should add, rather than substitute, the exploration of the predominant ego defenses, the re-enactment of old scripts in current self and object relations, and the specific character patterns of the person. By referring not only to the literature of classic psychoanalysis, but also to that of ego psychology, object relations theory, and self psychology for in-depth investigation, the analyst may then discover a more complete understanding of the patient's self aggrandizement and arrogance, as well as the corollaries of self-denigration and envy.

IV.

Because of the prevalence of the number of women in treatment, and because of women's socialization in a double standard society which encourages their devaluation (and sometimes overidealization), Dr. Strean's focus on the importance of resolving the unanalyzed positive transference is an especially useful and timely concept. Therefore, with the case of Marilyn, Dr. Strean offers an excellent introduction to the special problems of women.

It is reported that 89 percent of the 24,000 members of the American Psychiatric Association are male, but the majority of their patients, estimated at 80 percent, are female.[5] While the profession of psychoanalysis may vary somewhat from this statistical estimate, this trend is corroborated by most of the analysts in my sphere. In a society with a double standard, it is not unusual for women to have internalized a self-devaluating attitude which is accompanied by an unhealthy tendency to look for strength in others—particularly men—rather than themselves. This is further complicated by the reality that they have to rely on men for assistance at times, since men are more often in positions to facilitate their development (for example, in careers).

With regard to the analysis of Marilyn, a feminist analyst would take issue with the apparent overemphasis on her erotic life. Although Dr. Strean's careful analysis of the incorporated phallic wishes resolved the patient's sexual dysfunction, there is concern that without sufficient exploration of her character structure, and the re-enactment of the character patterns and critical events from her childhood in her current self and object relations, Marilyn will have only discharged and partially resolved her phallic aggressive wishes. Then she will remain stunted in her growth at a pregenital level with a regressive victim—castrator imago projected onto the screen of her self concept.

My recommendation would be for further analysis of Marilyn's alternations between her intensely erotic and positive wishes and the intensely violent and animalistic environment projected into the analytic environment. Unless the analyst has unresolved countertransference difficulties in this area, it ought to be possible to diminish and modulate, if not resolve and eradicate, her vacillating and extreme transference behaviors. Marilyn's seeming preoccupation with the sexual aspect of her life requires balancing from the analyst with a focus on the intellectual, cognitive, and character aspects of her life. Sometimes we analysts fall into the "trap" that love is all important, especially for women. We need to remember that the woman's internalization of the ego ideal and superego in the family has too often left her underdeveloped in other important areas.

It is possible to disagree with this position, however. Other analysts believe that women are appropriately frustrated in love relations because many men have been socialized to not find love sufficiently important.

As one of my colleagues stated recently, "More men should get on the couch and learn to love a little more, but since that is harder, women will just go on continuing to adapt and convince themselves that intellect, cognition, and character equal the thrills of romance, love, and sex."

In conclusion, Dr. Strean has stimulated my commentary on termination criteria, issues of the life phase, definition clarity, and special concerns in the analyses of women as they related to the unanalyzed positive transference. Dr. Strean has corrected an omission in the literature by raising this problem for reanalysis. This has led to a critical re-evaluation of the need for a thorough and balanced approach to the analysis of both the positive and negative transferences.

REFERENCES

1. Firestein, S. *Termination in Psychoanalysis*, New York: International Universities Press, 1978.

2. Ticho, E. "Termination of Psychoanalysis: Treatment Goals, Life Goals," *Psychoanalytic Quarterly*, 1972, 41:315–333.

3. Firestein, S. *op. cit.*, p. 230.

4. Ferenczi, S. "The Problem of Termination of Psychoanalysis" (1927), In *Final Contributions to Psychoanalysis*, New York: Basic Books, 1955.

5. "Update of 'Psychiatrists for E.R.A.' Boycott of A.P.A.'s New Orleans Meeting," *Behavior Today*, March 2, 1981, 12:8, p. 2.

DISCUSSANT: RONALD S. SUNSHINE

Dr. Strean calls our attention to a clinical phenomenon relatively undiscussed in the psychoanalytic literature, "the unanalyzed positive transference," and proceeds to analyze its effect in the analytic situation. He refers to two groups: patients in therapeutic analysis, and students in analytic institutes who are in training analysis.

I agree with Dr. Strean's criticism of social work education. I would extend that same criticism to the fields of psychology and psychiatry. Where the social worker tends to be too "feeding" in terms of support, the psychiatrist who readily dispenses medication actually does "feed" the patient, gratifying oral dependent wishes and joins the patient's resistances to understanding and working through the transferences.

In my own practice 80 percent of the patients currently in treatment have had from one to five prior therapeutic experiences. As far as I was able to determine from a careful examination of the patients' reports of their prior therapeutic experiences most of their previous therapists were not analytically trained. Some of these patients had negative therapeutic reactions in their prior therapies. However, a substantial number did experience what Dr. Strean refers to as "the unanalyzed 'positive transference'."

The first illustrative case which Dr. Strean presents is that of Marilyn. From the point of view of oedipal phase dynamics of this patient, I would agree with Dr. Strean's analysis. However, I view the patient's transference to both the first analyst and her transference to Dr. Strean as the patient's attempt to defend herself against her preoedipal longing for her mother. The material presented indicates that the patient had deep oedipal conflicts. Contrasted with Marilyn's experience with her "distant" mother was her eroticized relationship with her father. Dr. Strean reports that she had a very close, highly eroticized relationship with her father.

We are told that her father awakened her nightly during the ages from four to twelve years, brought her to the bathroom to urinate, and that he always wiped her. There is little information as to where the mother was when this was taking place. We are not told what the relationship was like between father and mother. We can conjecture from the above information that the father gratified many of his libidinal wishes through his relationship with his daughter. Of crucial importance in all of this is the effect that it had upon the patient. She may very well have felt that in her competition with her mother for her father that she was the victor.

Both of her husbands were "bright, dominating, successful businessmen with whom she was passionately in love at first but grew to resent their domination and sadism." It seems to me that the choice of these men in the first place stemmed from a strong unconscious wish for her father. And the divorces, in part, were necessitated by the fears of actually having achieved the oedipal victory: marrying father.

In order to understand the dynamics of the patient's transference gratification to the first analyst we need to refer to the preoedipal attachment to her withdrawn mother. The attachment, in my view, can be reconstructed by our analysis of the patient's comments about her first analyst, and the special meaning for her of the unanalyzed positive transference.

We are told that, although the patient is physically very attractive, she describes herself as feeling "unappealing, stupid, and not very engaging." Upon beginning her second analysis she was "in a state of active self-hate, depression and surprise." She described her first analyst as "wonderfully warm, . . . kind and supportive." She contrasts him with Dr. Strean in the following way: "He [the first analyst] never let me feel empty or vulnerable. He was always there. You [Strean] feel so separate and never part of me." The patient was in a panic-rage transference reaction to Dr. Strean. He became the "bad mother," not telling her what to do, letting her feel empty and vulnerable, whereas her first analyst, the "good mother," never let her feel "empty or vulnerable." Her wishes for a symbiotic merging with a loving, nurturing mother were, in my opinion, gratified by her first analyst. It seems to me that Dr. Strean was not perceived by the patient, initially, as the erotically involved father, but rather as the distant, separate, withdrawn mother. Her feelings of anger, despair, emptiness, and panic were a reliving of her relationship with her mother. Beneath the patient's manifest transference to Dr. Strean as father was the powerful latent transference of the distant, withdrawn mother. In her eroticized transference to both of her analysts, she was struggling to obtain the longed-for love of her mother through her relationship to her father. How could she not have eroticized the transference, given the nature of her relationship with her father from the age of four to twelve?

I am in agreement with Dr. Strean's analysis of the phallic and oedipal stage dimensions of his patient's unanalyzed positive transference and of her wishes to castrate her second analyst. However, in order for us to fully understand and analyze the defensive functions of the unanalyzed positive transference, I consider it essential that we examine the oral stage dimension. *There is always an oral, as well as an oedipal, component to the unanalyzed positive transference.*

We are told that the patient's mother was "a quiet person who seemed very much in the background." The patient's presenting symptoms in her first therapeutic experience seem to indicate that she experienced severe disappointment and frustration in her relationship with her mother. Her conscious wish to castrate the second male analyst who was "so separate and never part of me" is reflective of the patient's unconscious oral stage hatred of her withdrawn and distant mother.

It is essential that we analyze the patient's manifest sexual fantasies and experiences. When submitted to careful analysis we find that they can be used to express unconscious aggressive, dependent, homosexual, and oedipal wishes as well as superego conflicts.

The erotic longings for the analyst, which manifestly contain the oedipal wishes, are often used to conceal the latent wish for the mother. I would have asked the patient to reveal all the elaborate details of her fantasies. In effect, we ask the patient to tell us what an affair with the analyst would be like. After the patient reports her romantic sexual fantasies, she should be asked by the analyst, "What would happen after that?" or "What then?" In my experience what is uncovered in the patient's fantasies is the wish to reject the analyst after having had sex with him. This can be viewed as a seduce-and-reject mechanism. The patient's fantasies reveal two dynamics: her angry wishes to take revenge on men and her underlying attachment to her mother.

The patient, in my opinion, experienced her first analyst and the unanalyzed positive transference as a blissful union with a good mother, where she was loved, admired and fed. When she left her analyst, she experienced the same panic that a child experiences when the loss of mother occurs: anger, depression, despair, hopelessness and self-hatred. In short, for the child the world falls apart. I agree with Dr. Strean that, in this case, the unanalyzed positive transference was used defensively to ward off the negative transference toward the father.

In addition, I believe that the transference to the first analyst was used by the patient to gratify a deep unconscious longing for the mother. In one sense, we could say that, because the patient's needs for a gratifying mothering experience were not met in her childhood, and because of the overly eroticized nature of her relationship to her father, she was unable successfully to move towards men. The patient unconsciously tried to obtain her mother's love from her relationship with men. Marilyn's case is illustrative of how both oral and oedipal wishes co-exist and how oedipal wishes can be used as a defense against oral wishes.

Furthermore it appears to me that her first analyst's failure to analyze her frigidity may have been perceived by the patient in the transference both as her mother's wish for her not to acknowledge or to use her vagina and her father's wish for her not to have other men. The analyst's neglect of the frigidity may have been due to a countertransferential wish not to have this attractive woman love anyone other than himself.

It is the responsibility of the analyst to analyze all aspects of his patient's problems. Where this is not done as in the case of Marilyn's first analysis, it results in an incomplete analysis and is indicative of the analyst's unresolved countertransference.

In the second case discussed by Dr. Strean, the case of Jack, a student in psychoanalytic training, he offers us a rich piece of clinical material and brings to the fore a central issue of psychoanalytic training—the numerous conflicts involved in the training analysis. Jack's case is not unusual. He is a student in analytic training who is part child attempting through his personal analysis to resolve his inner conflicts, and part adult attempting to help his patients to resolve their problems. This perception of the analyst in training as a patient, somewhat further along the continuum of psychic well being than his own patients reduces the distance between the two. Where the traditional psychiatric diagnostic model is used, namely that of the sick patient in relation to the healthy analyst, it often serves unconsciously to increase the analyst's distance from his patient. I also believe that this is one significant unconscious factor in the resistance of analysts to being reanalyzed. [1]

In the illustrative case of Jack, Dr. Strean reports that he came for reanalysis one year after terminating his training analysis. Some of the presenting problems in the beginning of the second analysis were the severe aggression of Jack's teenage son and daughter, Jack's anger towards his colleagues, and his sexual impotence. It was hard for me to see, from Dr. Strean's description of the training analysis, what meaningful analytic work was accomplished. There was no working through via the transference of Jack's anger, dependency problems, his heterosexual and homosexual conflicts, and his punitive superego. Jack's anger towards his colleagues could be viewed as a displacement and splitting of the transference reaction to his first analyst and a reliving of his hatred towards his father and the personnel at the various orphanages and institutions where he was sent as a child.

The failure of his first analytic experience must have re-awakened in Jack many early childhood feelings of anger, despair, disillusionment, fear and panic. His lack of success with his patients stems from this same constellation of conflicts and feelings. He must have resented his patients' longing to be taken care of and loved, particularly since these wishes in himself had been frustrated and neglected in his first analysis.

I would have approached Jack's request for advice about what to do with his sexual excitement and longing for his patient somewhat differently than Dr. Strean. I would not have interpreted the patient's feeling of helplessness at that time, but would have asked that he tell me the specific details of his fantasy concerning the patient with whom he was infatuated. What was Jack's fantasy of how his patient would respond to his kissing her? How did he think it would affect her therapy? What did he fantasize would happen after he kissed her? How would their relationship change? Did Jack fantasize having an affair with his patient, and if so what would be the outcome of the affair? What was his fantasy of what would happen to his marriage if he had an affair? What did Jack fantasize would be his analyst's thoughts and feelings about his kissing a patient? I would have asked these questions in order to help make Jack's unconscious fantasies about his patient and Dr. Strean conscious, and therefore possibly helping him avoid acting out with his patient.

Jack's erotic yearnings for his patient were overdetermined. He was going to exploit and mistreat his patient as he himself had been mistreated by his first analyst, his father, and his childhood caretakers. Jack saw women as being either good or bad. His wife was the "cold, rejecting" woman and his patient the "admiring, tender and loving" woman. His anger and wishes to hurt and disappoint women were reflected in his impotence and lack of interest in sex with his wife and his acting out with his patient.

I agree with Dr. Strean's interpretation of Jack's strong identification with his female patients and of his homosexual transference. There is, however, an additional transference dimension to Jack's behavior with his patient which should be considered. In kissing his patient Jack was acting out his feeling of hatred for Dr. Strean through a defiance and spite transference. He was going to break a basic rule of analysis: an analyst does not have physical or sexual contact with his patients. In kissing his patient Jack was acting out powerful feelings of anger and wishes for revenge against Dr. Strean which genetically were derivatives of his feelings about his father and first analyst. Jack had a strong unconscious wish to defeat Dr. Strean, to prove him a failure as an analyst. These wishes must have been terribly frightening to Jack. He projected his wishes to Dr. Strean when he fantasized that Dr. Strean would throw him out of the training institute and the profession. In my view this fantasy expressed his wish to defeat Dr. Strean by denying him the achievement and pleasure of seeing Jack resolve his conflicts.

Jack acted out with his patient because his ego was able to deny feelings of healthy anxiety and guilt. This is to be contrasted with the fact that Jack simultaneously had an exceedingly harsh and punitive superego. The dichotomy exists due to a split in the ego. This phenomenon is seen in patients with a psychopathic personality structure.

The technical issue in the treatment and analysis of these patients is for the analyst to consistently point out to the patient that he lacks healthy feelings of anxiety and guilt in those situations where such feelings would be appropriate. In the treatment of these patients the analyst must have a deep understanding of the patient's early development and an appreciation of the power and tenacity of the infantile ego's primitive defense mechanisms. The analyst needs to be patient with these patients since it takes an extremely long time for them to give up their powerful infantile defenses. The unanalyzed positive transference perpetuates the split in the ego thereby maintaining a weakened ego structure which correspondingly results in increased aggression towards oneself and others, severe sexual conflicts, and an extremely harsh superego.

There is one statement which Dr. Strean made with which I am in disagreement. He said: "Freud found it very difficult to tolerate too much dissent and his wish to be considered the omnipotent God by his psychoanalytic children certainly seems evident." History does not corroborate this statement.

Freud arouses in both psychoanalysts and the lay public powerful emotional reactions. He is often seen as either a God or a Devil. In reality he was an extraordinary man, a genius who developed the psychology of man which, for the first time in the history of mankind, provided us with the knowledge and technique to help individuals to overcome their emotional pain and suffering. His fundamental discoveries are confirmed each time a patient and analyst meet.

It is, in my opinion, incorrect to say that Freud wished to be viewed as an omnipotent God. Objectivity necessitates that we carefully differentiate between Freud's personal attachments and conflicts with some of his followers and his role as the founding father of a new science which was bitterly and irrationally attacked by the medical and scientific communities of his day. There is a tendency to deny or underestimate the campaign of contemptuous primitive hatred and ostracism which was directed against Freud and the new science of psychoanalysis. Psychoanalysis was born into an extremely unreceptive and hostile environment. Freud functioned both as mother and father to his newly born science. He nourished it by developing and expanding the theoretical and technical foundations of psychoanalysis and simultaneously he sought to protect it and provide a safe passage from the numerous individuals and groups—medical, scientific, and lay—which wanted to destroy psychoanalysis. Ernest Jones,[2] in Volume II of his excellent biography of Freud, devotes a chapter to describing the irrational opposition to Freud and psychoanalysis.

It is therefore understandable that Freud's overriding concern throughout his lifetime was for the survival of his new science, psychoanalysis. The following statement reflects Freud's life long concern. "Analysis undeniably still has its enemies. I do not know whether they have means at their command for stopping the activities of analysts. I do not think it very likely; but one can never feel too secure."[3]

Freud was a strong man who developed and represented strong ideas; ideas which many medical doctors, scientists, and lay people in his time found to be very frightening and therefore responded with extraordinary contempt and hatred. Freud also encountered strong resistances and opposition to his views from his followers. This is most clearly illustrated by the powerful opposition by many medical analysts to Freud's views on lay analysis. Freud strongly supported lay analysis. He equated the survival and flourishing of psychoanalysis directly to the acceptance of lay analysis.

The extent of the medical analysts' opposition to Freud's views on lay analysis is seen in Freud's statement that ". . . the internal development of psychoanalysis is everywhere preceding contrary to my intentions away from lay analysis and becoming a pure medical speciality, and I regard this as fateful for the future of analysis."[4] Freud dealt with their opposition by rational discussion of the issue and by an analysis of the underlying resistances of doctors to lay analysis, as can be seen in his observation that their opposition to lay analysis was ". . . the last mask of the resistance against psychoanalysis and the most dangerous of all."[5]

There is no evidence available to support the view that Freud behaved in a manner which indicated that he wished to be considered an omnipotent God by his followers. That he encouraged independent thinking can be seen from the introductory paragraph of a letter Freud wrote to Edoardo Weiss, an Italian analyst who asked Freud's advice on the treatment of a patient. "It is very difficult to assume the responsibility in such a case. Therefore I must expressly refuse to advise you and I will tell you only how the case looks to me and what I would do according to my experience, without putting you under any obligation."[6]

In his paper Dr. Strean refers to the historic conflicts involved in the training analysis of analytic candidates. He calls our attention to the manifold conflicts in a training analysis where the training analyst is called upon to evaluate and to pass judgment on his candidate-patient's advancement in the institute. He indicates that this fuels the development of a "flattering identification"—transference—and that it intensifies the splitting of the transference to instructors, supervisors, and peers.

I am in full agreement with him, and research substantiates these views. In a recent study by Shapiro[7] on how frequently and for what reasons analysts undergo a reanalysis, a significant number of analysts who completed a training analysis cited the following problems in the training analysis:

> . . . difficulties arising from the training context of the analysis, severe countertransference problems on the part of the training analyst, and severe characterologic difficulties. A significantly larger number of the twice analyzed reported severe or major characterologic difficulty during their training analysis . . . dissatisfaction, however, seemed a spur, with 40 percent of those unhappy with their first analysis trying again . . . 13 of the 24 reanalyzed psychoanalysts returned to their former analysts . . . of the 11 who chose a different second analyst, seven had experienced unsatisfactory tranining analyses with their first analyst, with nine reporting serious and unresolved problems, eight reporting severe or major character problems, and one reporting "severe symptomatic problems." Eight of the 11 analysts cited difficulties that were ascribed to the training analyst or training context of the analysis . . . half of the respondents reported that they "experienced a sense of greater freedom (in the second analysis) as compared to the training analysis."[8]

In evaluating the reports of the analysts who participated in his study, Shapiro concludes that "the general impression may be accurate that training analyses tend to be pallid as compared to the emotionally heated transference reactions that often arise in analysis under nontraining conditions."[9]

The primary requirement for anyone who wishes to become an analyst is his own personal analysis. The analyst must have experienced deep personal analysis himself in order to prepare himself for the rigorous demands of his profession. He must free himself from his own conflicts, in order, as Greenson states, "that he be able to meet the unknown in the patients he treats, the strange and bizarre, with an open mind and not with aversion or anxiety."[10] Fine feels that the decisive factor in the therapeutic success of the analyst's personal analysis is the warmth and maturity of the analyst's own personality.[11] With these goals in mind, and with an understanding of the paramount importance of the analyst's personal analysis, I feel that all obstacles in an institute's training program which interfere with the personal analysis should be removed.

Analytic theory is often used defensively by students in analytic training. They often use the analytic defense of analyzing others as a resistance to being analyzed themselves. Some analytic training institutes further complicate the situation, and interfere with the confidentiality of a student's analysis, by requiring the training analyst to submit a report on the suitability of his analysand for advancement in the analytic training program. It seems to me that to ask the student-patient to incorporate his analyst as a reality superego figure through the course of his training analysis activates the danger that this kind of training analysis may defeat its own purpose. As Freud told us, "analysis can take place only in a situation where there is an adequate analytic atmosphere, that is, the analyst is non-critical, continually accepting, taking no role and uniformly consistent."[12] The training analysis must be conducted in this type of analytic atmosphere.

In conclusion, I feel that Dr. Strean's paper is an important contribution to the furthering of our understanding of the transference resistance phenomenon as we experience them both clinically and in our training institutes. His paper provides us with a valuable stimulus for research and thought.

REFERENCES

1. Sunshine, R. S. "Some Observations on the Analyst's Resistances to Re-Analysis," presented at the New York Center for Psychoanalytic Training's Symposium on Re-Analysis, New York Academy of Medicine, April 10, 1976.

2. Jones, E. *The Life and Work of Sigmund Freud.* Vol. II. New York: Basic Books Inc., 1955.

3. Freud, S. "The Question of Lay Analysis" (1926), *Standard Edition.* London: Hogarth Press, Vol. 20, 1959.

4. Jones, E. *The Life and Work of Sigmund Freud,* Vol. III. New York: Basic Books Inc., 1957.

5. Ibid.

6. Weiss, E. *Sigmund Freud as a Consultant.* New York: International Medical Book Corporation, 1970.

7. "Re-Analysis of the Analyst—How Often and Why," *Psychiatric News,* April 3, 1974, p. 14.

8. Ibid.

9. Shapiro, Daniel. "The Analyst's Own Analysis," *Journal of the American Psychoanalytic Association,* 24:5–42, Vol. 24, 1976.

10. Greeson, R. "That 'Impossible' Profession," *Journal of the American Psychoanalytic Association,* Vol. 14, 1966.

11. Fine, R. *The Healing of the Mind.* New York: David McKay, 1971.

12. Freud, S. "Analysis Terminable & Interminable" (1937), *Standard Edition.* London: Hogarth Press, Vol. 23, 1964.

Chapter 4

A FAMILY THERAPIST LOOKS AT "LITTLE HANS"

One of psychoanalysis's classics is the story of "Little Hans." Hans, a five-year-old-boy, was so paralyzed by his phobia of horses that he was forced to stay at home and not risk going outdoors for fear that he would be confronted by the castrating animals. His father, a non-professional student of Sigmund Freud's, decided that he would attempt to rid Hans of his phobia by utilizing the prescribed interpretive interventions of classical psychoanalytic technique developed by Freud for the psychotherapy of neurotics. Under Dr. Freud's guidance, Hans' father met with his son almost daily over a period of a few months and explained to the boy the reasons for the latter's suffering. Essentially, Little Hans was told that his phobia emanated from his oedipal wishes—that is, his strong erotic attachment to his mother coupled with his wish to displace his father and penetrate mother with his own "widdler" were causing him his difficulties. Hans was quite convinced that his desires toward mother would not meet with approval from his father; as a matter of fact, Hans feared that he would have to pay a steep price for his sexual fantasies toward mother and his competitive impulses toward father. The penalty for Hans' contemplated transgressions would be castration at the hands of his father! Unable to cope with his strong ambivalence towards his father, Hans repressed the hateful feelings, displaced them on to horses and then feared the horses' hostile retaliation rather than his father's.

Hans' recovery, according to Freud, was due to the boy's assimilation and integration of his father's interpretations which were mainly focused on Hans's oedipal difficulties. Eventually recognizing that his father would not punish him for his libidinal and aggressive wishes, Hans was

Reprinted by permission from *Family Process*, Vol. 6, no. 2 (September 1967), pp. 227–234.

free to resume his energetic life outdoors and enter areas where he previously feared to tread. [3]

The case of Little Hans has remained a classic to this day. Not only has it been utilized to demonstrate the metapsychology of anxiety hysteria, but it reveals poignantly the universal oedipal struggle which all children experience. In addition, the case of Hans has provided a colorful means of attempting to understand how psychoanalytic interpretations may lead to the uncovering and overcoming of a neurosis, particularly a childhood neurosis.

While studying Little Hans both as a student and as a teacher, this writer has either been asked or asked himself several questions pertinent to the dynamic diagnosis and treatment of this little boy which Freud apparently did not answer in this otherwise brilliant and stimulating treatise. "If the oedipus complex is universal, what is uniquely transpiring in this boy's life that can only be 'compromised' by the development of a paralyzing phobia?" is a query asked by many social work students. The treatment oriented worker has often inquired, "What is involved in the transference relationship of this boy to his father that induces Hans to accept virtually all of his father's interpretations?" Closely related to this last question is the following one, "Given the ambivalent relationship that Hans had towards his father, and granted that it was one typical of a five-year-old boy, why isn't Hans ambivalent towards his father as a therapist and why doesn't he respond to his therapeutic sessions ambivalently?"

Child guidance workers have pondered the influence of the parents' contemplated divorce on Hans' psychosocial development and on the unfolding of his treatment. "Does not a disturbed marital relationship affect or exacerbate a boy's oedipal difficulties?" is the most often repeated query. Other questions related to familial dynamics are the following: "When Hans' mother threatened the boy that his "widdler" would fall off because of his masturbating, hadn't she indirectly presented some of her own feelings about the penis and about men in general?" "Could not her sexual attitudes possibly imply a disturbed sexual relationship with her husband, reflecting her own feelings of castration and a wish to castrate?"

Recently, with the family more often the unit of diagnosis and treatment in social agencies, mental hygiene and child guidance clinics as well as among some private practitioners, family oriented workers, within the context of using the Little Hans case as a learning instrument, have asked questions like these: "When father enacts the role of therapist and mother is left out of the treatment plan entirely, what does this do to the family's homeostatic balance?" "Isn't father keeping mother away from the 'therapy' and possibly using the child for himself as a weapon against mother?" "What would have happened if mother and father agreed in advance on what to say to Little Hans and presented the 'interpretations' together?"

Just as Freud's case studies of Dora and the Wolf Man have been reevaluated in the light of new understanding and the development of new theory, so too, with the increments of knowledge that family oriented therapists now possess, it may be possible to refine and enrich our understanding of the case of Little Hans, considered by some as the first family oriented child guidance case in therapeutic history.

Buttressed and fortified by the findings of the social sciences and ego psychology, impressed with failures in individual therapy (particularly in child guidance treatment when only the child had been involved), and aware that post hospitalization recovery in mental illness has much more to do with the locus of the patient's residence and with whom he eventually interacts than with his diagnosis and prognosis, increased numbers of professional workers embracing several disciplines are subscribing to a family oriented approach in their diagnostic and therapeutic endeavors. The family, as currently viewed by many professionals, is a social system with several interacting parts and is governed by the principles of transaction, stability, and the communication of information,[4, 5, 6] When the family is viewed as a social system, it is contended that a change in one family member will modify the role interactions and transactions of the others.

As Ackerman,[1] Haley,[4, 5] Jackson,[6] and others have reiterated, the patient with symptoms is not only serving a complex function for the family through his expression of pathology, he is also satisfying the needs of family members by serving what Ackerman has referred to as a "scapegoat function."[1] As the displayed expression of family conflict, the patient is "holding the family together and providing a focus for its discontent."[4] Further propounded by theorists on family dynamics is that when the family member with the presenting problem improves, other family members exhibit distress and the dissolution of the family unit is threatened.[2, 4, 9]

Referring to the oedipus complex and its vicissitudes in connection with family interaction, Haley has stated:

... the permutations of such a triangle when seen as an actual situation are many, and the child raised in one kind of habitual triangular
pattern will presumably learn to behave differently from one raised in
a different one, even though the problem of such a triangle is universal. [4]

The family oriented practitioner or theorist in assessing the case of
Little Hans would therefore examine it not only from the vantage point
of the presenting problem; he would hold as axiomatic that the behavior
of one individual in a family exerts influence upon other family members and that a change in one member's behavior provokes responses in
the others. Consequently, the family therapist would be interested in
the interactions and transactions of Little Hans vis à vis his father and
mother as individuals—Hans' perceptions of their marital relationship,
the marital relationship itself, and the interdependence of the parent–
child, parent–parent, and spouse–spouse subsystems. In brief, then, if
we view Hans' family as a gestalt, we are compelled to not only analyze
Hans' oedipal fantasies but also learn what impact Hans' parents had on
their development. We would also wish to ascertain what conflicts
Hans' oedipal preoccupations induced in his parents as individuals and
into their marital subsystem.

Children's developmental problems activate unresolved childhood
conflicts of their parents. When a parent seeks assistance from a
therapist in relation to his child, through the child, he is also presenting
a part of himself which seeks help. [2, 7, 8, 9] When Hans' father went to
Freud, he may very well have been unconsciously communicating that
"I, Hans' father, have oedipal difficulties of my own which I can't
resolve. They are being stimulated constantly by my son. Please help
me and enlighten me!" It is of interest that concurrent with Hans'
developing sexual curiosity, we found that the father was curious about
the sexual theories of Freud and was attending Freud's lectures on sex.
Papa, in effect, was attempting to get sexual instruction from Freud
both in a group and in individual sessions. Based on Father's quests for
sexual information from Freud through the media of group lectures,
individual guidance and the literature, one may reasonably speculate
that Hans' father was having some sexual difficulties of his own.

If our hypothesis concerning the sexual difficulties that Father was
experiencing with his wife is correct, and if we consider the dearth of
communication that transpired between the mother and father
throughout the life of the case presentation, it would follow that Hans'
sexual curiosity could not be discussed by Mama and Papa together,

either with or without Hans present. Apparently, Hans' burgeoning sexual curiosity and attendant fantasies activated considerable anxiety for both parents. While we do not have factual data to confirm this, it would appear that Hans' erotic desires toward Mother were intensified by his sensing an increased sexual availability of his mother by virtue of Father's withdrawal from her. Furthermore, Father, who attended lectures on sex in his spare time and, from the available data, did not spend very much time with his wife, emerged throughout the story as a tender, maternal man. He was the type of father whose lack of aggressiveness could only strengthen a boy's oedipal guilt for an unaggressive father is a most difficult object towards whom a young boy can cathect his own aggression. Hence, Papa and Mama *avoided* each other, *avoided* discussing, as a couple, sexual questions with or about Hans, and interestingly, Hans developed a symptom which had as its major feature, *avoidance*. Because there was a dearth of *verbal communication* in the interdependent triangular relationship on sex, Hans squelched his feelings and thoughts on the subject and displaced his conflicts on to a safer and more convenient object, an object that could not *verbally communicate* at all, namely, a horse.

Freud, who saw nine or ten patients a day and then burned the midnight oil writing up his notes and studying them, could have felt a strong identification with Hans' father—they both were fascinated by the sexual theories on children but neither of them had, in all probability, an active heterosexual life. Freud did not explore the presenting problem of Hans' father and did not choose to see it as evolving from the father's inner distress; instead, both men discussed childhood sexuality.

Hans' father, like Hans, himself, was displacing his sexual curiosity on to safer objects. Hans' displacement took the form of horses; the father displaced his sexual curiosity on to the childhood sexual theories of Freud, who supplied the father with "horse sense" on children, and chose not to expose the father's sexual conflicts.

The relationship between Hans' father and Freud became recapitulated in the father's treatment of Hans. Childhood sexuality was again the topic of discussion. Considering that Hans' encounters with father transpired almost daily, we can tentatively conclude that the sexual discussions provided both partners with some sexual stimulation and sexual gratification. In the final analysis, father and son were having almost daily verbal sexual intercourse and excluding the mother. As Freud himself has taught us, when an oedipal conflict in a boy is strong (as we know it was in Hans' situation), a common defense is to repress his competitive aggression toward the father (as Hans was already doing) and deny the love attachment towards his mother. The boy then submits to father in a homosexual manner, his hostility goes underground, and a "love and beloved" relationship between father and son is formed. Father's sexual talks with Hans apparently seduced the boy into a submissive relationship with him and therefore, the "transference" became increasingly positive and Hans became more and more positively suggestible to his father's interpretations. To please his father Hans gave up the fear of horses, which was Father's main objective.

It will be remembered that as the case material unfolded and *not prior to the therapy*, Hans became increasingly effeminate and submissive, began to have fantasies of becoming a woman and dreamed that he was giving birth to a baby. Like his mother who had given birth to Hans' baby sister during his pre-oedipal phase, Hans became psychologically his father's wife and surrendered his own virility.

As we already know, Mother was excluded and probably excluded herself from the consultations with Freud. She did not attend Freud's group lectures on sex and was totally uninvolved in the treatment of Little Hans. Is there a possibility that the rage she felt in being a "*loner*" was conveyed to Hans when she admonished him for his masturbatory activity (which is performed alone) by threatening him with the loss of his "widdler"? Furthermore, as Mother was excluded so did she probably exclude and no doubt aided and abetted the intensification of Father and Hans' homosexual attraction.

As family therapists have convincingly demonstrated, when the family member with the presenting problem improves, other family members exhibit distress and/or the family unit can possibly be threatened with dissolution.[5] Hans' phobia was the displayed expression of family conflict, but like all phobias (e.g. school or work phobias) it held the family together and therefore preserved its equilibrium. When Little Hans, the family member with the presenting problem improved, the parents' marriage soon after was dissolved.

Utilizing a family orientation toward the treatment, the therapy of Little Hans, rather than representing a "working through" of Hans' oedipal conflict, can best be described as a "transference cure." The mutual avoidance pattern of both parents towards and with each other reinforced Father's attachment to his son wherein Hans became, psychologically, his father's wife. As mother became further alienated from her husband and son (and eventually bowed out entirely), Hans and his father drew closer, enjoying their sex talks more and more.

Father evolved into both a mother and father for Little Hans, was ascribed enormous omnipotence by the latter, and the patient was "cured through love." Hans, in his submission to father, complied with his father's prescription that was received from Freud, namely, that the "phobia is nonsense and is ridiculous to keep."[3]

The socio-psychological set of events that transpired in the treatment of Little Hans occurs frequently in current casework treatment and psychotherapy, particularly in the treatment of marital partners. One spouse forms a "love and beloved" relationship with the therapist—the latter becomes the "most important person" in the client's life—and the alienated spouse, no longer the loved object, withdraws further. Like Hans, who esteemed and idealized his therapist, many patients do likewise with their treatment partners who become psychological spouses for them. Hence, there is a certain grain of truth in the allegations levelled at various forms of treatment by the laity when they exclaim that "psychiatry makes the patient get a divorce." As in the treatment of Little Hans, where most of the boy's aggression went underground and little of it was cathected toward his therapist, likewise, many patients and therapists form a pact which is to "love, honor and obey" each other; the patient's spouse is either attacked by them in the therapy or else forgotten completely.

While it is not within the purview of this paper to moralize about the pros and cons of divorce and separation, it is of crucial importance for family therapists and all therapists to differentiate between divorce and separation achieved through the result of "working through" a series of conflicts as opposed to a divorce or separation induced by the transference–countertransference relationship of patient and therapist. When a "love and beloved" relationship is the consistent theme in the casework or therapeutic interviews, the patient cathects his libido in the direction of the professional worker, his aggression goes underground and instead of becoming part of the transference relationship where it would be available for ventilation and discussion, it is either repressed, acted out, or displaced towards the spouse. If Freud had adhered to the well proven child guidance axiom that the child and his functioning are expressions of the parents' egos, rather than giving Hans' father advice and sexual information (which was probably stimulating for both), he would have "begun where the client was,"[2] and explored the significance of the father's request. The results of the treatment, therefore, might have been different if Father's underlying need behind his request was responded to with real therapeutic understanding; his marital and sexual relationship with his wife could possibly have become the therapeutic focus eventually. Instead of recapitulating with Hans the kind of tête-à-têtes he experienced with Freud, Father could have emerged as more of a husband and more of a sexual partner of his wife's if he had been treated as a client in his own right. This would have possibly modified Little Hans' perception of his father and mother and no doubt, could have influenced his oedipal situation for the better. By the demonstration of maturer and more differentiated sexual roles through their behavior in real life situations Father and Mother could have perhaps helped Little Hans come to more of a resolution of his oedipal difficulties than he did through his stimulating sex talks with his father. In brief, a different chain of events could have taken place had Freud addressed himself to Father's therapeutic need. A discussion of Father's own sexual problems would probably have made Mother a subject or object of treatment which would have created a different oedipal milieu for Hans.

At the end of Freud's exposition on Little Hans, there is a postscript describing a meeting with Hans several years after the "therapy" was terminated, when Hans was 19. Freud's impression of Hans at the time was that the latter had grown to be a vigorous, mature, young man and free from the phobia of horses. Of interest is that there is no report on Hans' current sexual adjustment but a statement from Hans to Freud that both his parents were remarried after their divorce and that Hans was living alone. Further, Hans had no recollection of the therapy whatsoever. The sexual talks that Hans had with his father were "overtaken by amnesia."[3]

Although Freud mentions in his postcript that Hans was living alone for a number of years without either of his parents, he does not venture to assess the desirability or impact of this arrangement on Hans. Of definite interest, however, is that the three members of the system all went their separate ways. A family oriented therapist would conclude, therefore, that the phobic symptom had "held the family together and provided a focus for its discontent" and that "when the family member with the presenting problem improved, the family unit was threatened with dissolution."[4] In Hans' case, the family was not only threatened with dissolution when the phobia was dissolved but each of the three members eventually removed themselves from each other.

As family therapists we have observed in Little Hans an excellent illustration of how a symptom of one member binds and protects a whole family constellation. It enriches our understanding of the protective and defensive quality of symptoms and how their removal can intensify and exacerbate interpersonal difficulties rather than diminish them. Important for family therapists in particular and all therapists in general is to study the needs of a patient or patients and to comprehend the necessity, in many instances, for their maintaining symptoms, defenses, and resistances. Symptoms are, in effect, like protective layers of skin. When prematuraly pierced, blood flows.[9] Is it sometimes the lack of respect for and support of defensive adaptations of patients by therapists that stimulates what is frequently referred to as "a bloody mess"?[8, 9] Is it not possible to sometimes avoid "messes" by respecting the patient's right to maintain defenses as long as he needs them, since they protect the individual and sustain the family?

REFERENCES

1. Ackerman, N. W. *The Psychodynamics of Family Life*. New York: Basic Books, 1958.

2. Feldman, Y. "A Casework Approach Toward Understanding Parents of Emotionally Disturbed Children," *Social Work*, Vol. 3, No. 3, 1958.

3. Freud, S. "Analysis of a Phobia in a Five Year Old Boy," *Collected Papers*, Vol. 3. London: Hogarth Press, 1925.

4. Haley, J. *Strategies of Psychotherapy*. New York: Grune and Stratton, 1963.

5. _____. "Wither Family Therapy," *Family Process*, Vol. 1, 1962.

6. Jackson, D. "The Question of Family Homeostasis," *Psychiatric Quarterly*, Vol. 31, Part 1, 1957.

7. Sternbach, O. "Arrested Ego Development and Its Treatment in Conduct Disorders and Neuroses of Childhood," *The Nervous Child*, Vol. 6, No. 3, July 1947.

8. Strean, H. "Treating Parents of Emotionally Disturbed Children Through Role Playing," *The Psychoanalytic Review*, Vol. 47, No. 1, Spring 1960.

9. _____. "Treatment of Mothers and Sons in the Absence of the Father," *Social Work*, Vol. 6, No. 3, July 1961.

DISCUSSANT: ANN HARTMAN

Freud's classic story of Little Hans has been revisited time and time again by therapists, students, and those who would seek to gain new understanding and to reinterpret the extensive material presented in the case study. In the annals of psychodynamic literature, it remains, as Strean has pointed out, a poignant demonstration of a child's oedipal struggle as well as the primary exposition of the genesis of phobias in children.

In studying the original paper as well as Strean's analysis of the case and in trying to respond to either or both of these works out of my own perspective, it became apparent that truly useful interchange must take place within the context of a common frame of reference or a basic epistemological agreement. Given such agreement, discussion about the meaning of the material and the differing views of the particular dynamics of the case can be most useful. This is the nature of Strean's discussion of the Little Hans material. Little Hans is a classic presentation within the psychodynamic framework and Strean remains fundamentally within that framework. He broadens the view of the case to include the mother and father but primarily utilizes psychodynamic concepts to explain the unfolding events, searching for causes within the individuals involved and focusing particularly on the parents' as well as Little Hans' and even Freud's repressed sexual conflicts as the salient variables. Strean seeks to demonstrate how the sexual conflicts and longings of each family member affect and are affected by those of other family members. For example, he hypothesizes that father is experiencing sexual difficulties and that his approach to Freud for help with his son may well have signalled an unconscious desire for help with his own oedipal difficulties. He further hypothesizes that the daily discussions of sexuality between father and son were stimulating and gratifying to both and that in time Hans psychologically replaces the mother as the father's passive, effeminate partner, at which time he relinquishes his fear of horses.

Strean remains within the Freudian framework and even when highly critical of Freud's handling of this case, he turns Freud's own weapons back on the master, speculating that the case became an arena where Freud's own sexual conflicts were played out.

As a systems-oriented family therapist, attempting to comment on Freud's and Strean's work means that much of the common frame of reference and epistemological agreement is lost. Without this agreement, discourse and productive engagement around ideas is difficult as we speak in different languages, examine different data, and view different levels. Attempting to discuss individually-oriented material from a systems point of view leaves one in danger of confusing logical types. Whitehead and Runnel hold that a class and members of a class constitute different logical levels whose distinction must be maintained (Dell, 1981).

Within a systems framework, a family is not seen as a group of interacting individuals or even dyads but as a holistic entity, a self-regulatory system which controls itself according to rules formed over a period of time through a process of trial and error (Palazzoli, 1978).

The symptomatic behavior of family members is seen not as an expression of internal psychic conflict but as an effort to maintain the family or to solve another problem which may be destructive to the system. The first task in family systems therapy is to develop a hypothesis that includes all of the actors in the system and that reframes the "problem" as an attempted "solution" while identifying the problem that the "solution" is attempting to solve. As we turn to Little Hans, we ask the question, "What is the problem that the family is trying to resolve through the development of Hans' "problematic" behavior?

The difficulty in formulating a systemic hypothesis about the Little Hans case lies in the fact that the psychoanalytic frame of reference directed the inquiry and the gathering of data. We hear in detail about the fantasies that emerge in the discussions between Hans and his parents but very little about the circuit of transactions that take place around the development of Hans' problems. We would want to ask: When Hans first said he was afraid, what did mother do? What did father do? What did mother do about what father did? What were the transactions that preceded Hans' telling his parents he was afraid? How were those transactions different than a week before? Out of tracking the circular transactions of which the problematic behavior is a part, it is possible to formulate a hypothesis. Without this kind of systematic information, any systemic hypothesis must be highly speculative.

Some hints, however, about the context within which the symptoms developed lead me to succumb to the temptation to attempt at least a highly speculative hypothesis.

First, Hans reports on two occasions that he is afraid his mother will leave and not return. On another occasion he expresses a similar concern about the father. We also know that later the parents divorce. We can perhaps speculate that the parents' marriage was already in trouble. Perhaps the parents' attempted solution to the growing rift was to have a second child (Hanna).

A second piece of the puzzle concerns the fact that Freud asked his followers (and Little Hans' parents were among these) to observe and report to Freud evidence they might observe of their young children's sexuality and sexual fantasies. Father, long before the development of Hans' difficulties, began to send written reports to Freud detailing Hans' development and this was clearly a subject of discussion and interest between the parents.

It could be that the function of Hans' difficulties was to provide the parents with a shared interest and thus to help them with their growing distance. Certainly nothing could have interested these parents more than the development of a classic neurosis in their little boy. Although Strean feels that the mother was excluded from this preoccupation, there is considerable evidence that father and mother initially discussed Hans' sexual fantasies and behavior in detail and mother is reported to have been an active participant in the pursuit of Little Hans' fantasies and fears (Freud, p. 181). It may be that mother began to be excluded later on and it is possible that the family gave up Hans' symptoms because the parents were giving up on the marriage and because Hans became aware that he was no longer able to pull the parents together around his "stories" of falling down horses, over loaded carts, and so on.

A partial hypothesis could therefore be that Hans' problematic behavior was shaped at least in part by the parents' interest in following the little boy's sexual life. The development had encouragement of this behavior and was an unsuccessful attempt at the maintenance of the family system. If nothing else, at least this hypothesis is parsimonious.

Many aspects of the system transactions are, however, unknown to us. Freud himself clearly was an important actor in the system. He had treated Hans' mother prior to her marriage, and the parents were described as strong adherents of Freud's doctrines. Little Hans was so aware of Freud's importance in the system that he began to dictate things for his father to write down for "the professor." We do not know enough, however, to know how Freud fitted in.

We do know that Hans' symptoms made many contributions to the different actors in the system. For example, Freud was provided with information directly from a young child which served to substantiate his theories of infantile sexuality developed through his analysis of adults.

The parents or at least the father through presenting Freud with this fascinating case may have come to occupy a favored position among his followers.

A second area to be examined is the "treatment" of Little Hans by his father under Freud's direction. First, of course, the nature of the change effort is entirely antithetical to a family systems approach, based as it is on the view that change will occur through the development of insight by the little patient into the nature and source of his difficulties. The phobia is cured through the analysis of the child's oedipal conflicts.

Strean suggests that the father's sexual and marital difficulties should have been the therapeutic focus with the eventual inclusion of the mother, as either a subject or object of treatment. Although shifting to the parents, this intervention plan individually focused, locating the problem within the father and nominating him as the candidate for treatment.

If the tentative systemic hypothesis turned out to be accurate, the marriage could certainly be the primary focus for the intervention but a systems view would dictate that both partners are participating in the dysfunctional marriage and both should be involved in marital work. One hopes that as the couple began to engage around the difficulties in their relationship, Hans' symptoms would be less necessary to the maintenance of the marriage.

The other aspect of the therapy that is of even greater significance to a family therapist is the fact that the father acted as therapist. Freud comments that he felt it was the combined authority of the father and the physician that made it possible to apply the psychoanalytic method so effectively. A family systems perspective would question whether it would be possible for the father, as he is emersed in the system, to be able to act upon the system to bring about change. Of even greater concern to a family system therapist is the extreme boundary violation that takes place as both parents get into Little Hans' head pursuing his private thoughts and demanding access to his fantasy life.

On one occasion it is reported that the mother spent an entire morning attempting to get Hans to tell her his giraffe fantasy! At another point Hans pleads with his father to leave him alone. Neither Freud nor the enthusiastic parents seemed to respect the child as a separate person and showed no reluctance in using the power of adult, parent, and physician to intrude into the private world of this little boy. The intrusions were made doubly troubling as the parents, in their omniscience, told Hans what his thoughts *really* meant.

The rights of children were of little concern in the nineteenth century and a rereading of the Little Hans story surfaces a disturbing view of the child as without rights in an adult-dominated world.

Finally, Little Hans can provide parents who also happen to be psychotherapists with an instructive cautionary tale. It is often a great temptation for those who study the inner workings of the mind to use their knowledge in making interpretations to their children. Such interpretations violate the child's personal boundaries and exaggerate the child's sense of the parents' omnipotence. This can have serious consequences for the child's developing sense of autonomy and efforts to differentiate from the parents.

REFERENCES

Dell, Paul F. "Some Irreverent Thoughts on Paradox," *Family Process*, March 1981.

Palazzoli, Mara; Cecchin, G.; Prata, G.; and Boscolo, L. *Paradox and Counter Paradox*. New York: Jacob Aronson, 1978.

Freud, Sigmund. "A Phobia in a Five Year Old Boy," in *Collected Papers*, Vol. III. New York: Basic Books, 1959.

DISCUSSANT: LESLIE ROSENTHAL

In the introduction to his book *The Psychodynamics of Family Life*, Nathan Ackerman (1958) expresses his conviction that "the single, most encompassing reason for our conspicuous failure thus far to prevent mental illness derives from our failure to cope with the mental health problems of family life. We have somehow kept ourselves so busy, so preoccupied with studying and treating the suffering of individuals, that we have, in effect, blinded ourselves to the significance of the concurrent struggles of the family for mental health. I do not mean to imply that the treatment of the individual patient, the alleviation of the very real sufferings of a single human being, is unimportant. To the contrary. But I do question the effectiveness that does not take into consideration the sum total of this individual, which must of necessity include his environment and his interactions with it" (p. 9).

Ackerman pays tribute to Freud's "uniquely brilliant penetration of the individual psyche" but states that his investigation of social–psychological processes was wanting; that he sharply highlighted some aspects of family life while others were left in the dark. Ackerman adds the significant thought, "It is one thing to state the emotional needs of a child and another to make over the parents and family to meet these needs" (p. 9).

Dr. Strean has utilized the accretion of new insights, theory and perspectives developed in the field of family therapy within the last several decades to pose a series of provocative questions about this most famous of child guidance cases. These deal with Little Hans' family as an interacting system in which dysfunction is signalled by the child's dysfunction phobia. Addressing the threat made by the mother to Hans that his penis would fall off as a result of his masturbation, Dr. Strean asks whether this admonition was a vehicle for the mother's underlying attitudes toward the penis and toward men. He also speculates that the father's strong interest in Freud's sexual theories reflected sexual problems in the marital relationship which, when sensed by Hans, intensified his erotic desires toward the mother.

Freud himself alluded to some of the familial tensions in a curiously damning "defense" of the mother:

We must say a word on behalf of Hans' excellent and devoted mother. His father accuses her, not without some show of justice, of being responsible for the outbreak of the child's neurosis on account of her excessive display of affection for him and her too frequent readiness to take him into her bed. We might as easily blame her for having precipitated the process of repression by her energetic rejection of his advances ("that I be piggish"). But she had a predestined part to play and her position was a hard one.

It may be noted that ever since the analysis of Little Hans, Freud stressed the fateful conjunction for a little boy of an external castration threat with the observation of the female genitals, leading the boy to the conclusion that castration may really happen to him.

Dr. Strean suggests that the father's sexual talks with Hans constituted a homosexual relationship in which Hans submitted to the father. It is also inferred that this homosexual attraction was intensified by the mother's exclusion from the consultation with Freud and from the son's treatment. While it may have been largely true that the mother was excluded or excluded herself from the treatment, a specific entry in the father's treatment notes offers evidence that she was not totally uninvolved: "On April 24th my wife and I enlightened Hans up to a certain point. We told him that children grow inside their Mommy. . . ." Freud also informs us that both parents were fully in agreement that the treatment should be undertaken.

However, one cannot dismiss the telling point raised by Dr. Strean that children's developmental problems activate unresolved childhood conflicts of their parents so that when a parent seeks assistance from a therapist, he is also presenting a part of himself which seeks help. In accordance with this basic premise of child guidance clinicians, Hans' phobia was representative of the father's problem. From a family therapy vantage point, Hans' phobia represented the family's disguised request for help. It is not unreasonable to consider that careful investigation of the father's wish for help for Hans in terms of his own sexual adjustment and the inclusion of the mother in the exploration and subsequent consultations could have led to treatment and resolution of the marital problem. Dr. Strean also offers the interesting suggestion that Freud chose not to recognize or deal with the father's inner distress on the basis of subjective countertransference—the wish to avoid dealing with his own apparently inactive sexual life.

Another principle of family therapy effectively utilized by the writer in his analysis of the case is that of the complex function served by the family member with the identified problem in maintaining the family equilibrium as the "displaced expression of family conflict." Premature removal of the presenting problem may upset the family homeostasis and bring about fragmentation of the family unit. Thus we can only agree with the statement by Dr. Strean, "We would wish to ascertain what conflicts Hans' oedipal preoccupations induced in his parents and into their marital subsystem."

Dr. Strean has rendered a valuable service in offering this stimulating appraisal of Little Hans using the wide-angle lens provided by the insights of family therapy. He has expanded upon Freud's understanding of the case and deepened our appreciation of it. We are reminded that mental health (and illness) cannot be fully understood within the limited range of individual experience. A more inclusive approach to mental health must embrace the dynamics of the family and beyond that to the interrelations of individual, family, and community.

Chapter 5

THE CONTEMPORARY FAMILY AND THE RESPONSIBILITIES OF THE SOCIAL WORKER IN DIRECT PRACTICE

In September 1977, a five-year study conducted by the Carnegie Corporation concluded that the American family is in no great danger of disappearing. Once again a strain was created between colleagues in research and those in practice. What did those of us in practice declare after the research investigators thoughtfully and rigorously designed a study, worked arduously on it and then presented their conclusions about the family? We averred, "We knew it all the time!" (Fanshel, 1966).

Regardless of our field of practice, the setting in which we work, or the clientele whom we serve, social workers have a commitment, a deep interest in, and attachment to the family. And social workers do not stand alone. Since the beginning of recorded time and in all kinds of cultures, the family has existed as a bond that has taken precedence over other ties, and indeed, has often superseded the individual's own personal welfare and at times, even his survival. It is clear that families provide more social care to dependent members than do health and welfare agencies (Moroney, 1978).

The impact of the family is constantly reflected in our language, in our folk lore, and virtually everywhere. We speak of *homely* truths, *familiar* surroundings, and the *domesticated* in contrast to the primi-

Reprinted by permission from *Journal of Jewish Communal Service*, Vol. 56, no. 1 (September 1979), pp. 40–49.

tive. "Home Sweet Home," "There is no place like home," and "Home is where the heart is" are refrains most of us enjoy. Jews speak warmly of the "Meeshpoheh," and many synagogues and temples have as their name "Beth," which means "home." Almost every Jewish service begins with "Mah Tovu"—"How good it is for brothers and sisters to be under one tent!" A very popular Yiddish song is, "Alah mentchen zinen brider"—"Human beings are all brothers."

The need for a family is observed in the persistence of organized religion, for all religions may be viewed as psychological families. Jews and Christians have Fathers in Heaven and sons in the form of Moses and Jesus. The Holy Mother is an important symbol in Christianity and the Greek goddesses are well known for their fertility, creativity and capacity to nurture. Despite all of the obstacles imposed on them, Black slaves made many efforts to achieve and maintain family ties and much of the sociological research on Blacks points to more family solidarity than is usually recognized (Merton and Nisbet, 1966).

The family, whether we revile it, reject it, or renounce it, shapes us more than anything else does or ever will. We cannot resign from it. A number of research experiments have clearly demonstrated that the capacity to love, to respond warmly and affectionately, and later to socialize with others stems from early body contacts and emotionally gratifying communications between mother and infant (Bowlby, 1951; Erikson, 1950). Educators now are convinced that how well a child learns and how much pleasure he extracts from learning depends on how warmly and consistently he was taught the "do's and don'ts" by his parents and close relatives (A. Freud, 1965). How an individual relates to the opposite sex and how comfortable he or she feels in his or her sexual role evolves mainly from his observations on how his parents related to each other. Even sex therapists like Masters and Johnson have shifted their focus from an exclusive emphasis on bodily experiences to how people feel toward each other and feel about themselves. In their latest book, Masters and Johnson have joined those of us who work with people and their feelings pointed out that the capacity to enjoy oneself in physical expressions of love derive mainly from the observations the child makes as he witnesses how his parents greet, communicate, and resolve conflicts with each other (Masters and Johnson, 1970).

The child is a good team member if he has learned to tame his competitive and aggressive impulses by living in a cooperative family. The teenager copes better with the "Sturm und Drang" of adolescence if his family atmosphere is structured so that he may receive appropriate doses of autonomy while he concomitantly receives appropriate controls. It has been well documented that teenagers who resort to violence and impulsive behavior are subtly and tacitly, albeit unconsciously, encouraged by their parents to do so, and that those who champion love, work and consideration for others have been exposed to a loving and cooperative family (Ackerman, 1958).

In a recent book, *Adaptation to Life*, which studied the lives of 95 successful men (best selling novelists, cabinet members, scholars, captains of industry, physicians, teachers of the first rank, judges and newspaper editors) the author, Dr. George Valiant (1977), demonstrated that contrary to popular belief men who became successful had very happy marriages, enjoyable family relationships, and rich friendships.

Sigmund Freud, in a letter written in the early 1900s, said: "The announcement of my unpleasant findings had the result that I lost the largest part of my human relations. In this loneliness, there awoke within me the longing for a circle of select, high-minded men who would accept me in friendship in spite of my daring opinions. B'nai Brith was pointed out to me as the place where such men were to be found. The fact that you were Jews could only be desirable to me, for I myself was a Jew and I had always deemed it not only unworthy, but nonsensical to deny it" (Jones, 1953).

Here was the independent scientist Freud, the free thinker, the atheistic infidel, acknowledging that when the going gets tough, the tough turn to the familiar.

Dysfunctions and Stresses of the Contemporary Family

Although the Carnegie Study concluded that the family is alive—social workers and other professionals know it is not well. Actually, the family of the 1970s is in deep trouble. We now have a divorce epidemic in this country; in 1977 there was close to one divorce for every two marriages. Of marriages that sustain themselves, many can be characterized as full of one-upmanship fracases and pervasive friction. Teenage suicide has reached its highest level and has increased 250 percent in the last twenty years; suicide among children is also up. The drug culture is proliferating and the "battered woman" syndrome is now a well known clinical entity. In a recent book, *Wife Beating: The Silent Crisis*, Langley and Levy (1977) reported that one fifth of the married women in America beat their husbands, but that few of the men would admit it. We now

have deserting mothers as well as deserting fathers. The reported incidence of child abuse has soared. A new phenomenon has emerged
which is labeled, "child-snatching"—angry spouses who are divorced
perpetuate their vindictiveness by stealing their children when the other
is not looking. As households change or break up, children are increasingly under the care of one parent. In a growing shift from the past,
450,000 youngsters lived with their divorced or separated fathers in
1977.

The Jewish family is not exempt from conflict. Divorce statistics
among Jews have risen and recently a *New York Times* survey (January,
1978) reported one out of four orthodox Jewish marriages ends up in
divorce. Jewish alcoholism has risen and depressions, psychosomatic
ailments and obesity are all "popular" neurotic responses among Jews.
Philip Roth and other authors have portrayed the Jewish mother as an
all-consuming ogre. Even though this description of the modal Jewish
mother is exaggerated, Roth's books would not be so popular unless they
were striking a responsive chord that is ready to resonate with
vindictiveness.

Recently, one of the world's largest Jewish women's organizations,
Hadassah, had to affirm its "deep conviction that the Jewish family is
the Keystone of Jewish survival" and that "the Jewish woman and
mother serves as a central model." At this Hadassah convention was
Margaret Costanza, President Carter's former Special Assistant who had
to reassure the ladies present. She said, "Ladies, don't be ashamed of
ever having made the choice of being married and raising a family!"
When Hadassah women have to reaffirm themselves and receive assur-
ance that it is desirable to be a wife and mother, we can infer that the
contemporary Jewish woman is having some uncertainty about her
identity!

Narcissism and the Contemporary Family

The family, at one time so universally accepted as the mainstay of our
society is now facing stresses so serious that we need a Carnegie Commission to tell us that it is still a viable institution. Many factors coalesce
to undermine the contemporary American family, Jewish and non-
Jewish, but in this paper I would like to focus on one phenomenon
which contributes heavily to the weakening of the bonds that unite a
family. Psychoanalysts have referred to this phenomenon as increased
narcissism—self-love—and one analyst, Dr. Herbert Hendin, has

labeled our current era "The Age of Sensation" (1975) in which people want what they want when they want it and get furious when they don't get it.

Disruptive family life seems to reflect a cultural trend toward replacing commitment, involvement, and tenderness with self-aggrandizement, exploitativeness, and titillation. We now live in an age where we have unlimited expectations; many of us fantasize that Paradise can be regained and that the Garden of Eden can be located. We live in a culture in which anything done for another person must result in some immediate personal gain. As Robert Coles (1975), a Harvard psychiatrist, has stated, "In a highly secular, materialistic culture like ours, anyone who gets too altruistic is looked upon as 'kooky'." Young children are often seen as pleasureless burdens and older children frequently become extensions of the need to validate one's life. Witness Little League baseball games or basketball games between Community Centers where the fathers and mothers from opposing teams bicker while the children try, frequently in vain, to play ball cooperatively. Anthropologist Margaret Mead (1975) has said, "We have become a society of people who neglect our children, are afraid of our children, and find children a surplus instead of the raison d'être of living."

Many in our society are captivated by a B. F. Skinner who wants to avoid freedom and dignity and make feelings irrelevant through totally ordering and controlling experience or by a Timothy Leary who wants to escape beyond emotion through abandonment of control. To be a precisely constructed machine or a mass of waving sense cells reflects the common rejection of feeling, commitment and involvement (Hendin, 1975).

Those of us who work professionally with families frequently observe housewives berating themselves because they have failed to become an amalgam of an orgastic playmate, intellectual stimulator, emotional empathizer, cathartic absorber, and autonomous strong woman. Many of them seem to be aspiring toward a role set which is a cross between Madame Pompadour and Madame Curie. Not only does Mrs. 1979 desire a great deal for herself, but she expects as much, if not more, from her husband. He should be a willing provider of much money but enjoy her gainful employment; he should be a sparkling conversationalist but respect his wife's need for solitude; he should help with domestic chores but have a stable role as masculine father; he should be an appetizing sexual partner but tolerate his wife's flirtations with other men.

Husbands are in tremendous conflict and social workers observe countless numbers of them who often feel desperate in not being a complete sexual athlete, provider of profound wisdom and plenty of money. If they do not berate themselves, they are preoccupied with a fantasy that life could be more fulfilling if their wives were more motherly, tender, supportive, and feminine, but concomitantly their counterparts should also be ecstatically erotic, decisive, and brilliant.

Husbands and wives of the 1970s in effect, frequently expect of themselves and each other to enact the role of an omnipotent, omniscient parental figure. Unconsciously many people are seeking daily for the excitement of a Putin carnival and because they want so very much and feel so very deprived, many wives characterize their husbands as ogres and many husbands experience their wives as witches.

Because it is difficult for many spouses to achieve what they deem is sufficient fulfillment in a marriage, extra-marital affairs are not uncommon. Note the popularity of "swinging" and "switching" and the interest in encounter, sensitivity and nude marathon groups which renounce self and interpersonal understanding but champion instead physical holding and sex play. They all reflect a craving for blissful excitement which does not seem available within the confines of marital life. No longer does society frown as much as it once did on wedding ceremonies for other than two members of the opposite sex. Recently the *Des Moines Register* told of four-person marriages in which one husband-wife dyad married the other and shared sex and a home in staid Iowa.

Inasmuch as living in the 1970s has caused many to believe that blissful excitement is eminently and consistently attainable, a lot of people are in a state of frustration. This frustration activates hatred and has made the war of the sexes more acute than ever. Because men and women are so frequently locked in struggles, there are now accepted alternatives to heterosexuality—homosexuality and bisexuality. Mayors boast of Gay Pride Week and college officials get brownie points when they speak of increased attendance in gay groups on campus. Social workers have been quick to legitimize and organizationally support Gay Social Workers and Lesbian Social Workers without giving much thought to why these social workers fear heterosexual love and resist family life and procreation.

Testimony to our age of sensation and narcissism is what makes a book a bestseller in the 1970s. Bestsellers are frequently self-help books which place almost exclusive stress on gratifying the narcissism of the individual reader. His desires become rights and others should cater to him. Nothing the reader does should be considered wrong and guilt should always be suppressed, not understood.

In the 1970s parents' expectations of their children are excessively high. David should be a great ball player, a superior student and an expert socializer. But, he should also be able to tolerate failure with ease. He should be aggressive but conforming, autonomous but obedient, well groomed but modishly sloppy. To help him feel "secure" he should be given plenty of rewards and other indulgences. However, he should also take his parents' withholding very gracefully. Many young people, who frequently have been quite gratified if not over-gratified most of their lives, often rebel at the restraints that the responsibilities of incipient adulthood place on them and argue that their parents and other adults do not understand them sufficiently. Depressed because their powerful and frequently insatiable (but in their opinion justifiable) wants are frustrated, many of them look for the excitement which is absent but "necessary" by participating in the drug scene and in love-ins. There are now in this country close to a million teen-age alcoholics. The popular practice among young people of living together without being formally married reveals a wish for gratification, but without the responsibilities of a commitment. Their question is, "Why should I commit myself to one person when somebody or something else that is better might turn up?" Their fears of intimacy involvement and empathetic closeness go underground. Just as the parents of our young people feel that there is an available Paradise, young people find it difficult to commit themselves to one person, one occupation, or even one major in college. "I don't want to be confined or controlled. There is something better but I haven't found it yet!" seems to be the sentiment of many young people. It is a fight, of course, against the anxiety that punctured omnipotence and narcissism stirs up. As Bettelheim put it, "Whenever the older generation has lost its bearings, the younger generation is lost."

The urban and suburban dweller, in contrast to his rural antecedent is swamped by many primitive desires. Life contains very few limits and controls and even these can be challenged. Living can be much better, and if we can't find it in our job, marriage, neighborhood or community, we can switch. Similar to the young child, many adults believe that Paradise and constant joy can be achieved. It is somewhere and that is why we Americans are so mobile. Perfection in a job, mate, and sex is available. Many will travel miles to get it—it's there!

Because we want so very much that is unrealistic, our frustration

turns into desperation and our anguish becomes converted into a series
of rallying cries. If growing up in a family has been a horror, do away
with families. If intimacy is frightening, let us have open marriage. If
we are unsure about our sexual identities, let us attack the opposite sex
and if children seem like a curse, let's stop having them (Hendin, 1975).

Industrialized society with its unlimited opportunity structure has not
only made us think that constant bliss is eminently attainable, but that it
is just around the corner. One can be the recipient of love and admiration always—we just have to learn the right mechanical methods of
attaining them. Sex manuals, which often forget about love and
genuine intimacy but concentrate instead on steps 1, 2, 3, and 4, are
more popular than ever. We are constantly stimulated everywhere and
many of us are in a state of anxious excitation, wanting and wishing for
more and more. No wonder depressions, tranquilizers, suicides, divorces, power struggles and the rest are commonplace. If one does not
get his rightful due, something is terribly wrong with him or terribly
wrong with his spouse, relative, friend, or associate.

In a paper by Peter Glick (1977), executive director of the Columbus,
Ohio Jewish Family Service, entitled "Individualism, Society and Social Work," the author has documented how individualism as it is being
pursued today expresses itself in egocentricity and impulse-ridden behavior. Glick has effectively demonstrated how increased narcissism is
tearing the family apart and that the tremendous value placed on "doing
one's thing" is fostering the demise of the family unit.

The Contemporary Family and Social Work Intervention

Many of the families that confront today's social work practitioners are
unfortunately plagued by infantile, gradiose, and omnipotent desires
reminiscent of a young child and much of family life is a paradigm of
discontent because of the reduced capacity of men and women to give
and to feel protective and loving towards each other and their children.

Depression, dejection, anger and unhappiness in contemporary family is something that is not well understood even by contemporary
psychotherapists. Unhappy people *feel* deprived and angry but they
frequently are miserable because they want things which cannot be
attained—perfect looks, the perfect job, the perfect spouse, the perfect
supervisor, etc.—and frequently they are unwilling to expend the effort
to secure what is realistically attainable. As social workers who want to

strengthen family life, we have to face the fact that many of our clients do not know that one cannot expect to be understood and loved in a family or elsewhere without understanding and loving. Many of our clients do not know that one cannot expect cooperation from another without cooperating. In the families that we see, many of their members need help in understanding that they cannot expect "the other" to stop resenting them unless they first come to grips with their own contempt. Many of our clients have not learned that they cannot compete gracefully unless they allow for a loss. Some do not know that they cannot be heard unless they are also willing to listen. Many of our clients still believe that they should, can, and have a right to be considered at all times what Freud referred to as "His Majesty the Prince or Princess." Holding onto this conviction with tenacity, they become easily angered, and easily depressed.

We social workers sometimes get overly influenced by our hate culture and can forget our mission with married couples and families. Instead of using our knowledge of the unconscious and defenses to help a wife or husband who blasts the marital partner, we are too often tempted to join the client in his or her attacks—under the guise of enhancing assertiveness and freedom. When a husband or wife complains about the partner's sadism, stupidity, or lack of sexuality, we always have to ask, "Why does the client unconsciously want it that way? What protection does it offer the client when he or she experiences the spouse as a punitive superego, a half-dead mammal, or a ninny? In family therapy we always must ferret out why a particular member of the family is used as a scapegoat. What's in it for the goat and what's in it for members who are abusing him or her? Social workers must recognize that hatred is a resistance against love and that many of our clients feel humiliated, guilty, and weakened when they think of loving some one. They do not see love as liberating and leading to mental health. We as social workers must communicate our love, not by advice giving, not by reward and punishment, not necessarily by championing what the client champions, but by demonstrating our faith in his or her ability to look beneath the surface of his complaints and help him see how he writes in many ways his own self-destructive script.

Social workers who live in the Age of Sensation—which favors instant gratification over the reality principle, narcissism over interpersonal cooperation, and ventilation over introspection—have at times been too seduced by the encounter movement, the marathons, and the sensitivity movements. These so-called therapies all too often promote a type of aggressive foreplay—stimulating, exciting, but regressive and rarely ego building.

As Dr. Hans Strupp (1977) has recently pointed out, increasing numbers of people are entering a vastly expanding arena of therapies and quasi-therapies. Many of these innovative approaches to human problems depart sharply from the better known traditional therapies and capitalize upon sensationalism, promising substantial results in brief periods of time. Significant change in these therapies is often predicated upon an intense emotionally charged experience for the patient. Any massive assault on a person's defenses, as occurs in weekend encounter groups, marathons, primal therapy, Erhard training seminars and others, heightens the potential for uncontrolled arousal of powerful affects and the possibility of decompensation or other negative effects. Because of these hazards one might expect that close attention had been paid by researchers and clinicians to the study of outcomes from these therapies. This has not been the case and the few reports available are self-serving testimonials gathered by the proponents of a particular approach rather than objective and dispassionate investigations.

Even within the province of the more traditional therapeutic approaches, there is a movement toward brief interventions. Evaluations of results are focused on a narrow range of outcomes or changes in "target complaints" which fail to provide a complete assessment of the impact of these confrontative, short-term therapies on the client's total life.

Of course these new therapies "work." But, so does torture! The issue here is not the efficacy but the ethical and therapeutic dimensions of manipulative therapies. Short term symptomatic gains are achieved at the cost of sacrificing the client's long term developmental potential and as Robert Langs (1977) has said, "Many deviations in technique are not undertaken primarily because of the patient's needs, but are rationalizations of the extensive counter-gratifications they offer the therapist."

If one looks at the profession of social work historically one would have to characterize a good deal of current practice as regressive and fragmentary. In the days of Mary Richmond, although most help was limited to manipulating the client's environment and attempting to influence the client's "significant others" (Richmond, 1917), the friendly visitor was a disciplined professional who, though rigid and moralistic, had a clear focus in her diagnostic and interventive efforts.

When the friendly visitor learned that all clients did not respond positively to environmental manipulation and advice, psychoanalysis became a useful theory to undergird diagnosis and intervention. Psychoanalysis helped the social worker understand that while people may consciously want to change, they have unconscious wishes to preserve the status quo and can derive neurotic gratification from their suffering (Hamilton, 1958).

Although the metapsychology of Freud was and is helpful to social workers, his theory of treatment was misused and abused by many of them. It took social workers some time to realize that interpretations of defenses and unconscious wishes have to be done judiciously. Of more importance, techniques like free association and dream analysis, social workers slowly and painfully realized, are more applicable to middle class clients with observing egos and full stomachs.

The Depression and the War years helped social workers once again appreciate the fact that people live in situations and that all of the self-understanding in the world cannot rectify a dilapidated house, a decrepit neighborhood, or a chaotic welfare system. Social workers by the 1950s were actively talking about the person–situation constellation (Hamilton, 1951) and recognized that we cannot help a client unless we appreciate how and why his situation influences him and vice-versa.

I believe that the person-in-situation focus with its strong emphasis on study, diagnosis, and treatment, so widely adhered to in the 1950s, is what makes social work unique and what social workers should stress more today. Instead, practitioners have not taken sufficient pride in their understanding and skill in working with inner man and his environment, but have been unduly influenced by manipulative techniques like behavior modification, and other therapies which do not focus very much on person-situation interaction. All too often the social worker of the 1970s is too intimidated by the knowledge explosion and feels that his practice must be viewed in the language of system theory, role theory, organizational theory, and communication theory. To surround social work practice with a flock of theories that are not always applicable to the person-in-his-situation is not even a constructive intellectual exercise! The social worker of the 1970s always must ask of the new theoretical perspectives: "What is pertinent to practice?" "How will the concept help clients?"

As new modalities confront social workers such as task oriented casework, crisis intervention, and brief family therapy, they are too often experienced as panaceas and used indiscriminately. Insufficiently asked by social workers are the following questions: "What is the level of psychosocial functioning of the individual and/or family members that makes a particular modality the intervention of choice?" "What are the defensive patterns of the client or client system that makes one form of intervention threatening while another one is more palatable?" "How does the client experience the worker transferentially as he enacts the broker role, the crisis intervenor, short term therapist or advocate?" "Does the particular modality induce regression or progression, and what will be most therapeutic now?" In sum, there seem to be in current social work practice an absence of careful selection of modalities and an absence of a careful assessment of their usefulness for specific person-situation constellations (Neubauer, 1978).

Just as our Age of Sensation has induced much regressive behavior, more and more social workers seem to be attracted to regressive therapies like encounter groups, primal scream, and the sensitivity movements. More and more in the social work literature one notes the endorsement of therapeutic interventions which reduce the human being to an aggregate of stimuli and responses, devoid of hopes, dreams, fantasies, values, hurts, joys, and no unconscious mind. In our current era, the social work practitioner all too often overlooks the uniqueness of the person as he pigeonholes people into roles and subsystems and loses sight of the unifying genetic and experiential bases and the dynamic interaction of its parts. In many quarters social work's tra-ditional commitment to problem solving is whittled down from the person with the problem, to the problem. We are now witnessing a proliferation of specialists each confining himself to an artifically de-lineated and inevitably sterile area of practice. A number of experts converge on one family, each one nibbling in his domain, be it marital problems, child care, or employment (Grossbard, 1976).

As practitioners have become enamored with superficial interven-tions, as panaceas become popular like gurus are to young people, we have been witnessing more and more of what I have referred to as "The Flight from the Client" (Strean, 1978). In current social work we have a reward and punishment system which demeans practice. If a prac-titioner does good work with clients, he is promoted by removing him from clients and made a supervisor. In effect, the more ability the worker has, the more he'll be removed to the periphery of practice. The same phenomenon exists in our schools of social work where those who are nearest to practice and to clients, i.e., the field work instructors, have the least status. A social work educator, like a practitioner, is also rewarded by being removed from practice. If he does well as a field work instructor, he'll be transferred to the classroom and if he does well in the classroom, he'll become a sequence chairman or a dean and be further removed from practice.

As part of our current regression in social work, the modal practitioner is fast becoming a B.S.W. who is supervised by an M.S.W. with limited practice experiences; both are being educated by a D.S.W. who has worked with clients for only a short while, or who has not seen a client in years.

Social Work Intervention and Values

In order to help our clients—individuals, dyads, and families—our work must be guided by some values. We believe that man and woman, boy and girl can attain happiness through a way of living which involves love rather than hate, pleasure, sexual gratification, a feeling for life but which is guided by reason, an adequate role in the family, a sense of identity, constructive work, and a role in the social order. This is what Dr. Reuben Fine (1971) calls the "analytic ideal." If social workers strive for this ideal they serve as appropriate models for their clients— but not by imposing these values on them but by helping them look at what in them prevents them from having realistic pleasure and enjoyable interpersonal relationships.

Continual psychosocial growth and an enjoyable family life, whether it be for a child, man, or woman, not only implies realistic gratifications but experiences in coping with frustration. Most would agree that the maturation of a youngster not only requires the tenderness and nurturing of a mother, but eventual weaning must take place. Further growth inevitably requires frustrating the child's natural inclination to soil his diapers; toilet training is inevitable. Just as children need warm but firm training in giving up certain pleasures like the breast and soiling and learning to adapt to what Sigmund Freud called the reality principle, so too we must help our adult clients who have not grown up to recognize that there is no Garden of Eden. The idea of living in a Garden of Eden is pure fantasy and even Adam and Eve had their troubles there!

To help our clients enjoy marriage, and family life, we have to help them realize that their role partners can never supply them with eternal bliss. As therapists we know that bliss is always a momentary experience. But, our clients' lives can be fuller and more satisfying when they can truly accept frustration as an inevitable part of living. When they can assimilate and integrate into their daily interactions that their relatives, friends, colleagues and therapists cannot minister to their every wish, they are freer to enjoy their potentials. Furthermore, they are also helped when they can recognize that they cannot nor should not attempt to gratify each and every desire of their mates and friends. To aim for omnipotence, our clients should learn, is to court disaster. To accept reality as it is, permits much room for happiness.

Urban industrialized society does whet our clients' appetites. They often find themselves placed in a position similar to that of a young child in an immense candy store. They get overwhelmed by all of the niceties but find it difficult to forego pleasure. Yet, they can learn they do not have to eat everything in sight because if they do they'll get sick and if they even try, they might get nauseous. High on the list of the most common neurotic symptoms today are ulcers and obesity. These gastro-intestinal disorders are manifestations of psychological hunger. People want to devour everything in sight but simultaneously want to be svelte and have a well functioning stomach.

Our clients and we, too, are entitled to some inner peace, some pleasure from our confreres, some fulfillment from our pursuits and some feeling of stable identity. When Freud was asked how to achieve these precious ingredients, he answered tersely, "Lieben und Arbeiten"—"Love and work!" Those of his followers who wished to embellish on this prescription have offered rather simple but sage prescriptions. They have pointed out that a mutual love relationship involves listening to one's mate, not only being listened to. It involves absorbing his or her "no's" as well as being pleased with his or her "yes's" and it involves a concern for and understanding of his or her feelings and appreciating his or her attempts at same. Mature love requires an identification with "the other" so that his or her triumphs and disappointments, frustrations and joys are in some way ours as well. It involves the ability to light a candle rather than curse the darkness. That is the attitude that stimulates love, and a family without love between its members is really no family.

With regard to children, true love means not just vicariously enjoying their pleasures and achievements but absorbing and understanding their anger when they must be frustrated. It involves not only helping them enjoy the successes of which they are capable of achieving but helping them recognize that part of the human experience is encountering and living with failure in ourselves and others.

To function maturely in today's complex society requires of the individual sufficient autonomy so that the lack of praise or criticism does not crush him. When he can accept what he has rather than fantasize about what he doesn't have, he can better withstand the onslaughts of those who do not view him so positively.

Love, empathy, and work, though the hallmarks and necessary ingredients for a sound family life and sound mental health, never mean an endorsement of masochism. If marriage, parenthood, and the nurturing of children are viewed as unjustifiable self-sacrifice, then mutual self-affirming love will be replaced by resentment and an inability to communicate real love.

Winston Churchill once said that democracy is the worst form of government except for all other forms. Something similar might be said of the family. There is nothing better and we know that individuals who have renounced ties to a family are miserable, unhappy and angry individuals.

James Reston of the *New York Times* has written:

> If preachers are not to be believed and politicians are not to be trusted, and society as a whole is a jumble of lies and tricks, then the family may still be the best bet available, maybe even better than being liberated into loneliness.

Wrote James Baldwin:

> The sea rises, the light fails, lovers cling to each other, and children cling to us. The moment we stop holding one another, the moment we break faith with one another, the sea engulfs us and the light goes out.

REFERENCES

Ackerman, N. *The Psychodynamics of Family Life*. New York: Basic Books, 1958.

Bowlby, J. *Maternal Care and Mental Health*. Geneva: World Health Organization Monograph, 1951.

Coles, R. "The Cold, Tough World of the Affluent Family," *Psychology Today*, November 1975.

Erikson, E. *Childhood and Society*. New York: Norton, 1950.

Fanshel, D. "Sources of Strain in Practice Oriented Research," *Social Casework*, Vol. 47, No. 6, 1966.

Fine, R. *The Healing of the Mind*. New York: David McKay, 1971.

Freud, A. *Normality and Pathology in Childhood, The Writings of Anna Freud*, Vol. 6. New York: International Universities Press, 1965.

Glick, P. "Individualism, Society, and Social Work," *Social Casework*, Vol. 56, No. 10, 1977.

Grossbard, H. "Book Review of H. Strean's *Personality Theory and Social Work Practice*," (Metuchen, N.J.: Scarecrow Press, 1975), *Social Work*, Vol. 21, No. 4, 1976.

Hamilton, G. "A Theory of Personality: Freud's Contribution to Social Work," in *Ego Psychology and Dynamic Casework*, H. Parad, ed. New York: Family Service Association of America, 1958.

———. *Theory and Practice of Social Casework*. New York: Columbia University Press, 1951.

Hendin, H. *The Age of Sensation*. New York: Norton, 1975.

Jones, E. *The Life and Work of Sigmund Freud*, Vol. 1. New York: Basic Books, 1953.

Langley, R., and R. Levy. *Wife Beating: The Silent Crisis*. New York: Dutton, 1977.

Langs, R. *The Bipersonal Field*. New York: Jason Aronson, 1976.

Masters, W., and V. Johnson. *Human Sexual Inadequacy*. Boston: Little and Brown, 1970.

Merton, R., and R. Nisbet. *Contemporary Social Problems*. New York: Harcourt Brace, 1966.

Moroney, R. "The Family as a Social Service: Implications for Policy and Practice," *Child Welfare*, Vol. 55, No. 4, April 1978.

Neubauer, P. "Psychoanalysis versus Psychotherapy," *Bulletin of Washington Square Institute*, New York: The Institute, 1978.

New York Times. "Confronting Crisis in the Orthodox Jewish Family," January 25, 1978.

Richmond, M. *What Is Social Casework?* New York: Russell Sage Foundation, 1922.

Strean, H. *Clinical Social Work*. New York: The Free Press, 1978.

Strupp, H.; S. Hadley; and B. Gomes-Schwartz. *Psychotherapy for Better or Worse*. New York: Jason Aronson, 1977.

Valiant, G. *Adaptation to Life*. Boston: Little and Brown, 1977.

DISCUSSANT: ABRAHAM DAVIS

Dr. Strean's paper is compelling, provocative, insightful and tantalizing. He discusses the inherent value of the family and its fundamental importance to psychosocial development; the stresses and strains of the contemporary family; the symptomatic and destructive effects of narcissism on family life and individual development; the shift in social work theories and interventions from comprhensiveness to fragmentation. He concludes with some sagacious insights on how to help clients who exhibit narcissistic traits, which he primarily bases on the therapeutic intergration of the reality and pleasure principles.

While championing restraint, Strean at first glance is unrestrained as he attacks cultural, social, psychological phenomena and theories which he believes are endemic to mature development and in becoming a responsible family member. There is little that escapes his critical scalpel as he assails encounter and sensitivity groups, which he feels promote regression and stimulation without commitment; confronts individuals who search for new and different relationships based on omnipotent wishes and fantasies; challenges those who have unrealistic expectations of self, marital partners and children; criticizes self-help books which primarily cater to self-desire; opposes therapeutic theories, modalities and techniques which he claims are based on expediency, sensation and gimmickry rather than on understanding and differential assessment. He castigates the present model of social work education, and is contentious with those social workers who are consciously and unconsciously influenced by our narcissistic age and "hate culture" and its detrimental effects on their therapeutic endeavors.

Upon re-reading, Strean is to be commended for the courage of his convictions. His cogent analysis exposes the dubiousness of those lifestyles that promote self-fulfillment as the ultimate aim in life and therapies that promise instant resolution of individual and family conflicts. He unequivocally rejects a nihilistic framework and instead favors a clear set of values based on reality, reason, and understanding which social work practitioners can use to help family members live more productive and harmonious lives.

He effectively demonstrates that who we are and what we become is inextricably linked to our family upbringing; supports the desirability of wifehood, motherhood and eloquently favors cooperation and reciprocity in family interaction.

Strean is correct in inferring that the values and myths of our society with its stress on money, power, competitiveness and exploitation conflict with the idyllic belief that the family is considered to be the haven where love and comfort can be found, and where family members live cooperatively and supportively. These two contradictory aspects are particularly difficult for social work to resolve, since the profession has always struggled with its idealism and how to care and effect change in an uncaring society.[1]

Although he succinctly attempts to cover a broad range of issues, Strean's interpretations and conclusions stimulate controversy, and his limited elaboration of his many viewpoints raises as many questions as it answers.

He points out that the uniqueness of social work is its emphasis on the "person in situation" and "working with inner man and his environment," but the focus of his interventions is based on "inner man" with only passing reference to the "situation" and "environment." He powerfully describes and picturesquely captures the bleakness, emptiness and dysfunction of individual family members who are attracted to a narcissistic way of life, but his prescriptions hardly take into account society's influence on child-rearing patterns, the glorification of violence and the many different ways that society fosters individualism, narcissism, feelings of powerlessness and irrelevance.[2]

Strean's recommended interventions may help family members cope more realistically with frustration and inevitable limitations, but he does not consider how social programs have tended to replace family tasks and roles, rather than strengthening its capacities to perform its functions,[3] and how mental health disciplines have undermined parent–child relationships and hampered parents' confidence in their parenting capacities.[4]

I agree with Strean's suggestions that social work education and practitioners have departed from their traditional theoretic framework and have embraced new therapies, values and interventions, with shallow rationalizations and minimal consideration of their latent meaning. He is critical of theories and treatment modalities that deny individual differences and uniqueness, minimize feelings and experiences, and instead focus on the "problem" to be solved.

Although he attempts to be evenhanded, Strean favors a psychoanalytic approach to treat family dysfunction. While cognizant of and sensitive to family dynamics, he tends to deal with *individuals* who comprise a family. He makes only passing reference to family oriented practice. In highlighting the history of social work, he fails to sufficiently take into account that from its inception, the *family* was an integral concern of social work theory and practice.[5] In fact, the first professional practice journal was titled, "The Family."

Just as Strean points out that an individual is comprised of more than "stimuli and responses," a family consists of something more than its individual members. It is an emotional and social system with its own life cycle and governed by boundaries, rules, structure, space and time. A shift from an individual approach to a family focus may accomplish more dramatically what Strean envisions—which is to make "us more committed to values of fairness, cooperation, mutuality and harmony than to values of self-actualization, individual success and unlimited freedom."[6]

Although he is correct in pointing out probing questions that need to be asked before considering an intervention, he omits a crucial one: namely, if a child, adolescent or marital partner is involved in long term individual treatment, what impact and ultimate effect will this have on the client's family?

While Strean alludes to other factors that weaken the contemporary family, he prefers to primarily focus on one concept, "increased narcissism." The crux of his conception of narcissism is based on the idea that many people have been overgratified in early childhood, and therefore grow up with poor impulse control and with beliefs that the "world owes them a living"; others should always cater to their wishes and whims and their insatiable desire for newer and more stimulating experiences should not be frustrated. He incisively documents the tragic effects of those who can't get what they want—either because it is illusionary and unobtainable—or because they have not sufficiently developed the ego capacities of perseverance and mastery which would ultimately result in achievement and self-satisfaction. Instead, these people seek to reenact the omnipotent pleasures and fantasies of infancy without being able to integrate the responsibilities and task assignments of the adult life cycle.

We can readily recognize many clients who reflect these conflicts, but his analysis does not sufficiently distinguish the cultural and social effects of narcissism from its *clinical* diagnostic entity, and he therefore discusses its etiology from a limited framework.

Although clinicians posit a variety of explanations to account for the cause of narcissistic disorders, it is abundantly clear that it stems from many factors other than "overgratification."[7]

It appears to result either from a fixation or traumatization during the first year of life or during the separation-individuation phase, which impedes one's ability to internalize good interpersonal relations and to synthesize good and bad introjects. Thus the overinvestment and preoccupation with the "self" can be viewed as a defense against rage, powerlessness, weakness, inferiority. This results in people endlessly seeking objects to replace disappointing and/or rejecting parents or to unrealistically assert their grandiosity to convince themselves of their self-worth.

In summary, Strean has provided us with an illuminating analysis with which to view family problems and their treatment. While I have discussed additional considerations, his description of the "analytic ideal" is a model worth striving for—not only for our clients but for ourselves.

If indeed more family members than ever before are reflecting narcissistic disorders, social work practice with a focused integration of intrapsychic, interpersonal and societal phenomena is perhaps the best suited profession to combat family breakdown. As Jim Guy Tucker, chairperson of the White House Conference on Families, stated, "Our task is to insure that when government touches our families, it *helps* instead of *hurts*—that it *supports* instead of *undermines*."[8]

The same can, should and must apply to social work practice.

REFERENCES

1. Carol Meyer, "Social Work Purpose: Status by Choice or Coercion?" *Social Work*, 26 (January 1981), pp. 69–75.

2. Beatrice Simcox Reiner, "A Feeling of Irrelevance: The Effects of a Nonsupportive Society," *Social Casework*, Volume 60 (January 1979), pp. 3–10.

3. Christopher Lasch, *Haven in a Heartless World*. New York: Basic Books, 1977.

4. Christopher Lasch, *The Culture of Narcissism*. New York: W. W. Norton, 1978.

5. Ann Hartman, "The Family: A Central Focus for Practice," *Social Work*, Volume 26 (January 1981), pp. 7–13.

6. Seymour Halleck, "Family Therapy and Social Change," *Social Casework*, 57 (October 1976), p. 493.

7. See for example: Otto Kernberg, *Borderline Conditions and Pathological Narcissism* (New York: Jason Aronson, 1975); *Object Relations Theory and Clinical Psychoanalysis* (New York: Jason Aronson, 1976); Heinz Kohut, *The Analysis of the Self: A Systematic Approach to the Psychoanalytic Treatment of Narcissistic Personality Disorders* (New York: International Universities Press, 1971); Sophie Lowenstein, An Overview of the Concept of Narcissism, *Social Casework*, 58 (March 1977), pp. 136–142, and Anne O. Freed, The Borderline Personality, *Social Casework*, 61 (November 1980), pp. 548–59.

8. *Listening to America's Families*. Washington, D.C.: White House Conference on Families, 1980, p. 11.

DISCUSSANT: RALPH L. KOLODNY

A dirge such as Herbert Strean sounds for the present all too often becomes, by implication, a lament for the past. One must, therefore, regard it with some degree of wariness. To be sure, any thoughtful social worker reading his wideranging polemic against disorganization in the contemporary American family and the hedonism currently abroad in the land will find himself deeply stirred, and rightly so. This is a powerful statement of concern. One's inclination is, in response, to simply fall in behind Strean's banner of family integrity.

Certainly, this social worker, by the time he put down "The Contemporary Family and the Responsibilities of the Social Worker in Direct Practice" was ready to march. With Strean, he would take up the cudgel against epicureanism, irresponsibility, mindless divorce, the leap to a mechanistic view of man, the fear of commitment, brief treatment as a panacea for the psychological ills of families and individuals, homosexuality as a never-to-be-examined sacred cow, the intimidating influx of new social theories and their frequent irrelevance to social work practice with families, or to any kind of practice at all, quick-fix encounter groups, and those who would denigrate love and family's capacity to offer it.

As a social work educator who was a frequent target of students' attacks in their warfare on professors during the late 1960s and early 1970s—attacks whose parricidal overtones were all too apparent[1]—this reviewer warmed to Strean's castigation of the indulged generation, "the entitledniks" as they have been dubbed by friend and colleague, James Garland. Teachers who were involved can never forget the careless cruelty and self-and-other destructiveness of those who figuratively or literally took over their classrooms. They could only wonder then about the family life that spawned this excrescence.

Those who dared to reproach these college-age children for their behavior also remember casting about in vain for support from many of their colleagues. Often they were told by the more "advanced" of their fellow social workers and educators that they were over-reacting to what was, after all, legitimate, though perhaps excessive criticism of social institutions, such as schools and families, which had failed their missions. This writer also cannot forebear mentioning that those social work teachers who, like himself, had in their own youth been soldiers during World War II or Korea, found having to listen to cries of "oppression" from young people who had clearly been materially comfortable and physically undisturbed all of their lives particularly galling.

Even now, when verbal abuse and litigious carping by students have ceased, for the most part, educators continue to be concerned. As the new decade begins, it is the lonely, petulant self-centeredness of students they encounter that gives them pause. The subjects of Herbert Hendin's treatment and research, referred to by Strean, emotionally lost young adults, bent on immediate gratification of every whim, also continue to haunt some of our corridors. One moves from pity for these individuals to a scarcely disguised impulse to strike back at them. For it is they who would force the older generation to give up its notions of adulthood and its idealized version of family life. Thus, when Strean sounds a clarion call to save the family—rescuing the best elements in the family of the past—one feels immediately, "How good it is that someone with professional authority has at last spoken out on this matter and in such forthright fashion." Then he rushes to join Strean in his efforts to insure that, come what may, the family in its present form will survive.

Caution is the word, however, for although one may agree with the need to preserve the family idea, he may also find, on closer inspection, that some aspects of Strean's assessment of the social malady afflicting the American family may be somewhat askew. His "diagnostic" formulations may, to a degree, miss the mark. As a matter of fact, some of his views may be as much a part of the problem as those whose ideas and behavior he decries. It could be that the most fundamental of the inconsistencies and incongruities underlying contemporary parental behavior and family atmosphere are not of recent origin at all but have been deeply imbedded in our cultural ethos for centuries. The unconscious and double messages from parents, Strean cites, while important, may be considerably less important than other contradictory signals given off by the culture. Of these signals he seems unaware.

Actually, Strean appears to accept the "homely truths" on which this society has been built and from which much of our family life still takes its meaning. Such homely truths held to by an "older generation" that has "lost its bearings," however, may reflect other, deeper social and psychological splits.

Strean, for example, seizes on the matter of impulsive, aggressive behavior by today's adolescents. This he would have us understand mainly as a product of a parental need to mismanage, so to speak. The troubled parent, unloved and unloving, unconsciously encourages his child to act out violently. "It has been well documented," he writes, "that teenagers who resort to violence and impulsive behavior are subtly and tacitly, albeit unconsciously, encouraged by their parents to do so, and that those who champion love, work and consideration of others have been exposed to a loving and cooperative family." One can hardly quarrel with this general notion. But what leaves Strean most impressed is the fact that "successful" men come from these loving and cooperative families. It is noteworthy that he seems quite prepared to accept unquestioningly society's definition of successful and to see such "success" as good. He cites a study of the lives of 95 successful men, that is, "best-selling novelists, cabinet members, scholars, captains of industry, physicans, teachers of the first rank, judges and newspaper editors." The author, we are told, demonstrated that, "contrary to popular belief, men who became successful, had very happy marriages, enjoyable family relationships and rich friendships." We are left at sea as to whether, outside of close relationships, for instance in relation to employees or the socially disadvantaged, these are loving or humane men. The particular array he mobilizes leaves one in doubt. Strean apparently does not consider this fact important in this context, however.

Parental mismanagement, unconsciously motivated or otherwise, and parental double messages, are again held to account by Strean for the confusion and fierce narcissism of today's youth. The expectations of parents in the seventies and eighties, he writes, are "excessively high." The youngster is supposed to be a fine athlete *and* a great student. He must be *both* aggressive and conforming. He should feel secure and therefore must be indulged, but he is also expected to take his parents' withholding very gracefully. No wonder, says Strean, the products of such treatment in today's family "look for the excitement which is absent but 'necessary' by participating in the drug scene and in love-ins." And consider the fact of a million teen-age alcoholics.

Surely, however, double messages, contrary demands, and self-cancelling requirements of the sort which Strean correctly identifies are not new phenomena. Perhaps the contradictions with which all of us have to deal are even more profound. Perhaps central to our societal ethos, an ethos which Strean does not seem to question at its core, is a deeper tension, a vital disturbance, if you will, stemming from two opposing ideals in our culture. This tension was well described by the late Maurice Samuel over thirty years ago. There is space only to touch on Samuel's central thesis in the paragraphs which follow. He elaborates on this thesis in great detail in what was to be one of the last of his books, *The Gentleman and the Jew*.[2] The reader will find going through the entire volume a most rewarding experience.

If Samuel is correct, Western European and American parents, for centuries now, as carriers of Western culture, have been demanding of their children and of themselves that they live according to two diametrically and eternally opposed sets of values simultaneously: one stressing collaboration and love, and one, unabashedly violent, extolling competition and conflict. Furthermore, they remain unconscious of the contradiction involved.

The split—the contradiction in parental demands Strean described earlier—would seem to be susceptible of healing if only the parents would allow the child to be *either* more of an athlete *or* more of a scholar. Samuel, on the other hand, devotes some three hundred pages to explaining why these two ideals, the athletic and the scholarly, are irreconcilable. The former, he asserts, finds its ultimate expression in the person of the "gentleman" whose main objective, since life is a game, is to win, that is, to crush his opponent, although, it is hoped—again, since life is a game—that he will do so without hating him. This "gentleman" says Samuel, is the distinguished, well-tutored "courtly killer" who, once off the playing field—which, rather than becoming a means of sublimation, too quickly becomes the battlefield—is courteous and even kindly to his opponents.

The Judeo–Christian ideal, Samuel avers, in no way conceives of life as a game but is concerned with life as a search for moral fulfillment. The scholar, in this, the ancient Jewish sense, does not look for "success" but is a seeker with others after goodness. The gentleman, who is described approvingly in much of our Western literature, in Plato, in Castiglione's *The Courtier*, and in Shakespeare, is the noble athlete for whom life is essentially a contest. The overriding aim of his life is to come out on top, he is a seeker of power over others. War, itself, becomes the game par excellence, since it provides one with the greatest opportunity to exercise power. The gentle hero, the skillful warrior, who, in the words of Shakespeare's *Henry V*, "covets honor," but is not angry with his foes, and may even have friendships with individuals among them, remains perhaps the single most attractive figure in our culture. We tend to overlook the fact that what he stands for is in direct opposition to the teachings of the prophets or Christ, whom our society, including the non-religious, supposedly reveres. Above all, this "gentleman," and Samuel turns again to *Henry V*, is, for all his courtliness, desirous of "creating awe and fear in other men." Thus, finally, Samuel writes:

> And it is borne in upon us that the gentleman, the lover of honor, is essentially a killer! He must kill because in the last analysis "creating awe and fear in other men" calls for control over their lives, and this control must be demonstrated from time to time in its ultimate form—the taking of life.
>
> Behind the attractive hokum, then, behind the gallantry, the gentleness, democracy, the modesty, behind all these things, looms in control the ancient abomination. And this ancient abomination we must not confront, because if we do confront it—and I do not mean just intellectually, but in a naked *corps à corps* confrontation of complete, horrified understanding—all our world comes tumbling about our ears.[3]

Samuel serves up what may seem like exotic fare. His ideas, however, remain for this critic among the most penetrating and disturbing he has encountered. One cannot offer a critique of an institution like the contemporary family in America, and the behavior of its members, as Strean does, without taking into account the type of analysis of Western culture Samuel offers. Strean should consider the possibility that the American family which he seems to believe is newly in trouble has, like much else in our culture, been psychologically riven for some time. This condition, incidentally, antedates "industrial society," which Strean, at one point, singles out as a major contributor to family malaise, by many hundreds of years. Ultimately, Strean's notions in regard to the foregoing discussion may be criticized as being culture-bound. This is not so much because of the value conflicts which he discusses, but because of the more fundamental conflicts in values, such as those which Samuel ponders, which he overlooks.

The aphorisms of a Bettelheim, whom Strean quotes approvingly, are, of course, seductive. They do little more, however, than to thicken the atmosphere of nostalgia. To accept the idea that, "Whenever the older generation has lost its bearings the younger generation is lost" is to believe that the older generation not only had bearings of which they were certain, but that these bearings indeed protected them from becoming "lost."

One cannot help remembering in this connection, first, the slogan of a bygone era, "The family that prays together, stays together," and then the recent TV advertisement of a supermarket chain in the Boston area. This consists of playing a song with the words, "The basic things you used to know, were they so long ago? Where did those basic values go?" As this music is played, pictures appear on the screen of Norman Rockwell-like drawings featuring clean, tree-lined villages, complete with white church steeples and smiling apple-cheeked youngsters and adults of obviously impeccable lineage, dressed in clothes from the decade of the 1930s. The phrasing is awkward. The message, however, is clear.

Even granting that the family in America was once a more stable institution, however, a serious question remains. Did the fact that families were not "lost," in Bettelheim's sense, or "stayed together," or held to "basic values," make for a society which was any less troubled than today's? One wonders. Perhaps "the urban and suburban dweller, in contrast to his rural antecedent is swamped by many primitive desires," as Strean has it, with unfortunate consequences for him and for society, although this kind of Tolstoyan view can be challenged. It is necessary to remind oneself, however, that in the predominantly rural America of the past, in which family virtues were extolled, society tolerated and even perpetrated horrors of monumental proportions. Today's "flight from intimacy" is profoundly saddening; zero population growth is a worrisome notion, as Strean rightly emphasizes. The prevalence of violent crime is frightening and bodes none of us good. In earlier times, however, many individuals who were raised in reasonably loving rural and semirural as well as urban families saw nothing wrong, for example, with black semi-slavery in the South and the degradation of blacks in the North.

Anti-Semitism was even more of a staple than it is today, even though the "blessings" of rural family life were still to a large degree present. There are adults now in their fifties and sixties who can remember their fathers solemnly ushering the family into the living room on Sunday afternoons some 45 years ago to listen to the radio sermons of Father Charles E. Coughlin, who was easily the most popular radio orator of the day. These sermons included vitriolic attacks on Jews worthy of a Josef Goebbels. Millions of Americans in rural and urban America looked forward to his weekly broadcasts and listened to his outrageous ideas, apparently, in most instances, approvingly.[4]

The boys' books of the period extolled the virtues of life away from the city, in the forest or on the farm. They clearly supported the family ideal, along with those of nation and church. They also drove home several other sorts of values, and these would today have given some of us considerable pause. (The idealization of stable family life, by the way, apparently had no ameliorative effect on these more insidious values.) This reviewer, for example, remembers well a boys' book of the day which recounted the peacetime adventures of two young American soldiers stationed in the Philippines. At one point, while walking down the street, they notice a "native" eyeing a pretty American young woman. Says one to the other, "I just don' like a yellow man looking at a white woman that way." There was no lack of certainty here about one's sexual identity. Similarly, however, there was complete conviction on the part of the author and characters that, what we would consider the most vicious sort of race prejudice, was entirely proper, and, perhaps more importantly, would be accepted as such by their adolescent readers.

What Strean proposes by way of approaching the morass of problems facing the contemporary American family makes considerable sense, as far as it goes. It seems to this reviewer, however, that within the rather wide theoretical net he casts he fails to include a series of problems and methods that deserve consideration. Briefly put, Strean correctly emphasizes person-in-situation as a conceptual tool for assessment and treatment. After bowing only slightly in the direction of the latter— actually, about one paragraph's worth—he proceeds to treat it only as a backdrop to the person. The "situation" needs a much more extensive presentation and penetrating analysis than is afforded here.

Even setting aside the situation of the client and considering instead that of the worker, it must be remembered that the services or treatment Strean describes are still, for the most part, mediated by the agencies which employ social workers. The relationships between workers and the administrations of these agencies clearly affect service and treatment and, therefore, demand examination. In some parts of the country, historically, under the aegis of boards made up of prominent and well-to-do members of the community, some private agencies have paid social workers very low salaries. The salaries of workers in public agencies in many states, of course, also has never been commensurate with their efforts. The impact this has had on direct work with families—social workers resenting their low salaries and their low status dealing with families in turmoil—cannot be discounted. It is an integral part of the situation in which clients find themselves, along with other social realities with which they have to contend. Strean's discussion is remote from matters of this sort.

The failure of workers and agencies to pursue collaborative work also receives little attention from Strean. No matter how talented the individual worker, something close to arrogance is required on his part if he is to believe he can tackle by himself the tangle of family problems to which Strean devotes a dozen or so pages. The need is for networks of workers and agencies to be involved. Here, examination of the possibility of collaboration with a host of different types of agencies and various modalities is required.

The notion of modalities, as conceived of by Strean in this connection, unfortunately, remains focused on the one-to-one or one-to-family enterprise. Agencies like settlement houses and community centers which, ironically enough, were created one hundred years ago precisely to bring the presumed stability of village neighborhood and family life to the disorganized urban slum, may be as important as any other single agency, or more so, to the effort Strean calls for.

One finally does have the sense that in some respects Strean's comments, while applicable to one social stratum and a particular era in America, have not kept pace with the swift course of events. The urban industrialized society he writes of is one which "whets the appetites of clients" who "often find themselves placed in a position similar to that of a young child in an immense candy store. They get overwhelmed by all of the niceties but find it difficult to forego pleasure. Yet, they can learn they do not have to eat everything in sight because if they do they'll get sick and if they even try, they might get nauseous." The large numbers of urban families which, each winter since 1973, have been choosing between limiting fuel and food, and the inadequacy of whose housing is a national disgrace, are sick from other causes. And, indeed, when they are sick they are not very well taken care of. These cannot be the families about whom Strean writes.

Similarly, even individuals and families from other than the lower social strata might look askance at Strean's advice for the future. "To function maturely in today's complex society," he emphasizes, "requires of the individual sufficient autonomy so that the lack of praise or criticism does not crush him." Strean, therefore, counsels, "When he can accept what he has rather than fantasize about what he doesn't have, he can better withstand the onslaughts of those who do not view him so positively."

Alas, suggestions which have considerable merit when the problem is that of psychological hunger begin to take on an unreal quality when severe economic problems intrude. Social workers and social work agencies cannot deceive themselves that they are equipped to deal with these latter problems. Neither, however, must they deny that the families who will need them the most in the grim years to come will be those in which a major trauma will not simply be "not being viewed positively" but actually losing one's job. Those theorists who, in the past, have been responsible for so much of the creative thinking in social work had best set their minds to considering the problems that will arise when many families are unemployed. If not, much of their otherwise useful advice, unfortunately, will have a hollow ring. Strean has affirmed that, "a sense of identity, work and a role in society" are all essential to the psychological well-being of youth. For many of today's young, and the not-so-young, as well, these essentials may very well be scarce commodities in the decade to come.

REFERENCES

1. See Lewis Feuer, *Conflict of Generations*. New York: Basic Books, 1969.

2. Maurice Samuel, *The Gentleman and the Jew*. New York: Alfred Knopf, 1950.

3. Ibid., p. 43.

4. Ralph Kolodny, "Father Couglin and the Jews: A Reminiscence for Younger Colleagues," *Journal of Jewish Communal Service*, Vol. LIII, No. IV, Summer, 1977, pp. 309–319.

Chapter 6

A NOTE ON THE TREATMENT OF THE SCHIZOPHRENIC PATIENT

For over two decades I have been actively engaged in the treatment of and research on the schizophrenic patient. Like most practitioners and practice theorists, I have not only given much thought to the etiology of the schizophrenic process but have constantly modified my therapeutic orientation and therapeutic posture when clinical experience and clinical research have warranted alterations.

Over the years I have come to view psychoanalytic and psychotherapeutic technique as a constantly evolving set of procedures, rooted in theory and influenced by a growing body of clinical experience. Each therapist, I believe, develops greater precision, discipline and finesse in his or her work, as personal experience expands. As Waldhorn has recently stated, "The limitless diversity of our patients' productions, the absolute uniqueness of each individual's life and of each moment in time, make standardization of technique an impossibility and rigidity of style a handicap. . . . The avoidance of mistaken emphases and of undue preoccupation with any one aspect of analytic material over all others is a vital part of the self-critical, self-observant and self-enriching responsibility of the analyst."[8]

The enormous literature on schizophrenia so far seems to indicate that no one specific etiological factor can fully account for the process. As Spotnitz has noted, "A biologically inherited disposition for the illness seems to be of some importance, combined with constitutional and experiental factors. . . ."[5]

When I initially embarked on my work with schizophrenic patients, I

Reprinted by permission from *The Psychoanalytic Review*, vol. 64, no. 2 (June 1977), pp. 203–210.

was faced almost immediately with a serious therapeutic dilemma. The classical psychoanalytic method which I was slowly learning to master seemed to induce a great deal of anxiety in my severely disturbed schizophrenic patients when I used it with them. Attempts to make the unconscious, conscious and analysis and interpretation of resistance and transference phenomena often stimulated a diminution in the patient's ego functioning. One example that I shall always remember was a schizophrenic woman whom I treated twenty-five years ago. She had painful and prolonged migraine headaches and I was eager to help her get rid of them. Inasmuch as the headaches often appeared in the therapeutic hour and with greater intensity there, I made the interpretation that the migraine headaches were an expression of her anger towards me. The interpretation was correct and when the patient verbalized her wishes to spit on me, kill me, etc., the headaches did disappear. However, as she expressed her hatred she became more delusional, suffered from more hallucinations and manifested strong paranoid ideation.

With several experiences like the aforementioned, I began to alter my approach. In lieu of analyzing resistances and transference manifestations, I anchored the schizophrenic patient's productions to reality, tried to keep the transference positive, and steered clear of primary process productions. While this kind of orientation, which is still quite popular today among many practitioners[1] did not provoke the kind of terror and anxiety that I saw in my patients heretofore, I noticed limited therapeutic movement and strong dependent transference relationships seemed to be the rule rather than the exception.

In the late 1950s I became very much interested in and influenced by the work of Robert Lindner who took the position that the schizophrenic's delusions and hallucinations and other primary process thinking were very much part of his psychic world, and that a failure by the therapist to enter into the patient's psychotic universe was part of the former's countertransference and counterresistance.[2] The experience of helping patients tell me how I or others were poisoning their soup or keeping a gun ready for them often reduced their anxiety and did in fact lead to better ego functioning and ego integration. This type of therapeutic activity was quite similar to play with children which I had been doing with my young patients for some time and therefore the transition was not too difficult. Furthermore, Lindner's orientation seemed quite compatible with what I already firmly believed was necessary for good therapy with any patient—to meet the patient where he or she is and to permit him to experience the world and the therapist any way the patient wished to do so. I slowly began to realize that my fears of psychotic material had exacerbated the patients' fears and torturous feelings.

As I began to feel more comfortable and achieve better therapeutic results with my patients, I became quite intrigued with the work of Spotnitz[5] and then later with Marie and Ben Nelson's paradigmatic psychotherapy.[3, 4] These practitioners have emphasized not only the need for respecting the patient's narcissistic defenses when these defenses were needed to protect the patient against disintegration but like Lindner, they have taken the position that the patient's view of the world, albeit at times very distorted, must be experienced by the therapist as a psychic reality to be confronted in the therapeutic encounter.

As I learned to relate to schizophrenic patients with more discipline, as they felt my permission to be more and more themselves, could hate or love me when they felt so inclined, could resist or produce when they wanted to, as preoedipal and pre-genital fantasies were given more and more expression, the more conventional analytic model in later stages of treatment could be utilized and utilized well. Like little children they needed first to crawl and fall, stutter and stammer before they could walk or talk.

One of the important insights that I gained in my work and research with the severely disturbed patient was his ability to instruct me at times as to what he or she needed in the therapy. Often these patients harbor fantasies as to what they needed from parental figures; consequently, having them prescribe the therapeutic doses[4] and become my consultant[6] has been therapeutically advantageous at certain stages of therapy.

I have presented a cursory review of my own work and study of the schizophrenic patient, because the finding I wish to report on in this clinical note, *at first blush*, seems to contradict all of the clinical evidence, experience, and research that I have accumulated. As I have been supervising the work of other therapists during the past ten years or so, I have observed that some of the best and most effective therapeutic work done with schizophrenic patients has been performed by very inexperienced first and second year social work students!

When I first witnessed the results that students were achieving with patients diagnosed as schizophrenic, I was cynical and attributed their patients' therapeutic movement to chance or to some sort of combination of accidental factors. However, when successful case after successful case came to my attention and when I saw many schizophrenic patients leaving hospitals, taking on and sustaining jobs, relating reasonably well to family members and friends, I decided to study the therapy of these social work students more carefully.

A couple of vignettes of the students' work follows

Mr. A. was a thirty-nine-year-old hospitalized patient diagnosed as a simple schizophrenic. He had been a constant patient in a mental hospital for five years and had received electro-shock, vitamin therapy, psychotherapy, group therapy and an assortment of other interventions were also tried unsuccessfully. Mr. A. was hospitalized because of acute paranoia (he thought politicians were trying to keep him unemployed), delusions of grandeur (he referred to himself as an Emperor), vague psychosomatic complaints including insomnia, ulcer, and headaches. He had lost contact with his family and friends. Furthermore, he was described as an isolate by the personnel at the Veterans Mental Hospital.

As frequently occurs with patients on whom other professionals have given up, Mr. A. was assigned to a first year social work student, a male. The student had virtually no therapeutic experience and as a matter of fact, was considered "a risk" by the social work faculty because his undergraduate grades were mediocre and the reputation of his undergraduate college in the South was dubious.

When Mr. A. first met the student, he told his interviewer that he didn't want to have anything to do with him. He was tired of all those therapists who wanted to keep him in the hospital and away from a job. "You are all part of the military industrial establishment who want to keep me locked up and unemployed," said Mr. A. vehemently.

The student's response to Mr. A. was one of essential agreement. "Mental hospitals often *are* horrible places and often are run by incompetent people and that's why I want to get you out of here" he averred. The patient understandably responded, "How can I believe you?" and the student said "You can't, you'll have to wait and see if I can deliver the goods!"

At the second, third, and fourth interviews the patient and student talked about the kind of job the patient might be interested in locating. When the student reported, in response to Mr. A.'s doubts about the therapist's sincerity, that he was "dead serious" and felt his patient could work, the latter became panicky and said, "I'm an Emperor, I want something outstanding!" Here, the therapist replied, "Well, Emperor, what kind of outstanding job do you really want?"

In subsequent interviews the dyad arranged to visit potential places of employment and discussed their possibilities and limitations. At the twelfth interview Mr. A. stated with much feeling, "I'd like to confess something. I'm really scared about working and leaving the hospital. I'll feel insignificant on a job. Here, I am an emperor." The therapist told the patient that he was going to be available to him until he got

very settled on the job and into a home outside of the hospital. Mr. A.
responded, "You're my friend, not my enemy!"

Mr. A. did leave the hospital, sustained a job as a clerk, moved up
as an office manager, got his own apartment, began to fraternize with
men and after 16 months of treatment began relationships with
women. He remained in out-patient treatment with another therapist
after the student concluded his field work placement and maintained
all of his therapeutic gains. Delusions and other psychotic material
disappeared and Mr. A. frequently referred to "my new lease on life."

The vignette above of Mr. A. is typical of at least thirty to forty cases
of clinical work by social work students that I have carefully examined
during the past few years. What seems to have taken place with Mr. A.
(as with many patients diagnosed as schizophrenic) is that many professionals from many disciplines had given up on him. Furthermore, in
many ways Mr. A. had introjected the professionals' attitude toward
him, thus recapitulating in many ways, his own life history. To protect
himself against strong murderous feelings and an image of very low
self-esteem, he vacillated between grandiose fantasies ("I am Emperor")
and social seclusion. The student's genuine interest in him, the student's willingness to be turned away by the patient, his intuitive respect
for Mr. A.'s defenses as well as an optimistic outlook about Mr. A.'s
future seemed to bolster Mr. A. and helped him move from a very
isolated, immature, self-hating and hating man to a more responsible
and more object-related adult.

Miss B. was a fifty-two-year-old hospitalized woman who was also
diagnosed as schizophrenic. Like Mr. A., she had lost contact with
family and friends and had been hospitalized in a mental institution
for seven years. Miss B. had also been the recipient of various types of
therapy such as shock, vitamins, psycho-therapy and group treatment,
but all the therapies were to no avail. Her conviction that she was "a
horrible sinner" who deserved to be punished and killed continued no
matter what kind of treatment she had received. In the hospital she sat
and cried alone most of the time, bemoaning her fate. Miss B. often
took the position that she was born infected, probably had leprosy and
that if anyone got too near her, they would probably catch her leprosy
and some other diseases.

When Miss B. was greeted by her social work therapist who said she
wanted to get to know her, Miss B. responded with, "Knowing me is
to know a witch. You can do better things." The student, a young
inexperienced woman in her early twenties said that she had "never
met a witch" and even wondered whether they existed. But, I am

curious." Miss B. responded, "Well, here you are, dear, I am the first witch you've met!"

For a number of interviews the patient recounted how she had killed people—her mother, father, a brother and some friends. She described taking an axe and beheading them and furthermore Miss B. reported that there was no reason for this "horrible behavior" on her part. When the student said that though she was a very inexperienced professional and didn't know about many facts of life, she was "absolutely positive that nobody murders unless they are very angry."

Miss B. was able in succeeding interviews to describe how she was neglected by her alcoholic parents and given little gratification. She early in life thought that there must be something wrong with her inasmuch as she was so hated by her parents and other family members. "I started to believe that I had some infectious disease!" she remarked.

On the student telling Miss B. that when children hate their parents when the latter neglect them, the children criticize themselves because they need their parents, Miss B. wept and wept. "You are a doll. You really understand. My hatred is my poison. It has infected me, because I haven't let it out! I wanted to kill so badly that all these years I have believed that I have really done it."

As Miss B. looked at her past with a stronger ego and with the social worker's friendly and empathetic ear, she slowly was able to move out of the hospital and into her own apartment. She joined a group in her community and later went on to a job as a teacher's aid. Miss B., like Mr. A., was able to transfer to another therapist and be seen on an outpatient basis when the student left her field work placement.

As mentioned, the cases of Mr. A. and Miss B. are typical of many successful therapeutic outcomes by social work students that I have witnessed and researched during the past few years. The question that I have tried to answer myself is, "Why do inexperienced social work students very frequently achieve much more success with very disturbed patients than do their more experienced and trained colleagues?"

In reviewing with students their clinical work with patients diagnosed as schizophrenic, one theme has emerged quite consistently. The major impression I have had to date is that *social work internes do not consider patients diagnosed as schizophrenic, schizophrenic*. By this I mean, notions like "poor ego functions," "narcissistic object relations" and "narcissistic transferences," "oral fantasies," "unresolved resistances toward murder," and "hostile introjects" are not in their vocabulary and do not even cross their minds. In contrast to the more experienced practitioner who begins treatment with a concept of a serious disease process at work which frequently ignites latent counterresistances in him or her, the social work student optimistically and very humanely wants to help a real person in a real situation.

Unperturbed by previous therapeutic failures, unimpressed by the cautionary admonitions of his mentors, unencumbered by a bevy of therapeutic procedures swimming in his head, the social work student unconditionally regards his or her patient positively and truly accepts him or her where the patient is. In contrast to experienced professionals who often unconsciously communicate their therapeutic pessimism to the patient which then becomes introjected and incorporated by the latter, the student in effect says, "I want to help you and I think I can!" The patient seems to respond after some testing with, "Wow, no one has ever had faith in me before. That makes me love you. Let's work together." The student's benign and humane attitude seems to alter the vicious cycle and self fulfilling prophecy that has been perpetuated by experienced professionals, who have often unwittingly communicated to the patient the message, "You are crazy, pathological, and perhaps even a bit unhuman. I shall move cautiously with you because your prognosis is so guarded."

In one of the few empirical studies of psychotherapy,[7] which examined the effective ingredients in psychotherapy in psychoanalytic, client-centered, and eclectic theorists, some of the major findings that seemed to correlate very positively with successful therapeutic results were the therapist's non-possessive warmth, genuineness, and a type of empathy that conveyed the message, "I am with you." Furthermore, the researcher, Truax, not only demonstrated that accurate empathy or unconditional positive regard is higher for more successful cases than for less successful cases but that this relationship holds even more for severely disturbed schizophrenic patients.[7]

As we have examined the social work students' demeanor and therapeutic posture in their interviews with schizophrenic patients, Truax's findings seem to be borne out quite convincingly. Non-possessive warmth, genuineness, and empathy were consistently present in the students' therapeutic orientation.

In this journal (*The Psychoanalytic Review*), after almost a decade of practice, I wrote my first professional paper, which was entitled, "The Use of the Patient as Consultant."[6] I attempted to demonstrate there how severely disturbed patients can, at times, prescribe their own treatment. I ended that presentation with a statement of gratitude to my patients. I now find it quite timely to repeat the same statement to many of my students, "You teach me. I am ready to learn!"

REFERENCES

1. Arieti, S. "Psychotherapy of Schizophrenia," *Archives of General Psychiatry*, Vol. 6, 1962, 112–122.

2. Lindner, R. *Explorations in Psychoanalysis*. New York: Julian Press, 1953.

3. Nelson, M.; B. Nelson; M. Sherman; and H. Strean. *Roles & Paradigms in Psychotherapy*. New York: Grune & Stratton, 1968.

4. Nelson, M. "Effects of Paradigmatic Techniques on the Psychic Economy of Borderline Patients," *Psychiatry*, Vol. 25, No. 2, 1962, pp. 119–134.

5. Spotnitz, H. *Modern Psychoanalysis of the Schizophrenic Patient*. New York: Grune & Stratton, 1969.

6. Strean, H. "The Use of the Patient as Consultant," in *New Approaches in Child Guidance*, H. Strean, ed. Metuchen, N.J.: Scarecrow Press, 1971.

7. Truax, C. "Effective Ingredients in Psychotherapy," in *Creative Developments in Psychotherapy*, Vol. I, A. Mahrer & L. Pearson, eds. New York: Jason Aronson, 1973.

8. Waldhorn, H. "Dreams, Technique, & Insight," in *Currents in Psychoanalysis*, I. Marcus, ed. New York: International Universities Press, 1971.

DISCUSSANT: LAURA S. FUERSTEIN

My response to this paper contains both a broad underlying theme, and a more narrow focus on a particular area of psychotherapy. The overall theme is meant to convey the following message: the basic elements described by Strean as necessary for therapeutic success are found far beyond the specific relationship of inexperienced therapist and schizophrenic patient; these elements are inherent in almost any relationship which fosters normal ego development, and are rooted of course, in the primary dyad, mother and child. Moreover, the connecting thread which runs through these basic "growth ingredients" is human love. The specific area of discussion in the latter part of this response is supervision in the realm of psychotherapy. I shall attempt to demonstrate how the growth-producing elements referred to above can be applied both theoretically and clinically to the supervisor/supervisee relationship; an interaction which ideally should exemplify growth and learning.

The specific elements correlated with therapeutic success by Strean can be linked to the mother/child relationship. In the article the author asks, "Why do inexperienced social work students very frequently achieve much more success with very disturbed patients than do their more experienced and trained colleagues?"[5] A theme emerges, he states, which seems to lead him to an answer: ". . . social work internes do not consider patients diagnosed as schizophrenic, schizophrenic."[5] Furthermore, they take an optimistic and humane stance toward the patient and view him as a real person in a real situation; as opposed to the more experienced clinician who begins treatment with a preconceived notion of a serious illness at work.[5] I would like to know more about the population sample used for the study, and perhaps see similar studies done to further validate the findings. However, for the purposes of this paper, I shall accept these findings as valid, based on my own clinical experiences, readings, and discussions with colleagues.

Certain parallels can be drawn between the key factors defined in the article, and those deemed necessary to foster the normal ego development of a child. When the student therapist has a non-diagnosing, open view of the patient, this corresponds to the following attitude in the realm of mothering: a nonjudgmental, accepting view of an infant, and an adaptation to the child's needs which promotes and allows growth to occur spontaneously (this concept is incorporated in Hartmann's "average expectable environment" or Winnicott's "holding environment"). Furthermore, through dynamic processes such as projection and introjection, the normally developing child internalizes and integrates the parent's positive image of him, and in turn he develops a positive self–object representation. With this self-belief at hand, he can employ his identification with the parent in an effective way, and "separate and individuate" at his own pace (much as the patient can when the therapist believes in him).

A quote from John Sutherland, in an article about object relations theory, seems to restate much of the message of the preceding paragraph. He says, "What all of our theorists have come to is the view that the innate developmental potential has to be activated by an input of loving empathic care from the mother for it to become the proactive matrix with the positive enjoyment that developmental activity requires.

To be able to love and enjoy, the baby has to be loved and enjoyed. It is as if a 'positive field of force' is patterned as the core of the self system by the effects of the positive self-feeling at one pole and the expectation from a supporting figure at the other, at first external, then internalized."[6]

On the other hand, when the clinician focuses on the diagnosis of the patient, and views him as sick or defective, then symbolically a destructive mother/child relationship perhaps is being recapitulated. The unconsciously over-identified or hostile parent often scapegoats the child with judgments or accusations, for fear of seeing something undesirable or threatening about herself in her offspring; consequently the child introjects a negative self-object representation, and his ego growth is stunted. In the same way might the experienced but defended clinician, threatened by the schizophrenic's bizarre productions, frequently scapegoat the patient with a diagnosis. In this latter case, there is often an underlying hostile countertransference at work, and perhaps even the "unanalyzed psychosis" of the therapist. In sum, the "textbook view" of the patient may be employed as an intrapsychic dam against an overflow of the practitioner's own primary process thinking.

The key factor that permeates all the positive attitudes described previously, is human love. Reuben Fine, in *The Healing of the Mind*, conveys this concept most profoundly in terms of the therapeutic process. He states, ". . . the problem in the treatment of the schizophrenic lies in the first stage—establishing the relationship. Because of his history of rejection, his suspiciousness, his projections, his hostility, the schizophrenic makes it very difficult to establish any kind of relationship with a therapist. If the focus is on establishing a relationship . . . then eventually a relationship is established and the patient can be helped. If the focus is on attaching some diagnostic label to the patient, the result is literally to make the patient worse. Where we have a human being who craves warmth and interpersonal intimacy, he is given a harsh label. . . . "A more ludicrous and tragic situation would be hard to imagine."[3] Furthermore, Fine states, ". . . the therapeutic process involves a consistent overcoming of hostility toward the patient. The mental patient in our culture is viewed with scorn, derision, and hostility. . . . To be able to help him, the analyst must get over the culturally fostered feelings of hatred . . . . Thus, in both processes, the personal analysis and the growth of therapeutic skills, the same psychological growth is required: from hatred to love."[3] I would like to add here, in line with the theme of this paper, that this same process, from hatred to love, is required in varying degrees of almost anyone who is attempting to foster learning in a relationship. In short, if an individual feels loved, he can love and learn.

The ideas above can be applied to the relationship of supervisor/ supervisee in the field of psychotherapy. Yet, it is important to consider that there is more required of the supervisor than these loving attitudes, just as there are certain other requirements of the parent or the therapist, unique to each respective role, and dependent on the particular experience being considered. For example, the emphasis in mothering might be more on instinctiveness, than on "book knowledge"; whereas the therapist and supervisor must acquire a broad base of theoretical and clinical knowledge, while also employing an intuitiveness in their work. Keeping these ideas in mind, the fact remains that the foundation for professional development in the supervisee is largely formed with the help of the supervisor's humane attitudes toward him.

My main inspiration for focusing on this subject has been my own positive experiences as a supervisee. I feel that many of the basic "growth elements" which are inherent in a positive mother/child relationship, therapist/patient interaction, or any other relationship characterized largely by learning have also been reflected in these rewarding supervisee experiences of my own.

When a supervisor has shown a basic acceptance of me, has maintained an optimistic view of my work, has empathized with me, and has supplied me with constructive criticism, he or she has therefore encouraged my natural creativity to grow. It is most often with these experiences that I have felt the greatest surge of professional development. Perhaps a study might be done to validate this personal finding, if it were not such a subjective issue; however, my informal discussions with many colleagues have confirmed it. Moreover, colleagues seem to be in agreement with me on the following: It is at periods of initiation into a "psychotherapist's training ground" (i.e., the first practicum experience of social work school, or the first internship program) that the humane attitudes of the supervisor are most crucial.

Unfortunately, more often than not the ideas stated above are not incorporated in the supervisory experience. Instead, a paradoxical situation appears to exist: Just as the infant and the schizophrenic, who are in the most vulnerable positions with "caretakers," are often provided the worst treatment, so does the most inexperienced supervisee often receive the least helpful, and at times destructive supervision. My own observations and discussions with students who have attended graduate schools of social work and psychology have often revealed this unfortunate situation. Many of my peers have described experiences with supervisors who displayed doctrinaire, unempathic, nonsupportive, and defensive qualities.

I recall being told of a supervisor who required process recording in great detail of one patient's sessions, ignoring the supervisee's great need to discuss his strong areas of difficulty with several other patients. Another supervisor would focus only on certain areas in which she felt comfortable or knowledgeable, and would repeat the same phrase for the supervisee to use at each session (i.e., to say to the patient, "You are acting hostile"), even when this seemed to be some acting out of anger on the supervisor's part. When the supervisee confronted the supervisor with the feeling that this technique was distancing the patient, she was defensive and attacking of the supervisee. She then used the supervisee's countertransference difficulties as a vehicle for her own power-play.

Countertransference, which is perhaps the greatest problem area for many therapists, is often at its peak of difficulty for the student–therapist. With this in mind, the supervisor should be supportive, help the supervisee to recognize the problem, and perhaps encourage him to confront it in personal therapy. Unfortunately, the majority of supervisors seem to avoid discussion of this problem area and often comment with isolated, "superego" statements when a countertransference issue is at play, without further exploration of the problem (i.e., "Why didn't you tell the patient that he is acting out?" etc.). Perhaps in this case, the supervisor is revealing the same fear of his own instinctual impulses, much as the mother with her acting-out child, or the therapist with his schizophrenic patient, as discussed previously.

With the preceding paragraph in mind, parallels can be drawn between the three relationships which are the focus of this paper. I have briefly mentioned how the internalization and identification processes are important in the child's relationship with the parent and the patient's relationship with the therapist; and how separation–individuation is influenced by these processes. These same dynamic phenomena can be applied again, this time to the supervisory experience. The supervisee's belief in himself and capacity to grow professionally, while developing his own "style," can be affected in varying degrees by the supervisor's view of him.

In the supervisory vignettes offered above, the "misuse" of the internalization and identification process stands out quite prominently. Jacob Arlow states in "The Supervisory Situation" that identification with the supervisor is the most effective pedagogical influence; the supervisory work is addressed to the observing portion of the therapist's ego and conveys information, understanding, and a realistic appraisal of the psychoanalytic process.[1] If this concept is accepted, then there is further proof that the supervisors' qualities described above act as negative factors in the supervisees' development. It might be concluded that two major results will occur when such qualities are displayed in the supervisory relationship: first, to some extent (although naturally not to the same degree as an infant or patient with his respective "caretaker"), the supervisee will internalize the supervisor's negative view of him; second, through identification he is provided with a negative paradigm for work with his patients, and the same inflexibility, etc., with which he has been treated, will be conveyed back to them.

In sum, I feel that the findings in "A Note on the Treatment of the Schizophrenic Patient" can have both a specific and general application to the supervisory relationship which integrates the basic theme of this paper. The specific application is the following: If inexperienced therapists display an inherent strength working with schizophrenics (or if any supervisee reveals any natural ability for that matter), why not, as supervisor, encourage this quality to grow spontaneously, rather than squelch it with a didactic or judgmental approach. There is an implication here that supervisors should be more on guard for their own intrapsychic conflicts affecting their supervisory work, and moreover, should be more aware of the possibility of their own need for therapy or renewed therapy.

The second, more general application of the article's findings is in the realm of the so-called "parallel process" in supervision. Eva Kahn states in "The Parallel Process in Social Work Treatment and Supervision": "The concept of the parallel process refers to the simultaneous emergence of similar difficulties in the relationship between social worker and client, social worker and supervisor, and postulates a link between these two relationships, whereby emotions generated in one are acted out in the other. . . . Margery Doehrman, in her research study on the parallel process, emphasized the intensity of students' reactions to their supervisors and the considerable effect rather ordinary actions by the supervisor could have on therapists' feelings about themselves and upon the way they conducted their therapy."[4] I feel that this parallel process and the identification process incorporated within it, must be understood and integrated into any successful supervisory experience. Furthermore, the relationship of the social work interne and schizophrenic described in Strean's paper, can serve as a type of paradigm for this parallel process. Again, the importance of the supervisor's self-understanding and need for therapy is underlined.

I would like to conclude with a quote from Winnicott, found in Bowlby's *Separation*, in a chapter entitled "Growth and Self-Reliance." I feel that this quote most effectively helps to convey the basic message of this paper. The author states: "Maturity and the capacity to be alone implies that the individual has had the chance through good-enough mothering to build up a belief in a benign environment. . . . Gradually the ego-supportive environment is introjected and built into the individual's personality, so that there comes about a capacity actually to be alone. Even so, theoretically, there is always someone present, someone who is equated ultimately and unconsciously with the mother. . . ."[2] In the final analysis, whether the internalized object is the mother, therapist, or supervisor, the capacity to "be alone" and to grow as an autonomous being, is founded on the same basic elements.

REFERENCES

1. Arlow, Jacob A. "The Supervisory Situation," *Psychoanalytic Quarterly*, Vol. 33, 1964, pp. 576–594.

2. Bowlby, John. *Attachment and Loss*. Vol. 2, *Separation*. New York: Basic Books, 1973.

3. Fine, Reuben. *The Healing of the Mind*. New York: David McKay, 1971.

4. Kahn, Eva M. "The Parallel Process in Social Work Treatment and Supervision," *Social Casework*, Vol. 60, 1979, pp. 520–528.

5. Strean, Herbert S. *Crucial Issues in Psychotherapy*. Metuchen, N.J.: Scarecrow Press, 1976.

6. Sutherland, John D. "British Object Relations Theorists," *Journal of the American Psychoanalytic Association*, Vol. 28, 1980, pp. 829–860.

DISCUSSANT: SHERMAN MERLE

Strean's paper raises an issue that has been a matter for comment and discussion for the long time that there has been interest in how one individual influences another.

Specifically, his "Note on the Treatment of the Schizophrenic Patient" addresses the issue of the therapist's capacity to help those who have been clinically assessed as "schizophrenic." Among the many points made in this paper is the "dramatic"—one might even say "heretical"—comment that ". . . social work internes do not consider patients diagnosed as schizophrenic, schizophrenic." This I would suggest presents a dilemma or at least an anomaly for clinical practice and most importantly for the clinical instructor and learner.

The two cases presented in the paper evidence clearly—one could say blatantly—a "schizophrenic" picture. Certainly it would be fair to assume that these "internes" would have had—even in the most unsophisticated and cursory way—some clinical/psychopathological information and education to recognize the "classification" of the bizarre behavior present in both these cases. What then is meant by Strean's "dramatic" assertion quoted above? I think that what happened in these situations was that these students transcended the "diagnosis"; that they did not become "the captives of the diagnosis" or make that fatal error in any therapeutic endeavor of consciously or otherwise forcing the person manifesting his pain via a symptom or behavior "picture" onto the procrustean bed of diagnosis. Herein lies the anomaly: How does one teach a basic content (psychopathology) and a set of social casework skills and yet leave the student free to avoid being so absorbed (Strean says fearful—counterresistant) by the pathology that the therapist's humanity (responsiveness—desire to enable) finds full expression.

I believe that anyone who has had extensive experience teaching in the clinical context knows how very difficult this kind of teaching/learning is. In a recent volume on the teaching of psychotherapy, Dr. Basch, in reporting a supervisory session with a resident, informs us about this when he says to the resident:

> . . . One of the problems in our field which you have already run into is that textbook descriptions are high-level abstractions that don't take into account the individual circumstances that usually confuse what one sees in a given instance. That's why it's so frustrating when you try to apply these abstractions. Indeed, though in retrospect we justify our diagnoses by matching them against lists of symptoms and signs, that is not the way we actually arrive at them.

And the resident asks,

> "What did I do wrong?" and the clinical instructor responds, "Nothing really. Actually you were on the right track. Mr. Clark was referred to you with the label 'depression' already attached to him. That means

you met him with a ready-made pattern of expectation—a pattern based on your past experience. . . . However, when you actually saw the patient and tried to fit him into that category, you felt that somehow he didn't match the expectations that the diagnosis mobilized in you. What you have to do then is to see what *does* occur to you as you continue to talk to and examine the patient. Sometimes a testable hypothesis comes to you . . . . Other times . . . you end up not knowing what's going on."[1]

The challenge in this clinical dilemma is to provide the learner with the information needed to have some understanding of the phenomena being observed, but also to help the student to remain open, responsive, and apply the abstract of diagnosis to the particular—the person in his life space.

I would suggest that the students' work presented in Strean's paper, rather than demonstrating that the social work internes did not consider their patients schizophrenic, demonstrated a fine therapeutic capacity to *really* understand the psychodynamics of the patient diagnosed "schizophrenic" and to employ a treatment plan that fully *considered* the schizophrenic process. That consideration, however, did not become absorbed in the morbid or pathological aspects of the situation (paranoia, delusions of grandeur, psychosomatic complaints, "sinfulness"). Rather, the student became absorbed in doing what the best of all sophisticated social casework practice has always done so well. A basic acceptance was established and the focus and attention of the treatment was to find and nurture those strengths that were there: to "stay with the client"; yes, to "listen attentively" and inform oneself about what the pained person was saying; and "to move at a pace that the pained person could tolerate." To do this is an excellent social casework, a therapeutic intervention that has been codified and rooted in the practice of social work.

Strean had in another paper made a valuable contribution to our fund of therapeutic interventions when he showed us the way he uses the person being helped as a consultant.[2] I would suggest that this paper—though focused on the treatment of the schizophrenic patient—is really a further, though subtle, illustration of this treatment technique.

If one examines carefully the students' work in both these cases there is considerable evidence to support the view that the students indeed did "consult with" the person they were seeking to help.

"At the second, third, and fourth interviews the patient and student talked about the kind of job the patient might be interested in locating.";

"Well, emperor, what kind of outstanding job do you really want?"
....
"You are a doll. You really understand. My hatred is my poison.
It has infected me, because I haven't let it out!"

I would suggest further that what Strean has demonstrated in this paper is an essential and basic truth in all therapy: The genuine concern, warmth, and empathy of the helper is the "motor" that generates the latent strength in *any* person seeking help in a therapeutic context. Indeed, Strean documents this point with his reference to Truax's empirical findings in this regard. But those of us engaged in clinical teaching have always known of the not unusual phenomenon of the uncanny ability of the "beginner" to have some remarkable successes where the more experienced (possibly jaded or less invested) have "failed." Is this not further evidence of the power of genuineness, warmth, empathy?

Finally, it is to Strean's credit that he acknowledges his own limited results in applying a "... classical psychoanalytic method..." with his "... severely disturbed schizophrenic patients.... " I credit him for these frank acknowledgments, for it does take a certain quality of security and courage to admit our errors and "failures" in therapeutic interventions. But I would add that social casework practice has known for some time that the treatment of choice with the person caught up in a schizophrenic process was best served by avoiding the attempts to "... make the unconscious conscious..." and to "... [anchor] the schizophrenic patient's productions to reality... keep the transference positive, and [steer] clear of primary-process production." Farber,[3] Varley,[4] Marcus[5] and Nelsen[6] have all discussed this at length and it has been in the social work literature at least since 1958.

In summary these notes on the treatment of the schizophrenic patient yet again force us to critically examine that which is effective in our clinical practice. It is not redundant to have another clinical report that substantiates the value of basics; genuineness and interest and seeking and responding to the troubled person's strengths in a therapeutic environment of non-possessive warmth are powerful and necessary conditions for effective psychotherapeutic interventions.

To come full circle, then, the students' work was effective not because they did not "consider patients... schizophrenic." They may have known this very well. Their effectiveness was related to the fact that they did not get caught-up in the "craziness"—neither frightened by it, morbidly intrigued by it, nor discouraged and apathetic by the "clinical diagnosis." Their work illustrated that they went beyond the diagnosis and helped the individual bring forth the ego capacities that were part of the whole person being worked with.

REFERENCES

1. Michael Franz Basch. *Doing Psychotherapy*. New York: Basic Books, 1980, p. 89.

2. H. Strean. "The Use of the Patient or Consultant," in *New Approaches in Child Guidance*. Metuchen, N.J.: Scarecrow Press, 1970, pp. 53–63.

3. Laura Farber. "Casework Treatment of Ambulatory Schizophrenics," *Social Casework*, Vol. 39, No. 1 (January 1958).

4. Barbara Varley. "Reaching Out Therapy with Schizophrenic Patients," *American Journal of Orthopsychiatry*, Vol. 29, No. 2 (April 1959).

5. Esther Marcus. "Ego Breakdown in Schizophrenia, Some Implications for Casework Treatment," *American Journal of Orthopsychiatry*, Vol. 31, No. 2 (April 1961).

6. Judith Nelsen. "Treatment-planning for Schizophrenia." *Social Casework*, Vol. 56, No. 2 (February 1975).

Chapter 7

SOME REFLECTIONS ON
THERAPEUTIC WORK
WITH THE COLLEGE DROPOUT

For more than a decade a plethora of literature has appeared which has attempted to unravel some of the psychosocial determinants that induce an intellectually capable student to drop out of college. Sociological explanations from scholars like Keniston[7] have referred to the covert rejection of society by the dropout, and Riesman[11] has utilized the term "inner emigration" when describing him. "Inner emigration" is a term broad enough to include not only those young people who consciously absent themselves from what they see as the "American way of life," but those who remain inwardly silent, apathetic, loud and uncommitted, even while outwardly going through the motions of participation.

Other sociological attempts to explain the dropout phenomenon have alluded to the advances of industrialization. Industrialization, it has been contended, contributes to making the adult realm so unappealing to the young person that he resists entering it. College, it has been alleged, provokes a "cultural discontinuity" for the young person and he feels alienated from his environment.[14] This appears to be particularly true for Blacks and members of other minorities.[11]

The myriad sociological analyses on the college dropout—which have consisted of hypotheses that range from affluence to unemployment, political apathy to incipient revolution, peer group over-stimulation to insufficient stimulation by the group[2]—are matched by hypotheses of clinical investigators who have focused their attention on the dropout's psychodynamics.

Difficulties in adapting to college life have been attributed to faulty

Reprinted by permission from *The Psychoanalytic Review*, vol. 66, no. 2 (April 1979), pp. 201–214.

resolution of oral, anal, and phallic–oedipal conflicts. The dropout, it has been averred, cannot "swallow" the adult's knowledge because he has so much aggression towards authorities, and incorporating their knowledge is like taking in bad food.[3] Not only has the dropout been poorly nourished according to some investigators but he has also been described as a negativistic person who is interested in spiting his teachers and other parental figures.[8] Furthermore, the dropout has been described as one who must avoid a powerful impetus towards successful competition with the parent of the same sex.[4]

It would appear that every phase of psychosocial maturation has been linked to the etiology of the dropout phenomenon by those who utilize a psychoanalytic perspective. The dropout has also been equated with the latency school phobic who fears new situations,[8] and the phenomenon has also been related to the turbulence, ambivalence, and generalized hostility that occurs in adolescence.[15]

Ego psychologists such as Menaker[10] have reported on the dropout's regressive desire to prevent separation and individualization. Menaker has concluded that the success of work life in college "will be correlated with the degree of separateness of the ego from the personalities of the parents."[10] Family therapists have alluded to the narcissistic and controlling parents of the dropout[4] and role theorists have pointed out that there is tremendous divergence in role expectations between the dropout and his teachers.[14]

There is no doubt that all of the social and psychological dynamics referred to in the foregoing brief review can exert a force, and at times a crucial impact, in contributing towards the dropout phenomenon. There are probably many other psychosocial variables operative that have not been mentioned and perhaps some are even unknown. Yet, the dropout continues to attract attention from parents, college officials, social workers, therapists, psychoanalysts, college administrators and many others.[1, 4] Furthermore, many of these "significant others" have offered prescriptions designed to retard the increasing numbers of college dropouts in society.

Sociologists have discussed the necessity of modifying the college system and other negative inputs from the sub-systems of the dropout's culture.[2] Social psychologists have called for role modifications and changes in role expectations that tend to propel dysfunctional student-teacher interactions.[14] Family therapists have suggested that the dropout is frequently utilized as a scapegoat in his family and parts of the familial interaction between him, his parents, siblings and extended family have to be rearranged.[4] Other clinicians have recommended all kinds of therapy ranging from intensive psychoanalysis[13] to short term casework and "crisis intervention."[5]

Background of this Study

This paper is a report of a study made on the diagnostic and treatment processes of 50 cases of college dropouts* who either sought by themselves or were referred for treatment to a student mental health center, a social agency, or to private practitioners. The clinical data upon which the observations and hypotheses presented in this paper are based are from presentations to the writer from student social workers at the Rutgers Mental Health Center, social workers from the Jewish Family and Children's Service of Paterson, New Jersey, supervisees of the writer who are in private practice, and from the writer's own private practice.

The College Dropout at Intake
(The First Few Interviews)

More often than not, the college dropout whom we worked with did not seek help on his own. Most of the time he or she appeared at the clinic, agency, or private practitioner's office because he had been urged, begged, or cajoled into doing so by parents, teachers, or guidance personnel. When he initially presented himself, his failure to cope with college was something that had somehow just happened to him, and as he perceived the situation, he had limited if any responsibility for what had transpired. "They are teaching stuff that has no meaning. Philosophy and psychology are wastes," blurted out Abe in his first interview. When asked why he didn't arrange to take other courses, he responded, "Most of the faculty are 'fuddy duddies' who don't know what life is all about!"

Not only was the dropout severely critical of his teachers, the administration, and the university system in general, but he or she was invariably confident that he had the ability to do college work and to do it well. "I know I'm very bright but I don't feel like working for people if I have little respect for them," remarked Bob. This notion that he, col-

---

* By "dropout" we are referring to patients who dropped out of college, were in the process of doing so, were threatened with it, or asked to drop out of college.

lege dropout, had the ability to do college work was almost a universal phenomenon and was frequently fortified and buttressed by sentiments of parents and other figures.

In several instances the dropout presented his failure to cope with college life as motivated by professors' unfairnesses and biases. Either the professor was threatened by the patient's ideas or else he had inappropriate and subjective reactions to the patient's modus vivendi. Stated Barbara, "He didn't like my figure and my clothes. If I were more 'square' he would have passed me!" Like Barbara's reaction which was typical, so was David's. Said David, "If I didn't make it clear that I was a follower of Laing's, he never would have flunked me!"

Although many of the young people whom we observed "turned off" their teachers and course work, some engaged in rather severe power struggles with their instructors. Of those that engaged in "one-upmanship" fracases with their mentors, most frequently tried to find some vulnerable area of the professor and attacked him constantly for it. "He seemed like such a know-it-all and such a pompous ass that I had to show him that he wasn't boss all of the time. I knew he hated it when I knitted so I purposely did knit," argued Jane in a very self-righteous manner.

The attempt to "put down" professors was frequently extended to many other figures in authority, particularly the patient's parents. Parents were frequently presented as "square," "unrealistic," "Living in another world" and "too demanding." Remarked Sam, "My old man expects me to study two hours a day and that's ridiculous. I'm young and it is time for fun!"

Although the parents of the dropout were usually described by our patients as too demanding and too limiting, with complaints of parents ranging from not getting enough money from them, not having a car all to themselves, insufficient parental tolerance when it came to smoking marijuana or taking other drugs, the parents were typically presented, nonetheless, as being active and attentive in the patient's life. Often the young person opined that his or her parents were *too* active and *too* interested in his life. "She's always asking me how things are going. I wish she wouldn't be so interested in me," remarked Sally when referring to her mother. Said Henry of his father, "He really means well. He always wants to get together. I liked going to ball games with him in the past, but holy smoke, let me have a breather!"

As the patient presented salient aspects of his history, parents were invariably described as being consistently involved with their children in most aspects of the latter's lives from birth onwards. They freely gave of their time and could praise their youngsters with ease. In most of the cases it was quite clear that the parents indulged their children, rationalized their children's failures, and ascribed most disappointments that the patients experienced to negative forces in the environment rather than to their children's limitations or provocativeness. Most of our patients came from intact and small middle class families and in many situations, they were the only and much loved offspring.

In almost every situation that we reviewed, the patient demonstrated above average or superior academic work in grammar school and high school. Furthermore, in over 80 percent of the population that we examined, the patient pointed out that he or she did not study very much in high school. The young person could get by on his native intelligence and charming demeanor. Often the patient was active in extra-curricular activities and in a few cases graduated as "All Round Student," valedictorian or salutatorian.

Frequently our modal patient contrasted high school life with college. "The teachers in high school really cared. They laughed and played with you and here they just want to teach dry stuff. I felt at high school the teachers were my pals, my equals. Here, they are like big bosses!" remarked Irv. Not only did the patient contrast his high school teachers with his college mentors, but the patients' peers at college appeared remarkably different, as well. Complained Joan, "At high school they liked to bowl and dance. Here they're too damned intellectual."

More often than not the young person showed a cluster of symptoms indicative of a rather pronounced depression.[13] Not only did the patient complain of feelings of depression, crying jags and apathy, but in a number of cases had suicidal fantasies. In over half of the cases, the patient was on drugs. As part of the depressive constellation, the patient was not eating or sleeping too well, found it difficult to concentrate, and spent a lot of time fantasizing, listening to music, reading novels, masturbating or reading exotic literature.

In most instances the patient was asocial in his interpersonal relationships with peers but there were a few of our cases who were involved in very intense love affairs in which their partners consumed much of their time and energy. In some of these cases, the students cut classes together and mutually decried and demeaned college, courses, professors, and the university environment in general.

Although most of our subjects were vehement in their criticism of college personnel and did not take much responsibility for their plights, projecting most of their difficulties on to parents and other figures of authority, they were *not* poorly motivated when it came to the idea of receiving therapeutic help. "Although I know college is not for me, I'd like to learn more about myself and make some decisions" was a very typical remark in one of the first few interviews. "I feel depressed and maybe this will help." "There's something wrong when I have insomnia all of the time." "I don't trust 'shrinks' but I'll come" are modal statements of the group of students that we studied.

Some Diagnostic Considerations on the College Dropout

As has been mentioned, although our sample of fifty cases is drawn exclusively from one area of the country and therefore may not be representative of college dropouts nationally, some of the diagnostic considerations that evolved from the study of our population might be pertinent to other groups of young people who become college dropouts.

As the material that evolved from the first few interviews with the dropout attests, the patient does appear to be an emotionally immature person. Projecting most of his difficulties onto others, his arrogance, contempt, and self-centeredness tend to imply that he is a rather narcissistic individual who expects to give little of himself to most people and situations but expects a great deal for himself.

Frequently indulged by parents and significant others who found it quite difficult to impose demands and limits on him, the dropout is often moved by immature cravings such as fantasies of omnipotence and grandiosity, exhibitionistic wishes, and strong dependency needs. Prior to coming to college, life was very easy for him; others often anticipated his wants or else he would manipulate others to supply him with a life that closely resembled a Paradise.[16]

Dominated by the pleasure principle, having not recognized that coping with frustration is part of living, not having much belief that there is a reality principle which implies that work and giving to others are facts of life, the college atmosphere with its requirements of work, submitting to others' demands and absorbing frustration induce in the patient rather profound cultural and psychological shocks. The college and its demands severely frustrate and certainly do not gratify his egocentric and self-aggrandizing propensities.

Instead of being given to, the student in college is expected to put out in the form of studying, writing term papers, taking exams, and mastering concepts that do not always come easily. Instead of being the center of attention as he was at home and in his community, he is forced to share with others and not be in the limelight so constantly. Instead of having adults cater to many of his whims, he frequently has to compete for their attention with students who are as equally capable as he. Instead of dominating discussion, he is often required to be a listener to material that is not always that simple to comprehend.

Unable to relinquish his omnipotent and grandiose fantasies which have been gratified for so many years heretofore, our patient is at first very angry. Since compliance, submission, putting out extra efforts are not part of his narcissistic orientation, he does battle with his teachers either overtly or covertly. His involvement in either fantasied or verbal power struggles with his mentors are expressions of his unwillingness to relinquish the childish position of "His Majesty the Prince." However, because the patient has never had to struggle by himself for himself—because he is basically a passive individual—he gives up the fight, suppresses and represses his aggression, and becomes depressed and sorry for himself.

To buckle down to work, to see his teachers as people who may know more than he does, to acknowledge limitations in himself is too great a blow to his narcissism. Instead, like an angry child, he takes the position that college is not his cup of tea. He could do the work if he wanted to, but he does not want to. It's beneath the dignity of his inflated self-image and idealized self. He rationalizes his defeat by proclaiming that the college or university has a different value system than his and that the work is dull, boring, and not for him.

To cope with his depression and declining sense of self-esteem of which he is only dimly aware, the patient escapes from reality and reads novels, listens to music or attends movies without doing much work at all. To bring excitement into his depressed life, he takes drugs which often contribute towards a deeper depression.

Although the idea of treatment is usually not something that the dropout thinks of on his own, because again it is viewed as a potential narcissistic injury, he does welcome the complete focus of attention that he can receive from the therapist and does get involved in a therapeutic encounter.

Some Considerations in the Treatment of the Dropout

In the cases that we have studied, we achieved rather remarkable success when we formulated our treatment programs around a few related but crucial issues. As we began to assess our typical patient, we felt that the corrective emotional experience that we could and should offer him or her was essentially a *frustrating* one. Inasmuch as the patient is dominated by the pleasure principle, is constantly bombarded by immature cravings designed to gratify his infantile omnipotence and narcissism, we concluded that it was necessary to demonstrate to him in the therapeutic relationship that we would not cater to his powerful dependency wishes. Rather, in contrast to his parents and significant others who frequently admired him and gave him quick rationalizations for his failures, our approach to the dropout was the constant message that he was the conductor and arranger of his own script and that his inability to do college work was because he wanted to remain a passive and indulged child.

Our research and experimentation led us to the conclusion that because the patient under consideration is, from a psychosocial point of view, a regressed child and one who is symbolically seeking the breast incessantly and determinedly, treatment should provide an experience in which the client will be successfully weaned.[16]

The process of effective weaning does not mean that the therapist is an angry, arbitrary frustrator; he listens to the patient's cries of frustration and angry outbursts, does not reject the patient when he damns the therapist, but does *not* offer sympathy or rationalization for failure. The emotional weaning in the therapy implies that the patient has some ability to take on some frustration and the therapist is not ambivalent about stating this.

The therapist, in loco parentis, helps his son or daughter to lessen the latter's symbiotic attachment to parental introjects by *not* anticipating the patient's wishes or requests. When the patient asks questions or seeks advice or sympathy, the therapist firmly takes the stand that the patient should explore his own thoughts, his own fantasies, and examine his alternatives. As the therapist stimulates autonomy rather than gratifies dependency, as he encourages the patient to examine himself and his environment, and as the patient finds himself having to use his own resources rather than the therapist's, he at first becomes sullen, angry, and sometimes even more depressed.

When this treatment crisis occurs, the therapist must not appear sorry or guilty but realize that the patient is once again attempting to manipulate others to take care of him. We found frequently that although the patient threatens to quit the treatment, he rarely does so. If he does, it is only for a very brief time.

Because this rather narcissistic patient is swamped by excitation and undischarged tension due to the primitiveness of his still remaining infantile dependency wishes, he eventually welcomes the therapist's attitude that, "What you want gratified is unrealistic for a young adult, but as long as you keep persisting you'll end up depressed and failing!" Coming to therapy at a time when his grandiose and omnipotent orientation to life is not working, he seems, after fighting the therapist for a while by manipulation, testing and depression, to accept the possibility that the therapist has a way out for the patient's dilemmas.

As the therapist champions autonomy in and out of the therapeutic situation and does not capitulate to the patient's demands, the patient slowly tries to experiment with self-initiated activity. When he clings less, demands less, and criticizes others less, he begins to feel stronger, feels more capable, and becomes more productive. As his infantile impulses master him less and he masters them more, the patient's self image and self esteem rise and there is more energy available for constructive activity.

The weaning paradigm[16] that we have formulated for the treatment of the college dropout implies not only helping the patient to renounce certain infantile pleasures, but it also implies that the therapist must assist the patient toward the recognition that parental figures are not omnipotent and perfect. When the therapist anchors himself to the reality principle, by not indulging the patient's complaints and projections, by not joining him in his criticisms of the college and its environment, by not responding to pressures for advice and other kinds of gratification, but by helping the patient explore himself and others, something important happens. The patient's emotional need for a parental figure becomes less intense and separation and autonomy become more easily achieved.

In addition to his willingness to examine and understand his patient's wishes, the therapist must feel quite secure in frustrating the patient's demands. If the patient senses the therapist's discomfort, he can exploit the therapist by making more demands as he could with his own parents. Although confident of his role in defining reality, the therapist must present himself as *not* knowing all the answers because if the patient is going to enhance his own functioning, he has to eventually come to the conclusion that quick gratification and all-giving parents are not that available. As the young person finds that the therapist is not an all-giving dispenser, he begins to utilize his own resources and gradually achieves some autonomy.

In brief, treatment with the dropout is a weaning experience in which the patient learns to cope with more frustration and to rely less on others. As his narcissism, grandiosity and infantile omnipotence are given limited if any gratification in the therapy, the patient achieves stronger self-esteem, less depression, and more autonomous ego energies become available to him so that he can apply them constructively to more mature love and work. This, of course, is predicated on a therapeutic orientation in which the therapist understands and studies without rejecting; frustrates without being too aggressive and limits without feeling guilty.

A Case Illustration

Joe, a 19-year-old young man, was referred for therapy because he had failed most of his grades in his freshman year. As was true in a number of other cases, Joe was directed by college officials to take a year off from college, get treatment and if the therapist advised the college that the patient was psychologically able to return to college he could do so.

Besides his failure in college, Joe was day-dreaming incessantly, attending porno films daily, masturbating compulsively, was on drugs and was very depressed. His relationships with people consisted of a weekly chat with his father, who gave him a handsome allowance of $150 a week, and visits with some call girls and prostitutes. Joe mentioned rather early in treatment that he was the teacher's pet in grammar school and high school but now that he was in a large metropolitan university where he was not individualized too much, he had little desire to study. Joe's history reflected that he had succeeded in getting to be many people's "favorite."

After presenting salient features of his current and past life, Joe attempted to manipulate the therapist by assuring the latter that he, Joe, could do college work. If the therapist wrote a letter right away, Joe could return to college and all would be well. When the therapist asked Joe how either of them could be sure that Joe could do the work well, Joe instead of answering the question became sullen, depressed and quiet.

When the therapist joined Joe's silence by being silent himself, Joe bitterly attacked the therapist by saying that the latter was supposed to help people and instead he appeared like an army sergeant. If Joe were the therapist he would have written a letter a long time ago. The attacks on the therapist continued without retaliation from the latter until Joe saw that he could not intimidate the therapist or induce much guilt in him.

Joe then moved on to a new tactic. He told the therapist that he thought that the therapist didn't like him and it made him "feel lousy." As a matter of fact, Joe was getting more depressed from the treatment and using drugs more. Joe asked, "Aren't you worried about me?" And, he reported a dream that he was lying in a hospital bed suffering and crying and the medical attendant was merely studying him. When the therapist remarked that it seemed that Joe was more interested in being pitied and fussed over than understood, Joe went on another tirade. He told the therapist that the latter was a "cold stiff," "a sadist," and a "non-humanist." He looked at a big picture of Freud above the couch and said, "If he were alive, Strean, he'd be ashamed of you." Of course, as aggression towards the therapist was verbalized Joe became less depressed.

Joe pointed out over and over again that he was much brighter than the therapist, his professors, and parents and was sure he could do college work. His narcissism was quite punctured when the therapist pointed out that Joe was merely rationalizing away his failures and that it was quite possible that Joe wasn't college material in the first place. He certainly hadn't demonstrated this to the therapist who he knew was a college professor.

Joe talked about his wonderful successes in high school without studying. He had several dreams of wanting to be back there which were interpreted as such. The therapist further told Joe that he didn't doubt Joe's successes in high school but college required work and Joe didn't seem to be able to do this. After debating with the therapist, "to prove you wrong," Joe took a part-time job and enrolled in a community college and took three courses.

He did reasonably well on the job and in the courses but started to get depressed again and after several weeks on the job and in college, he threatened to quit the job, the community college, and therapy. He mentioned that in all three places, he felt very unappreciated and again blasted the therapist for his unsympathetic attitude. Here the therapist pointed out that it was quite clear that Joe would have an extremely hard time making it in college or in any job because like a child he seemed more interested in being admired than in anything else. This was followed by a dream in which Joe was happily gazing in a mirror in the nude and a worker from H. Strain's Moving Company altered the mirror so that Joe looked less handsome.

After several months of therapy, Joe, for the first time, acknowledged that therapy was having its impact. He recalled that all of his life he was given to by everybody, loved it, and did not realize that "as you get older you do have some responsibilities to others, I guess." At this time he saw an article of the therapist's on the newstands, purchased it and said he enjoyed reading parts of it.

Joe began to examine more seriously his relationships to adults and peers and gave one vignette after another to substantiate the notion that he had never considered alternatives other than one single possibility, that is, that he be His Majesty the Prince. With his increased ability to renounce some of his egocentrism, narcissism, and omnipotence, Joe was able to finish a successful semester at the community college and continue his job. He returned to the university and got A's and B's in his courses. From a near recluse he began to date girls, from a contemptuous student he began to enjoy his professors as well as the course content, and from a depressed boy he became a rather spontaneous and warm young adult. I saw Joe in a follow-up interview three years after treatment. He'd received his Ph.D. in philosophy, was happily married, and was about to teach as an Assistant Professor in a well-known university.

Summary and Conclusion

Although there are myriad sociological and psychological factors that contribute to the etiology of the dropout phenomenon, this study singled out one primary dynamic factor for explication. From our research on fifty cases, it became quite clear that the intellectually capable college student who drops out is typically a very immature person, narcissistic, egocentric, passive, and with many grandiose and omnipotent fantasies. As one who has been catered to and indulged, college with its requirements for study, hard work, frustration and some submission induces a psychological shock. With many of his infantile wishes not gratified, the dropout becomes depressed and resorts to excessive fantasy and other regressive behavior.

The college dropout, to be helped in treatment, needs a relationship in which he is emotionally weaned. As his narcissism and dependency wishes are frustrated in the treatment, as his failures in the past or present are not rationalized by the therapist, as he is expected to think through alternatives, his ego functioning increases and his autonomy is furthered. Because he has been given to in the past and likes exclusive attention, the patient enters into treatment reasonably easily. Although the frustrating weaning approach is initially very unwelcomed, he slowly identifies with the therapist's championing of the reality principle, and after a period of anger and testing, begins to rely less on infantile satisfactions and builds on his ego functions.

REFERENCES

1. Berman, G., and M. Eisenberg, "Psychosocial Aspects of Academic Achievement," *American Journal of Orthopsychiatry*, Vol. 41, No. 63, 1971, pp. 406–415.

2. Coleman, J. *The Adolescent Society*. New York: Free Press, 1961.

3. Colm, H. "Phobias in Children," in *New Approaches in Child Guidance*, H. Strean, ed. Metuchen, N.J.: Scarecrow Press, 1970.

4. Halpern, H. "Work Inhibition in Children," *The Psychoanalytic Review*, Vol. 51, No. 2, 1964, pp. 5–21.

5. Josselyn, I. "Etiology of Three Current Adolescent Syndromes: A Hypothesis," in *Adolescent Psychiatry*, Vol. I, S. Feinstein and P. Giovacchini, eds. New York: Basic Books, 1971.

6. Keniston, K. "Youth as a Stage of Life," in *Adolescent Psychiatry*, Vol. I (see reference 5).

7. Keniston, K. "Alienation and the Decline of Utopia," *American Scholar*, Vol. 29, 1960, pp. 164–179.

8. Kesten, J. "Learning for Spite," in *New Approaches in Child Guidance* (see reference 3).

9. Lanvin, D. *The Prediction of Academic Performance: A Theoretical Analysis and Review of Research*, New York: Russell Sage, 1965.

10. Menaker, E. "Clinical Aspects of Work Inhibition," Paper presented to New York Society of Clinical Psychologists, May 1959.

11. Riesman, D. *Individualism Reconsidered*, New York: Free Press, 1954.

12. Smarr, E., and P. J. Escoll. "The Youth Culture, Future Adulthood and Societal Change," in *Adolescent Psychiatry*, Vol. II (see reference 5).

13. Sternbach, O. "The Pursuit of Happiness and the Epidemic of Depression," *The Psychoanalytic Review*, Vol. 61, No. 2, 1974, pp. 283–293.

14. Strean, H. "Role Theory," in *Social Work Treatment*, F. Turner, ed. New York: Free Press, 1974.

15. Strean, H. "Some Difficulties Met in the Treatment of Adolescents," in *New Approaches in Child Guidance* (see reference 3).

16. Strean, H. *The Experience of Psychotherapy*. Metuchen, N.J.: Scarecrow Press, 1973.

DISCUSSANT: ARTHUR BLATT

Dr. Strean has written an article focused primarily on the "how to do" of psychotherapy and has only peripherally glanced at the "how come" of psychotherapy. Yet his paper touches on universal theoretical questions related to the quantity and quality of effective, meaningful parenting.

Why do some adolescents and/or young adults who are intellectually capable not follow the usual paths set out by society? Why do they not follow the prescribed model dream of their parents and their peers? The German youth in the "flegejahre" of the 1800s, roaming over the countryside; the beatniks of the 1950s; the flower children of the early 1960s; the hippies of the late 1960s and the young drifters of the 1980s all attest to the insistence, prevalence and universality of the young adult who rebuffs the parental dream. Dr. Strean has reflected on this problem and has insightfully explored the treatment dynamics appropriate to this population. Wisely, he initially avoids the Scylla of sociological exposition and the Charybdis of casual causal psychological explanation as the exclusive dynamics of the dropout. He does recognize that external social and psychological forces do contribute to the dropout phenomenon but singles out the inner dynamics and fantasies of the behavior of the dropout as being essential for the therapeutic amelioration of this condition. On this note, it is interesting to see the parallel conclusions arrived at by Felton and Biggs in a paper entitled "Teaching Internalization Behavior to Collegiate Low Achievers in Group Psychotherapy." They saw internalization as a process wherein the person sees and accepts his behavior as being within his own control. They used a Gestalt therapeutic orientation which focused ". . . on the use of a language of responsibility and on responsible behavior" (p. 281). For example, where Dr. Strean writes of the patient's need to be emotionally weaned, to frustrate his narcissism and dependency wishes, and to not rationalize his past and present failures, Felton and Biggs write of the patient's need to confront himself, to orient himself to the present, and to use a language of responsibility.

Although Dr. Strean's paper incisively describes the clinical symptomatic behavior of these patients, it does not delve into the question of why an ". . . only and much loved offspring" becomes a dropout. What is presented is a paradox. On the one hand, we have an intellectually superior adolescent whose parents were active, attentive, and loving and who was highly successful in high school (the type of student who most of us would believe would succeed in college) and then the same adolescent in college complaining of depression, crying jags, apathy, and suicidal fantasies. This behavioral chasm has to be bridged and explained. For example, what percentage of these students went to a college campus away from home? Also, at what point in their college career did they drop out? Information about these two questions would enable us to determine whether separation anxiety from their parents was a causative factor in dropping out of college. More information is needed in order to assess whether there was something about the quantity and quality of parental loving that was amiss.

C. P. Adatto in a paper, "On the Metamorphosis from Adolescence into Adulthood" found that in working with adolescent patients ". . . in their fantasies, affective actions and transference manifestations reflected not only regressive trends but also active attempts at newer forms of psychic synthesis, even if grossly maladaptive" (p. 414). One wonders whether the patients in Dr. Strean's paper were expressing behavior which although grossly maladaptive, was an attempt to redefine the parent-child relationship. Success in college for these patients had to wait until success in growing up (separation-individuation) had occurred. The dynamic that unites these 50 cases is not that of dropping out of college but that of immaturity. The roots of this immaturity were probably as varied and unique as the external factors that eventually forced them into observable behavior. External factors as diverse as the standards set by the college they went to; the roommates they encountered; the vagaries of individual professors; the stress of romantic and sexual encounters and certainly the absence of the time-worn phrase "in loco parentis."

REFERENCES

Adatto, C. P. "On the Metamorphosis from Adolescence into Adulthood," *Journal of American Psychoanalytic Association*, Vol. 14, 1966, pp. 485–509.

Felton, G. S., and Biggs, B. E. "Teaching Internalization Behavior to Collegiate Low Achievers," *Psychotherapy: Theory, Research and Practice*, Vol. 9, No. 3, Fall 1972, pp. 281–283.

Kneeland, D. E. "Young Drifters in America: Who, Where and Why," *The New York Times*, Wednesday, April 15, 1981, Sect. A, p. 28.

DISCUSSANT: MARGARET G. FRANK

We have come to understand through the growth of ego psychology that man is an organizing and synthesizing being who is drawn to order the world and classify experience. The article "Some Reflections on Therapeutic Work with the College Dropout" attests to the high order of these capacities in its author. Dr. Strean reflects on phenomena of great concern to clinicians, families, and society at large. He groups observations of adolescents exhibiting a range of similar behaviors and suggests certain common dynamic and genetic issues. There follows a therapeutic approach which is informed by the author's dynamic formulation. The extent to which the suggested treatment enabled his group of "dropouts" to reengage in their studies and the direction of their lives is impressive and attests to the accurate directions of his formulations.

Dr. Strean is quite clear that he is not attempting an exhaustive study of the dropout phenomenon. He offers only his own observations and experiences set forth in a primarily psychoanalytic frame of understanding.

My own comments on this article are informed by my study of

psychoanalytic developmental theory which leads me at one and the same time to admire the thinking offered in this article and to point up both omissions and dangers in the presentation.

Diagnostic Considerations

The expansion of psychoanalytic theory into developmental studies of self, ego, the drives, affect, cognition and object relations has confounded our ability to classify or diagnose our patients. No longer can we group similar behaviors and assume similar dynamics.

The phobia, once viewed as the hallmark of neurosis has been observed clinically to be present in psychotics, borderlines, etc. As knowledge of early development is refined, the field is moving toward descriptive developmental diagnosis. Here the focus is more upon discerning structure and the organizing capacities of the ego and less on behavior. Dr. Strean's patients are presented with marked similarity in *behavior:* antagonism to professors, the system, etc. These verbal attacks are assumed to be projections and an inability to "own" the autonomy and responsibility of the situation. But I have heard these same remarks made by a young woman (a bright, well endowed young woman physically separated from home for the first time) in a desperate attempt to prevent engulfment and loss of her fragile sense of self. For her, success in school endangered her early attachment to home and mother. The point I wish to make is not to question the accuracy of Dr. Strean's formulations but to urge the reader to take care not to look at behavior without the context of assessing structure.

Adolescence: Stage of Development

I am concerned that Dr. Strean gave so little note of the developmental stage of his patients. It would be beneficial to look at all college students as adolescents and to remind ourselves that early developmental (preoedipal and oedipal) issues are *normally* reworked during this period. While society, families and colleges would be content if there were less or no disruption, I believe Anna Freud once warned aloud, "Beware of the adolescent who does not appear adolescent." This remark can lead us to wonder about all the students who never come to our attention because "all goes well." Perhaps too well.

Margaret Mahler's studies have provided a view of development in the realm of object relations: the process forming a psychically separated and individuated self based on the nature of early parenting. Dr. Strean's patients sound quite similar to the rapprochement child who must master a crisis in order to promote structure and attain psychological birth. This crisis involves the loss of the sense of omnipotence experienced in the practicing sub-phase of both self and parent. The child must deal with accepting the more real self and the realities of his parents. Passage through rapprochement involves not only loss, and disillusion, but rage. The rage is directed at the self and the parent. If the child could give voice to his experience he might be saying, "How can I be so small and helpless when I thought myself to be so powerful?" And to the parents, "What's wrong with you that you cannot fix this? I thought you were all powerful!" The parent who can be available through the rage, disillusion, and loss aids the child in accepting the realities of self and object. Dr. Mahler's writing notes clearly the difficulties of the child's developmental tasks. She makes further note of the profound challenge to the parent. I am leading to the conjecture that the patients studied here were reworking rapprochement issues and came to college and treatment with more adequate parenting than meets the eye.

Treatment Considerations

The "weaning" approach offered in this study could be seen as one in which the therapist aids the reworking of rapprochement. He withstands the rage of disillusionment and promotes the functioning of the ego capacities. It seems to me that only the young person with well-formed structure, with a predominance of positive object experiences could use and respond to this approach in a relatively short period of time.

What we call the "border-line" patient who is struggling with earlier issues of separation and attachment must be understood and treated differently. One may do harm to try to wean a starving patient.

Dr. Strean's presentation offers a thoughtful therapeutic approach to a group of young people reworking similar developmental issues in adolescence. They share a common behavior—that of dropping out of college. The reader must be clear that behaviors cannot tell us diagnosis. Diagnosis is ascertained only by a careful view of developmental issues and structure. It is the diagnosis that informs the treatment.

It is no wonder that so many theories (sociological and clinical) prevail around this phenomenon. It is a behavior deriving from multiple dynamic and environmental conditions. The focus on the pleasure–reality principle needs the expansion which can be provided by object relations theory.

Chapter 8

THE EXTRAMARITAL AFFAIR: A PSYCHOANALYTIC VIEW

The last decade has witnessed a rather strong modification of traditional sexual practices. Premarital cohabitation and sexual intercourse, instead of being shunned, are accepted by most. "Swinging," "switching," and "group sex" among the married are far from taboo in many sectors of American life. Homosexuality, instead of being considered morally and legally reprehensible, is now more legitimized as a way of life, and the American Psychiatric Association recently struck "homosexuality" from its psychiatric nomenclature. Many dynamically oriented therapists now advocate premarital and extra-marital sex as avenues to mental health and some have even opined that such sex activity will enhance ego functioning and sexual maturation.

Those of us engaged in the practice of psychotherapy and psychoanalysis are also active participants in society; we, therefore, are influenced by modifications of traditional sexual practices. The growing popularity of sensitivity groups, "touching" encounter groups, nude marathons, etc. reflects the pervasive influence of societal values and practices on psychotherapeutic modalities.[11, 23]

Psychoanalysis has long contended that behavior in and of itself can not be fully understood or evaluated unless a comprehensive meta-psychological orientation is utilized to unravel its significance. Unless the patient's history, structural components of his personality, dynamic unconscious, object relations, fantasies, and other features of his complex psyche are taken into account the meaning of behavior can, at best, be only hypothesized.[10] Therefore, the dynamically oriented therapist is not ready to say upon immediate observation that sex not practiced in the marital bedroom is neurotic, acting-out, or "sick"; neither is he

Reprinted by permission from *The Psychoanalytic Review*, vol. 62, no. 2 (June 1975), pp. 211–219.

willing, at first blush, to term the behavior mature, healthy, adaptive or object-related.

Despite the fact that the psychoanalytically oriented therapist, in particular, and all therapists in general spend much of their professional energy assessing the meaning of their patients' erotic lives and analyzing many of the components of their patients' premarital and extra-marital activities, there has been little systematic psychoanalytic attention given in the literature to these phenomena. Although it must be stated at the outset that the sexual behavior of a patient in conflict may have different connotations and implications than the behavior of an individual who is not in treatment, we know from Freud's work and from those of others[2, 9] that an understanding of our patients' complex metapsychologies can lead to a more enriched understanding of the modal "normal" human being.

During the last ten years or so I have witnessed in my own practice, and in the practice of colleagues and students, a sharp rise in the incidence of "extra-marital affairs." Close to forty of these phenomena have been subjected to psychoanalytic study both in the consultation room and in several supervisory discussions. This preliminary report is an attempt to extract the major themes, conflicts, and fantasies of those patients who subjected their extra-marital behavior to psychoanalytic investigation. It is hoped it will stimulate others to report on other psychoanalytic dimensions that this research has not unearthed, so that a phenomenon that has been shrouded in too much secrecy may be better clarified and conceptualized.

A Note on Some Problems of Today's Spouse

Our society is an affluent one and opportunities for "expansion" of our income, status, and psyches always exist. Our appetites are constantly being whetted and new excitement is always around the corner. Instead of averring that where there is id there shall be ego, we live in a society that is constantly inviting us to enjoy new id pleasures—massages, porno movies, erotic literature, to name but a few.[11]

When appeals to our narcissism, grandiosity, and omnipotent fantasies are ubiquitous, our frustration tolerance tends to decline.[4] It is more difficult for today's spouse to remain "loyal" in marriage than it was for his forebear, now that more loving communication, more attentive comfort, and more exciting sexual possibilities seem quite available.

The drudgery of washing the dishes, listening to boring details of the day's happenings, resolving conflicts among the children are more than obviated in the regressed but exciting atmosphere of the motel, hotel, yacht or borrowed apartment.

The extra-marital "date" takes the lover away from the realities of frustrating routines, delibidinized interaction, adult work, and into an arena that champions the pleasure principle. Because the husband or wife today, more than at any other time in our civilization, finds so many media stimulating his or her narcissism, erotic hunger, grandiosity, and in addition bears much advocacy of the "open marriage" and other alternative ways of relating sexually, we should not be too surprised that swinging, switching, and the rest are commonplace.

The institution of marriage, rather than promoting regressive excitement that exists in an affair, often requires challenges to our maturer ego functions—high-level judgment; object-related interaction rather than narcissistic joy; frustration tolerance rather than instant pleasure; mature reality testing and deferred gratification; acceptance of criticism rather than adulation, etc. These are jobs or tasks which many of us shun. The affair, with its island of bliss, excitement and devilish abandon, can offer more libidinal pleasure, but usually not without some conflict.

The following clinical examples are of patients who did not necessarily come for treatment because they were in conflict about their extramarital affairs. Rather, the extra-marital activity became an object of analytic investigation during the course of treatments which were often sought for other reasons. It should also be stated that of the four categories of patients presented, these categories are not mutually exclusive, i.e., it is quite possible for the extra-marital relationship to be an over-determined affair.

1. The Spouse as Incestuous Object

One of the difficulties of marriage is that in our search for the omnipotent mother and/or father, we come face to face with the incest taboo.[6] Particularly in American society where the spouse is often expected to psychologically assume a parental role and "comfort," "nurture," "understand" and "love," it is quite easy to arrange for the spouse to unconsciously be mother or father. With the spouse as mother and/or father, sex is experienced as incestuous and therefore prohibitive.[5, 6, 7]

Mr. A., a thirty-five-year-old man, sought treatment for several reasons. He was dissatisfied with his poor job performance as a stockbroker, was insomniac, depressed on frequent occasions, had difficulty in most relationships where he would get involved in power struggles, and had several psychosomatic complaints.

Fairly early in his treatment, Mr. A. complained about his wife. He described her as warm, pleasant, kind, good to the children, but unexciting. He felt marriage was like "having a noose tied around my neck" and he had to break out of it. He blamed his sexual impotence with his wife on her "unexcited" behavior in bed. He found her statements of love to him "abominable"—"she sounds like my mother who wants to envelop me." To prove that his impotence was his wife's "problem," Mr. A. boasted of his big erections and sustained potency with an un-married girl friend who was "exciting," "stimulating" and "never controls me."

During the course of treatment Mr. A. reported that he decided to take his girl friend away on a vacation to a motel. However, part of the deal was that the girl friend would cook and assume other traditional chores of a wife. While the first day or two of the vacation were blissful, Mr. A., to his surprise and indignation, became impotent with his girl friend. As he later said in treatment, "As soon as a broad becomes like a wife, I make her into a controlling mother. She even begins to smell like my mother and I want to run."

It is quite clear in the case of Mr. A. that because he had a strong oedipal attachment to the maternal introject (and, in fact, unconsciously wanted to have incestuous sex with her), the patient had to split the woman into two, i.e., the virginal mother and the whore. [1,5] As long as he did not have a living, day-to-day relationship with the woman, he was safe. Living with a woman and then making her into a mother stimulated a feeling in him of being controlled and attached by "a noose."

The following case with a similar theme is that of a woman patient, Mrs. B., aged 40, who came for treatment for several reasons. She had difficulty getting along with an aged mother and wondered how much time she should give her; she had identity problems and felt insecure on her job as a librarian; interpersonally, when involved socially or professionally she often got involved in sado-masochistic quarrels. In her marriage, she had a lot of resentment towards her husband who acted "like a know-it-all," "considers me beneath him," and "screws like a naive boy."

In the treatment, as Mrs. B. began to voice more resentment towards her husband for being a "bossy know-it-all" whom, of course, in her mind she had to castrate by making him a "naive boy," she moved into an extra-marital affair with a married man. In contrast to her husband, this man was not "a know-it-all" but a "man of the world," and although most of their sex was pre-genital (fellatio and cunnilingus), her paramour was described as a "great lover." In contrast to Mrs. B.'s husband, whose statements of love "make me sick" and "engulf me," her lover's cool detachment "turns me on."

When Mrs. B. and her boy friend went on a camping trip for several days, the relationship "cooled." The couple engaged in Virginia Woolf dialogues, had all kinds of one-upmanship arguments and the love and bliss which previously characterized the relationship broke down. Mrs. B. ambivalently declared after returning from the sojourn with her lover, "When I was with him over time, everything lost its glamour. We fought and never got anything settled."

Mrs. B., like Mr. A., needed her marriage. Like young children, they wanted the ministrations of parental figures but, of course, could not tolerate sexual expression to or from their spouses. Sexuality was experienced as overwhelming, controlling, and debilitating—much as a child would experience sex if he or she participated in it with an adult parent.

Extra-marital partners for both Mr. A. and Mrs. B. were experienced as love objects whom they could enjoy only so long as the patients did *not* have to live with them on a sustained basis. As soon as they did live with their partners for even a few days, their incestuous wishes became activated and the bliss of their extra-marital affairs deteriorated in many ways.

One of the reasons, no doubt, that "open marriage" or no marriage at all can be helpful to many people is that these individuals can avoid the on-going living relationship inherent in a traditional marriage. Avoided is the anxiety that is stimulated by a dependent, incestuous attachment which they crave but fear.

2. Fighting the Superego

Not unrelated to the type of conflict described in Category 1 is the patient who transfers many of his superego commands onto his or her spouse and then has to defy the latter by rebelling against controls which the patient has ascribed to the spouse.

As has already been implied, most individuals bring into the marital relationship residues of childhood attachments, particularly attachments to parents.[1] Those of us who observe patients in marriage often note that much of their energy is expended in trying to please the marital partner, much as a child tries to seduce and ingratiate himself with a parent. As the patient engages in activity that will appeal to his spouse's narcissism, so that the marital partner (mother or father figure) will reward him and gratify him, he begins to resent the position he has created for himself. Not only does he hate himself for feeling so small, powerless and dependent, but he also resists the very omnipotent position in which he has placed his spouse. Feeling a victim of abusive power, unappreciated as a mature man or woman, and defiant, much like an adolescent whose autonomy is challenged, the patient can retaliate against the superego figure, his spouse, and do what he feels will diminish his partner's elevated position and enhance his own.

> Mr. C., aged 45, sought treatment because he was depressed, had various gastric disorders and other psychosomatic complaints, insomnia, and unexplained temper tantrums. He was married to a woman three years older than himself whom he consciously revered for her warmth, kindness, and ability to mother their children. Easily intimidated by his wife–mother, he would hide when he smoked because "she criticizes me too much." Like a defiant boy, he enjoyed cursing and then having mother-wife yell at him to cease and desist. Although his wife was not too interested in sex, he handled her resistance with only mild protest.
>
> For years Mr. C. was a "good boy" with his wife, who in his mind stood for law and order. He could defy her by cursing and smoking but basically he was quite compliant. By the time he came into treatment, he had allowed himself to be seduced by an aggressive married woman who enjoyed his cursing and loved his rebellious and seeming self-confident worldliness. In contrast to his mother–wife, his mistress was one who wanted to be educated to sex because her own husband was too "moralistic" and not sufficiently exciting. Mr. C. complied and dutifully became her mentor.
>
> Mr. C. and his girl friend, like two rebellious adolescents, flaunted their new-found power. Their relationship became known to many individuals in their neighborhood but this didn't faze them. They were, in effect, saying, "Superego figures, we hate you, we'll have our thing!" not realizing, of course, that they had created and induced their spouses to represent and symbolize their own punitive superegos which they found too taxing and controlling.

As is true with patients with powerful superegos, like Freud's "Criminal Out of a Sense of Guilt,"[8] Mr. C. unconsciously arranged for his extra-marital activity to be ascertained by his wife, and was severely admonished by her for several months afterwards. Like the guilty boy who rebelled against mama, he could "enjoy" eventually suffering and hating himself.

The conflicts provoking the extra-marital affair for Mr. C. could be compared to an adolescent's problem with autonomy, emancipation and identity. Projecting his own powerful superego commands on to his "mother–wife," he then fought her controls. Because his affair was merely an erotization of his aggression rather than a genuine libidinal and object-related experience (as is true for many adolescents), the guilty child had to get caught and punished. When caught and punished he could feel a sense of relief and begged his mother-wife for forgiveness.

The following case of a thirty-four-year-old married woman reveals the same type of conflict that was noted in Mr. C.—a fight or rebellion against the superego.

> Mrs. D. was the wife of a prominent minister and had been married to him for over fifteen years when she sought treatment. Very early in the treatment she brought out her resentment towards her husband, who always stood for "propriety." "He is always helping people, never hurting others, and is another Jesus," she complained. Mrs. D. objected to these qualities in her husband because, "after all, Jesus never liked sex!"
>
> Although further investigation revealed that Mr. D. enjoyed sex and often wished Mrs. D. would be less inhibited and more spontaneous, Mrs. D. was convinced that to have sex with her husband was really "dirtying" him. Treatment revealed that actually it was Mrs. D. who was quite uptight and that sex could only be exciting for her if she were fighting society's mandates. "Motels and the woods are great; there is something so sterile about the marital bedroom," she declared.
>
> Like Mr. C. in the last case, Mrs. D. found another rebel like herself, a married man who resented his wife's controls, and had an affair with him. Again like an ambivalent adolescent, Mrs. D. could enjoy rebelling against her superego–husband's restraints. However, this was always followed by guilt reactions. Often, after she completed sex with her paramour, Mrs. D. sought in her head for her husband's forgiveness. Like Mr. C., of course, Mrs. D. had to arrange for her husband to learn of her extra-marital activity and could then punish herself "for upsetting him so much."

From cases like those of Mr. C. and Mrs. D., we learn that an extra-marital affair might be engaged in by rather repressed people who actually condemn their own sexual impulses. They tend to find spouses who might give them some reason or reasons to reinforce their own guilt and anxiety over their libidinal wishes. Rather than analyzing their own superego commands and lessening their impact, these patients, like adolescents, project their superego commands onto their spouses and rebel against them, thus externalizing and acting out the conflict. Because these patients also feel guilty about their rebellious activity and fantasies and often need their dependent attachments to their spouses, they unconsciously arrange to "get caught" and be punished by these superego figures.

3. Expression of Bisexuality

As the psychoanalytic literature has impressively revealed, within all of us are active and passive aims and wishes to be members of both sexes.[2,9] However, when the bisexual conflict is rather profound, it often expresses itself in and invades a marriage. The man, for example, who suffers from much castration anxiety enjoys but cannot tolerate his passivity, and can protect his feeling of vulnerability by "proving" that he is a man. This he can do through Don Juan–like, promiscuous extra-marital activity.[6] Similarly, the woman who is dominated by phallic strivings and wishes to castrate and compete with her husband can prove her "femininity" by outside sexual activity. The bisexuality can be preserved for these patients as they gratify one part of themselves in an affair and another in a marriage. This is often why many individuals need ongoing relationships with two members of the opposite sex. It may be noted that bisexuality is probably also at the base of the rather recently popular sexual practice of having three people in bed—one man and two women or one woman and two men. All participants are probably gratifying their bisexual orientation under the guise of "enrichment," "excitement" and "stimulation."

> Mrs. E., a thirty-six-year-old married woman, sought treatment for her six-year-old boy who was described as "very effeminate, sissyish, passive and much too girlish." As she elaborated on her son Andy's difficulties to his therapist, it became quite obvious that Mrs. E. attained quite a bit of gratification in seeing Andy as "a weak boy."
> As time went on Mrs. E. moved into a discussion of her marriage and it became quite obvious that she had formed a similar relationship with her husband as she had with Andy. She described with scorn and contempt how her husband is "fragile," how she, Mrs. E., was more adept at mechanical and athletic pursuits, and how when she derided her husband, he seemed so hurt.
> Mrs. E.'s phallic competition with her husband and son was rationalized by her as their inability to accept and feel secure with

their own masculinity. Consequently, she could easily justify her extra-marital affair with an older married man who was "truly masculine, adept in athletics and mechanics and a great lover." When she was asked why she didn't marry her paramour, Mrs. E., without insight, averred, "I get much security out of my marriage. My husband and son are always there. They both accept all of my *mishegas* but Jerry [her lover] makes me feel like a woman. I need both."

Mrs. E.'s bisexual conflict was clear. At home with Mr. E. and Andy, she could be the phallic aggressive woman. However, she had a great deal of discomfort in seeing herself in this role exclusively, despite the fact that she could rationalize her activity with her son and husband, and ascribe her aggression to their vulnerabilities. Instead of attempting to strengthen her son and husband, she continued to deride them and in her extra-marital affair could be "the woman." As Mrs. E. herself implied, because of her bisexual conflict she needed to be a woman with her paramour and, in many ways, a man with her husband and son. A similar conflict may be noted in the following case of Mr. F.

Mr. F., a thirty-nine-year-old salesman, was in treatment because of poor job performance, phobic reaction to cars, subways and airplanes, psychosomatic reactions, and generalized depression. In his marriage he felt rather intimidated by his wife but rather than assert his own wishes, he often submitted to her commands. Sexually, "my wife calls the shots as well as the positions with her usually on top." Furthermore, Mr. F. also mentioned that his wife didn't want sex too often.

To compensate for Mr. F.'s feeling of low self-worth vis-à-vis his wife, he sought an affair with a younger married woman who had many sexual difficulties. However, in contrast to his passive position with his wife, Mr. F. enjoyed educating his girl friend to sex. He felt "very much the man" as he dominated her, and enjoyed her admiration of him. Yet, when Mr. F. was asked why he didn't marry his girl friend, he praised his wife, who, "although asexual, is wonderful." Mr. F. humorously but insightfully commented, "It's good to have two women. It makes for a fuller life. With one, you are the boss and with the other you're the servant. A rounded life, eh what?"

Although many individuals with bisexual conflicts can justify their behavior in an affair by pointing to their spouses' lack of responsiveness, it is interesting that in cases like those of Mrs. E. and Mr. F., both clung rather tenaciously to their marriages. This should not surprise us, for the patient with a bisexual conflict needs two partners, one whom he experiences as masculine and the other whom he experiences as feminine.

4. A *Defense Against Symbiosis*

A rather common marital dyad is the symbiotic union. Here, two very dependent individuals find each other and "share everything." Feeling shaky about their own self-images and identities, they constantly seek each other out to reaffirm themselves. As often occurs in this complementary pattern, a mutual attempt at domination occurs in order for them to cope with feelings of vulnerability and anxiety. Both partners become critical of each other, feel constantly insulted and humiliated, and attempt to humiliate each other.[1]

Because both members of this dyad have an intense longing for dependency, they become very sensitive to criticism and lack of affection. Each wants to win a victory over the other and assert his or her omnipotence. One means of breaking away from the symbiotic tie, attaining a victory, and assuming some feeling of autonomy is by having an extra-marital affair.

> Mr. G., forty-six, was married for about twenty years when he came for treatment. He complained that his wife was very distant, cool, critical and didn't share in any of his pleasures. "For years I have tried to get her to love me and approve of me but she hardly even gives me a gum-drop," Mr. G. stated. Despite his wife's lack of responsiveness, Mr. G., for many years, was convinced "she has it to give" and tried to extract maternal love from his wife.
>
> Mr. G. described many arguments with his wife. It turned out that both partners resented each other's lack of loving response to each other, competed with each other for approbation from friends and their children, and constantly derided each other. Yet, Mr. and Mrs. G. could never be emotionally separate from each other and had to share every detail in each other's life. However, these discussions often broke down into arguments because each resisted the other's advice and attempts at support, experiencing them as derision.
>
> Mr. G., in an attempt to "proclaim my independence, show her that I don't need her that badly and have some pleasure from a woman," chose an unmarried young woman for a girl friend. He enjoyed "telling her all about my life" without receiving so much criticism. Because she was a younger woman, he could also enjoy dominating her and instructing her in the ways of the world. Despite the fact that many of his symbiotic needs were gratified in his extra-

marital relationship, his attachment to his wife remained strong. Eventually, he gave up the affair and with much humiliation and guilt confessed his "bad ways" to his wife. "I have to be loyal to her, it feels so much better," Mr. G. concluded.

Like the child who resents his dependent attachment to a parent, the symbiotic marital partner utilizes an affair to proclaim his independence. However, just as the child who feigns pseudo-independence needs his parent, so too, patients like Mr. G. have to return to their "mama-wife," declare their guilt, and continue the symbiosis. The same pattern may be noted in Mrs. H., the next case illustration.

> Mrs. H., a thirty-eight-year-old woman, was the wife of a physician. She came to treatment because she felt "that I have no identity of my own." Wherever she went she felt she was labelled 'Dr. H.'s wife' and she resented this. During the fourteen years of her marriage she consulted Dr. H. on most of her major decisions and usually abided by his advice. However, she always resented her dependent position and often retaliated by withholding sex from Dr. H. In her treatment she talked about feeling like a second-class citizen with her husband and in the community, found it hard to like anything of her own doing and was frequently depressed.
>
> While engaged in some P.T.A. work at her daughter's school, she met one of the teachers who lauded her work and expressed admiration of her talents. When the male teacher arranged for Mrs. H. to head a committee, she felt extreme pride in herself and was most grateful to her admirer. Soon the two were involved in an affair and as Mrs. H. described it, "I don't feel I'm just an appendage. I'm an independent person in my own right. That's different than the way I feel with my husband."

In the cases of Mr. G. and Mrs. H. we have two very dependent individuals who vacillated between wanting childish omnipotent desires gratified by their spouses and then arranging for their spouses to be their omnipotent parents. When they felt humiliated, lowered, small and impotent vis-à-vis their spouses, they attempted to assert their independence through an extra-marital affair. Like the youth who resents his dependence on the parent or some other authority, the individual in this category tries to renounce his dependency on the "spouse–parent" and becomes dependent on someone else. The conflict, of course, does not get resolved this way, but the patient through his extra-marital activity feels a certain sense of new-found autonomy and independence, although still maintaining the relationship with the marital partner.

Summary and Conclusion

Living in an age of affluence with many opportunities to whet our appetites, the frustrations of marriage can be somewhat obviated by the gratifications and pleasures in the regressed atmosphere of an extra-marital affair. Although this study focuses on individuals in psychoanalytic treatment, it is felt that some of the dynamics that have been unearthed in our subjects may offer some understanding of extra-marital behavior in general.

Four categories evolved from our research on forty patients who were involved in extra-marital affairs. It is recognized that when the spouse is experienced as an incestuous object, a punitive superego figure, a partner in bisexual conflicts, or in a symbiosis, an extra-marital affair is one means of externalizing the conflict. It was further emphasized that these categories were not mutually exclusive; theoretically incestuous, bisexual, and symbiotic fantasies could exist in one person who concomitantly can experience his or her spouse as a superego figure.

It should be noted that with further study of the vicissitudes of oedipal and pre-oedipal fantasies, maturational fixations, and other meta-psychological data of patients involved in extra-marital activity, further categories in addition to the four reported in this study may evolve. Although we cannot at this time state with conviction that all extra-marital activity is maladaptive, we are inclined to concur with Fenichel, who wrote: "Marital infidelity has more frequently than one believes a neurotic origin; it is not a sign of liberty and potency but of the opposite."[2]

REFERENCES

1. Eidelberg, L. "Neurotic Choice of Mate," in *Neurotic Interaction in Marriage*, V. Eisenstein, ed. New York: Basic Books, 1956.

2. Fenichel, O. *Psychoanalytic Theory of the Neuroses*. New York: W. W. Norton, 1945.

3. Ferenczi, S. "Gulliver Fantasies," *International Journal of Psychoanalysis*, Vol. IX, 1928, pp. 283–300.

4. Freud, S. "Introduction to Narcissism," *Collected Papers*, Vol. IV. London: Hogarth Press, 1953.

5. Freud, S. "Contributions to the Psychology of Love: The Most Prevalent Form of Degradation in Erotic Life," *Collected Papers*, Vol. IV. London: Hogarth Press, 1953.

6. Freud, S. "Contributions to the Psychology of Love: A Special Type of Choice of Object Made by Men," *Collected Papers*, Vol. IV. London: Hogarth Press, 1953.

7. Freud, S. "Splitting of the Ego in the Defensive Process," *Collected Papers*, Vol. V. London: Hogarth Press, 1953.

8. Freud, S. "Some Character-Types Met with in Psychoanalytic Work," *Collected Papers*, Vol. IV. London: Hogarth Press, 1953.

9. Freud, S. *New Introductory Lectures in Psychoanalysis*. New York: W. W. Norton, 1933.

10. Rapoport, D. "The Structure of Psychoanalytic Theory: A Systematizing Attempt in Psychology," in *Psychology: A Study of a Science*, S. Koch, ed. New York: McGraw-Hill, 1959.

11. Strean, H. "Social Change and the Proliferation of Regressive Therapies," *The Psychoanalytic Review*, Vol. 58, No. 4, 1971, pp. 581–594.

12. Strean, H. "Choosing Among Practice Modalities," *Clinical Social Work Journal*, Vol. 2, No. 1, 1974, pp. 3–14.

DISCUSSANT: POLLY CONDIT

In this article, Dr. Strean has addressed what is perhaps one of his particularly controversial subjects, or at least one which seems to have stimulated a wide variety of very strong reactions. The extra-marital affair is both a popular and yet unpopular subject. It seems to be a form of behavior which is increasingly discussed, studied, and written about; yet, curiously, there has been almost no investigation of this phenomenon in the psychoanalytic literature. Most recent material about the extra-marital affair has been written from a sociological, behavioral, or descriptive point of view. Case material has been drawn from research oriented interviews, and questionnaires, or sometimes small group discussions. These studies describe the conscious reasons people choose to have affairs, and how they feel this behavior has affected them and their marriages. Conclusions are then drawn about the dynamics, benefits, and problems of extra-marital relationships. Many of these studies indicate that extra-marital affairs are healthy adaptations to the unhealthy state of monogamous marriage, that they enhance personal happiness and sexual functioning, and that the problem lies primarily with the institution of marriage.

A point is often made in these studies that their subjects are normal, i.e., as far as can be determined by interviews and sometimes psychological testing, they show no signs of neurotic illness or other psychopathology. This method of determining "mental health" or good adjustment is questionable, as anyone who really takes a look into people's inner lives understands.

As Strean points out, his study is based on material gained solely from people in psychoanalytic therapy, and it is true that, in psychoanalytic tradition, we believe that what we learn from our patients can be applied to our understanding of all human beings. For those who would say that Strean is using a skewed sample, I would state that these are people who are not so very different from any of us, except perhaps more courageous about facing their inner lives. And what better way is there to gain an in-depth knowledge of the meaning of a type of behavior than to study it in the context of an individual's personal history, dreams, fantasies, and other unconscious processes? Only in this way can we begin to fully understand behavior, with its complex interplay between individual psychodynamics and current life circumstances.

There is an issue which seems important to consider when looking at material gained from therapy sessions. Anything which transpires during treatment, whether an action outside of the consultation room, or associations which come to mind during the hour must be looked at in terms of transference and resistance issues. Thus, the analytic understanding of the affair must include also the understanding of the affair as possibly an expression of transference wishes, and resistances, to the analysis. As Strean makes very clear, marital relationships are influenced by a complex array of parental introjects, infantile conflicts, and defenses. The same dynamics are recapitulated in the transference, and, thus, the affair might be an expression of transference frustrations as well as marital dissatisfactions. Although I see this as an important dimension to take into consideration when studying any behavior by psychoanalytic investigation, I don't think it refutes the premises put forth in this article. It does pique my curiosity to know more of these cases, however.

As Strean pursues his theory that unconscious conflicts within the individual lead to the seeking of extra-marital affairs, he risks being experienced by us as a critical and punitive "analytic superego" figure. No one particularly likes to have to consider that maybe a piece of behavior—as socially acceptable, tempting, and gratifying as an affair can be (so nicely described by the author)—might be a result of a neurotic conflict, or an infantile need. Perhaps that is one reason that this increasingly common manifestation of modern marriage has not been studied very much by psychoanalysts.

We've long known, from Freud's vivid writing on the subject, of the impact of incestuous fixations on the choice of a love object; i.e., the attraction of illicit sexual relationships, the need to separate affectionate and sensual feelings, and the meaning of jealousy. Strean has described these problems in his patients, and, in addition, has looked at a variety of other oedipal and pre-oedipal conflicts which lead to unhappiness in the marital relationship and need for an affair. He relates specific kinds of problems in a marriage to the occurrence of an affair, and sees the affair as the product of these particular conflicts. For instance, in the dynamic formulation of the spouse who projects his superego onto his partner, it is specifically the need to defy that superego figure which leads the person to seek an extra-marital partner. Then there is the equally compelling guilt and resulting need to be caught and punished, which these two cases illustrate rather graphically. Strean here makes another important point which is that people find spouses who fulfill certain needs, or express one side of a conflict. A person with much guilt about his sexual feelings may choose a mate who plays the part of a forbidding parent. Strean shows, in all his case examples, the importance of understanding an individual's unconscious wishes which are being expressed in his choice of marital partner. The type of person chosen as an extra-marital partner, and the way that person is perceived, is also determined by these factors. The marriage and the affair are two sides of the same conflict.

In the cases illustrating incestuous fixations as the primary dynamic, certain aspects are expressed quite dramatically, perhaps more so than we find in most of our patients. These two people were able to get enough of their desired lovers, and, discovered, in short order, that the same problems arose that existed in the marriage. It is well known that sexual pleasure, either in fantasy or reality, seems more pleasurable to many people when the partner is not available for a day-to-day relationship. With these two people, it seems clear that any close sexual relationship would break down rather quickly due to their unconscious conflicts. Because they were in treatment, they were apparently able to begin to look at the fact that the problem was not necessarily in the other person, but some process taking place within themselves. Because having an affair allows a person to externalize his conflicts, he may not subject this behavior to psychoanalytic scrutiny unless he happens to be in treatment for other reasons, or, as we sometimes see, the affair begins to cause too much pain.

Strean's theory of the affair as an expression of bisexuality again looks at early conflicts as an important factor in the need so many people have for two or more sexual partners. Here he addresses the very crucial issue of why a person may need to continue a marriage which by all accounts is so generally unsatisfying. Over and over we see people who are stuck in unhappy marriages, and though there are always conscious reasons to explain this (i.e., money, children, guilt, a comfortable lifestyle), it is very important to understand the unconscious gratifications which the marriage provides.

Although in this article Strean only presents four categories of marital conflict leading to affairs, he refines these and adds many others in his book *The Extra-Marital Affair*. This extensive work also includes studies of the spouse whose partner seeks affairs, something which one must wonder about when reading this article.

Strean's approach to studying the extra-marital affair is as much a thorough study of marital relationships as it is about the dynamics of affairs. Perhaps in looking at why people choose to have extra-marital relationships, we can learn much more about what it takes to have a successful marriage.

Certainly the tasks of marriage are formidable. Strean enumerates some of the more developed ego functions required of a marital partner and contrasts them to the very stimulating and promising environment in which we live. In addition, sexual roles are changing rapidly, and men and women are expecting much more from one another. In his case studies, more requirements for a good marriage are described. A person should be able to tolerate dependency wishes, be relatively free of incestuous fixations, have a benign superego, be unconflicted about sexual identification while able to enjoy active and passive sexual impulses, have a good self-esteem, and a sense of separateness and autonomy. No wonder marriage is such a difficult proposition.

It seems to me that the very issues that can cause such serious problems if left unresolved before a person enters a marriage are also stimulated by the condition of marriage itself. In a relationship where one lives in relative isolation with a partner who is supposed to meet all sexual and most emotional needs, every oedipal and pre-oedipal yearning must be stirred up, such as in the search for the omnipotent parent as noted in the article. Strean talks of the regression of the extra-marital affair, but the regressive pulls which are activated in a marriage are equally important.

The advent of children brings another dimension to the marital relationship, and must also, I would think, be an important part of the dynamic constellation leading to an affair. Two people who have attained some measure of equilibrium must make room intrapsychically for one or more new persons. Identification with the child and the role of parenthood stimulate many wishes and conflicts concerning one's own parents, and childhood. Experiencing a spouse as mother or father to one's own child, competing with each other and the child for love, and living through each of the child's developmental stages are just a few of the stresses which must profoundly affect the marital relationship. In one of Strean's cases, dynamics concerning a child are important, but in several others, children are mentioned only in passing. I think this is an aspect of marital dynamics which we need to know more about.

Another issue which I would like to examine within the dynamic framework presented in this article is the question of how an affair might serve as a means towards individual growth and increased self-awareness. For most of the people discussed in this article, the affair provided an opportunity to experience a part of themselves which previously had been quite unavailable to them. As I think over some of my patients who have had affairs, I realize that often the question of just when the affair occurred, what particular conflicts were being expressed at the time, and what changes followed are all very crucial in understanding the affair. For instance, a woman who had been painfully inhibited about sex became less frightened and had an affair. For the first time in her life, she experienced orgastic pleasure. This experience then led to her being able to more fully understand what went wrong between her and her husband. In several of the cases in this article, it seems that the affair was in part both a result of growth in the individual and was also stimulating further development. I also wonder if an affair might sometimes permit a person to maintain a marriage which, though not without problems, brings real meaning and satisfaction to his or her life?

To avoid just superficial conclusions, these questions, too, will have to be looked at carefully, as Strean has done, with the help of the people who come to therapy. His view of the affair as an expression of conflict within the individual must increase our understanding not just of the extra-marital affair, but of marital relationships as well.

DISCUSSANT: JEROME B. ROSEN

> "For the first time in my life I feel like a real woman."
> "Sex with my wife is better since I've had this affair."
> "He's more interested in pleasing me . . . not like my husband."
> "My wife doesn't suspect a thing."

If you are a psychoanalyst, social worker, or counselor, you have heard one of the lines above or combinations of any of these in reference to the extra-marital affair from any number of your patients.

The psychoanalyst is constantly dealing with the patient who is involved in or fantasizing about an extra-marital affair. Yet there is very little in the literature that addresses this common phenomenon. Dr. Strean has filled this long delayed need in his paper published in *The Psychoanalytic Review* (Spring 1976) and in a subsequent book, *The Extra-Marital Affair* (New York: Free Press, 1980).

The original version included in this collection of Dr. Strean's papers speaks eloquently in the amount of space allotted for such a wide ranging subject. It would be unfair to you not to include in this review at least some of the subsequent findings in the book which goes beyond the scope of the present paper.

At the beginning of this paper Dr. Strean states, ". . . the dynamically oriented therapist is not ready to say upon immediate observation that sex not practiced in the marital bedroom is neurotic, acting out, or sick; neither is he willing, at first blush, to term the behavior mature, healthy, adaptive, or object-related."

We now know that we are in the presence of a psychoanalyst who is about to take us on an exploratory journey. In the paper it is a bird's eye view. Dr. Strean states that it is a preliminary report and hopes that it will act as a catalyst for other psychoanalysts to report their findings. He calls for clarification and conceptualization of this phenomenon that has been "shrouded in too much secrecy."

It is evident that Dr. Strean in the intervening four years has taken the task upon himself with notable success:

> I believe that many people who get married are psychologically still children, seeking gratification of childish wishes to merge, to domi-nate, to rescue, to be demeaned, to compete, etc. Furthermore, be-cause unresolved childish wishes cause anxiety, many married indi-viduals must defend themselves against intimacy because it conjures up wishes that they cannot tolerate.

In that single paragraph from the book, Dr. Strean has encompassed the dynamics of the majority of our patients and has isolated the infan-tile wishes that people bring into their marriages, and also, incidently, into their psychoanalysis. In this paper he can only postulate the search for the omnipotent mother or father and of coming face to face with the incest taboo.

In the book he demonstrates with remarkable clarity the infantile wishes, which, when unresolved from earlier developmental stages (the oral, anal, etc.), operate and create unrealistic expectations within a marriage. When fulfillment of these wishes is frustrated, as it must be, the marriage falters and an extra-marital affair is often the result.

In the paper before you, Dr. Strean touches upon a goodly measure of what he elaborates on in the book. Just as he clearly states the problem, he is able to conceptualize the ideal for the individual in a happy marriage:

> It is a person who can be dependent on someone without wishing for a merger .... can accept frustration without feeling sadistic or masochistic; can enjoy sex without being bombarded with competitive or incestuous fantasies; can admire a partner without over-idealizing and can be autonomous without resentment. He or she is a relatively happy human being who will want to devote him or herself to another happy human being.

That person may not exist, but the clarity of the ideal sums up the analytic goal that reaches beyond the scope and subject of the paper and book. One reads Dr. Strean with the growing awareness that we are indeed in the presence of a psychoanalyst who is that rare phenom-enon, a truly creative teacher.

To illustrate the depth of his understanding of the psychoanalytic process and his ability to teach us how to think with the psychosexual model always before us, I would like to discuss "The Agony and the

Ecstasy: A Psychoanalytic View of Psycho-Sexual Development," a chapter from the book. In this chapter Dr. Strean uses each of the designations oral, anal, phallic, oedipal, latency, pubertal, adolescent and genital period of development to illustrate that how well or badly one has resolved the psycho-sexual tasks appropriate to the various stages of childhood affects one's ability to fail at or sustain a loving and sexual marriage.

In the oral stage he points out how the experiences of the first year of life can influence how comfortable one is when involved in an intimate sexual relationship, how trusting one feels, how expressive one is and how much pleasure one derives. The attitude that the mother demonstrates in the feeding process is the attitude that the child is likely to associate with food, feeding or the nursing process. Frequently, the individual who cannot trust another human being in a sexual relationship has been extremely frustrated during the first few months of life. Under the subheading "Oral Frustration," Dr. Strean writes about the frustration every infant experiences and the need for instant gratification. If the child has been indulged and not appropriately weaned he will tend to approach a love relationship as would a demanding baby.

So Dr. Strean begins to deal with the archaic roots of some people involved in extra-marital affairs. There is a broad spectrum of ideas, clinical observations and conclusions all based on the oral stage and what this could possibly mean for the infant who forty or so years hence may be "fooling around."

> A consistent and mutually gratifying mother–infant relationship leads the child to seek out emotional attachments to people for the rest of his life. If his first emotional attachment has been emotionally gratifying, he will have resolved the first psychosexual task and thus will later be able to enjoy mutually gratifying love relationships [says Dr. Strean].

Throughout this chapter we are re-educated to psychoanalytic theory. Each developmental stage is discussed with the same consistency, insightfulness and authority until one is convinced that failed marriages may be traced back to the failures in these early developmental stages.

Early in the book he states, "Anything other than a monogamous marriage is immature and unhealthful," and, "A happy marriage is composed of two happy people." Upon these two statements Dr. Strean builds his theoretical pyramid and he reinforces this pyramid with unarguable psychoanalytic truths:

1. "The husband or wife involved in an extra marital affair is unable to relax in a mutually dependent relationship because of fear of rejection, abandonment or engulfment...."
2. "The person involved in the affair unconciously fears a monogamous marriage.... They are tormented by feelings of distrust, self doubt, inferiority, a shabby self-image, and uncertain sexual identity.... He or she needs a lover to bolster low self-esteem."

... and the eloquently simple:

3. "Since the essence of romantic love is idealization of the beloved, it cannot withstand the confrontation with reality that day to day married life entails."

If you are an experienced analyst the book will reaffirm what you already believe. If you are a neophyte you will be shown that there is indeed a path that is strewn with fewer obstacles than anxiety had allowed you to comprehend. Reading most contributions to psychoanalysis is a chore. We are inundated with convoluted paragraphs of jargon: objects, significant others, borderline states, etc. For most of us it becomes a matter of translating the printed word into a meaningful clinical concept for ourselves.

There is no such problem with Dr. Strean's writings. Whether we agree with his conclusions or not, what is stated for the reader is clearly and logically expressed. What you see is what you get to understand, to argue with, or to agree with.

One question I have for Dr. Strean is about his omission of the homosexual affair. He discusses unconscious homosexual dynamics and defenses including the marriage as a defense against homosexuality, but offers us no examples of those cases in which the extra-marital affair is a homosexual relationship. I wonder what Dr. Strean can contribute to our understanding of this phenomenon.

Having treated a number of homosexual males who have had relationships with married men, I have often wondered about the dynamics of their sexual partners. From the data in the book, I assume that one of the factors involved for some married men would be the breakdown of the defenses against the forbidden homosexual wish. But under what conditions do these defenses break down and what are the underlying dynamics of some of the others involved in extra-marital homosexual affairs?

Those of us who were fortunate enough to read both the paper and the book gained a privileged glimpse into the creative process at work—the awakening of the idea, the problem, the struggle to state the possible conclusions and finally everything falling into its place. This psychological document based upon the cornerstone of psychoanalysis and its formal process stands before us complete and theoretically sound.

Chapter 9

A CLINICIAN LOOKS AT INTERMARRIAGE

Any clinician who dares to offer his assessment of the psychological and interpersonal dynamics involved in intermarriage must do so with some humility and several misgivings. The topic appears overwhelming for it involves discoursing on two complex phenomena—love and religion—which for countless decades have pained, anguished, and absorbed poets, philosophers, social scientists, psychoanalysts, and many others. In the literature of both Jews and non-Jews, one finds many statements to the effect that "the way of a man with a maid" is beyond human understanding; rabbis and other clergymen often tell us that marriages are made in heaven.

Despite the fact that marriage counselors of all persuasions are doing a booming business, many individuals believe that only God knows why A marries B and whether the marriage will work out (Arlow, 1966). To ponder the whys and wherefores of how come two people love each other and eventually marry is a difficult enough task. When one adds to that seeming perplexing question still another one, "Why do two people from different religious denominations decide to marry each other?" solving this puzzle can appear onerous.

Yet, intermarriage is a fact of contemporary life and the rising rate of dual-faith wedding ceremonies is confounding religious leaders. Although only a handful of clergymen of most established faiths will officiate at such weddings, and only a minority will welcome two-faith families into their communities, it is nonetheless clear that today one in three Jewish marriages involves a non-Jew and about half of the Catholic and Protestant marriages involve a non-Catholic or non-Protestant (Kaye, 1980).

Reprinted by permission from *Journal of Jewish Communal Service*, Vol. 58, no. 1 (September 1981), pp. 342–352.

In other times and places, the hostility of the surrounding society was a major factor in keeping Jews within their own group; consequently intermarriage was a rare event when anti-Semitism was so strong. Few of us need to be reminded of the long history of Jewish persecution, highlighted by events ranging from the twelfth-century pogrom in York, England, which led to the banishment of Jews from that country until Oliver Cromwell readmitted them in the seventeenth century, to the Spanish Inquisition of the fifteenth century, to the pogroms of Russia in the early years of this century. Those of us who lived in the 1940s will never forget the Second World War when Hitler's rise to power in Germany led to the destruction of a thriving and apparently well-assimilated German Jewish community. To Jews steeped in these stories, non-Jews can rarely be seen as people to be trusted; they are Goyim or outsiders and often are viewed as potential persecutors—certainly not potential partners in marriage.

Although the fear of the Goy still persists in some quarters, in contemporary America the ghetto walls have broken down and have given way to an openness which makes it virtually impossible to re-create the tightly cohesive Jewish communities of Europe's past. Comparative community studies of middle-sized American cities indicate that there are relatively few areas of economic life from which Jews are excluded. In addition, there has been a growing participation by Jewish leaders in general civic causes and community service activities (Dean, 1960). In an intensive sociological study, Polsky was able to demonstrate that only a minority of the members of Orthodox synagogues carry out—in their personal lives—basic requirements of Jewish law. He further documented the widespread secularization of religious observances that is taking place among Jews all over America. Acceptance, rather than resistance to cultural change is becoming the norm (Polsky, 1960).

In the Eastern European "shtetl" communities, rituals were integrated into everyday religious and secular life. From the moment he arose in the morning the "shtetl" Jew entered into a regimen of ritual practices which did not cease until he closed his eyes in sleep at the end of the day. In the ghetto or "shtetl," the Jew had been relatively isolated from the influence of scientific rationalism. The Jewish school, which was for most East European Jews the only kind of school they attended, was primarily an institution for the transmission of traditional learning and values; science played no role in the curriculum. Not until the Jew was permitted to move freely in the general society—in Western Europe as early as the eighteenth century, but not until the twentieth century for Eastern Europe—did he feel the full impact of scientific rationalism. This influence has been especially strong in American society, where the virtues of modern science are daily extolled in the schools and in the mass media. Many Jewish people living in the twentieth century find it difficult to reconcile the teachings from biology, physics, and psychoanalysis with biblical and other religious teachings. Skepticism which results from exposure to scientific rationalism is, of course, not limited to a questioning of the Bible's accuracy; it tends to be diffused through other religious beliefs and practices as well (Rosen, 1960).

Living in a twentieth-century society that propounds equalitarianism makes it increasingly difficult for many Jews and non-Jews to endorse the concept of God's "Chosen People." As Myrdal has noted in *An American Dilemma*, equalitarianism is part of the American Creed (1944). In American society the equality theme stresses the similar intrinsic value of every man and woman and is combined with a resentment of any claim to social distinction or special status not earned or based upon particular merit—a factor which the social psychologist Geoffrey Gorer argues, militates especially against the Jews (1948).

Marshall Sklare (1960) has pointed out that perhaps the single most disruptive force to American–Jewish Orthodoxy has been the position of women. Female subordination constitutes an important violation of Western norms and many Jewish women have contended that they should be part of the minyen, should be rabbis and cantors, and should not be treated as a discriminated against minority. One of the results of these new attitudes toward women in religion together with the growing emphasis on autonomy for women is the growing number of interfaith marriages.

While changes in society, in family structure, in traditional religious beliefs and in the role of women have helped to create a trend toward many dual-faith marriages, the move toward intermarriage is rarely without conflict. Despite the fact that in the liberal, ethical, and equalitarian society of today, religion is often dismissed, the influence of traditional religious ideas quietly, often invisibly, permeates many areas of our lives. The majority of Americans have been brought up in one or another of the traditional religions, and the values that they have learned in their churches or synagogues, as well as the customs, rituals, and ceremonies, still influence their attitudes and thinking. Americans are among the most religiously aware citizens in the Western world, with more than half of the total population belonging to a church or synagogue. Total church or synagogue membership is estimated at around 131 million people; in a typical week about 40 percent of adults in America attend a church or synagogue, compared to 26 percent in Greece, 20 percent in England, and 18 percent in Uruguay (Kaye, 1980).

From a psychosocial perspective intermarriage immediately poses a conflict between two values that concomitantly exist in all of us. Very few Americans—Jews and non-Jews—will not endorse equalitarianism, enhancement of the role of women, the breakdown of ghetto walls, and open communication between all races and creeds. Yet our teachings in childhood and the ideas we have absorbed from family, teachers, and friends about religion instill in most of us a subtle mistrust of those who are not part of the same group. Terms like "goy", "shikseh" or "shaygetz" are rarely used benignly. We know members of our own religious group while the others seem like outsiders. The term "goyim" actually means "other nations."

Judaism is especially strong in instilling what Bruno Bettelheim has referred to as a "paranoid fear of the Goy" (1951). The legal definition of a Jew, according to rabbinic authorities, is a child born of a Jewish mother. Converts are frowned upon, and the Orthodox regulations for conversion are designed to deter all but the most persistent.

Is Intermarriage Neurotic?

Because intermarriage frequently poses a conflict for an individual as he assimilates and therefore moves away from his own religious group, the question is often asked, "Is intermarriage pathological?" As I intend to demonstrate in this paper, intermarriage can be healthy or unhealthy, pathological or mature, or can consist of a combination of mature and neurotic motives. However, in assessing intermarriage, we must distinguish between a psychological assessment and a value judgment. From the point of view of the organized Jewish community, intermarriage is undesirable for it threatens the perpetuation of the group identity which is an important means of sustaining traditional values, folkways, and mores. Because so few newcomers are welcomed into Judaism, it is essential for the preservation and future of Judaism that its young people marry only other Jews. This is why the pressures on young people to marry within the faith—"within the Tribe," as it is sometimes expressed—can sometimes be extreme (Kaye, 1980; Arlow, 1966).

From the point of view of the mental health of the individual, intermarriage is not necessarily undesirable. It cannot always be considered as evidence of pathology that every Yid who marries a Shikseh or every Yidneh who marries a Shaygitz is "meshugeneh." A happy marriage consists of two happy people. It is quite possible for a mature Jew to marry a mature Gentile and have a happy marriage. It is equally possible for two immature members of the same faith to choose each other as marital partners and be miserable. In effect, intermarriage is a religious and moral problem; it may or may not be a mental health problem.

To understand in more depth the phenomenon of intermarriage from a psychodynamic point of view, we should explore some of the factors in the choice of a mate, and some of the unconscious factors in sustaining an identification with a religious group and maintaining a belief in its dogmas and rituals.

On Choosing a Mate

Marriage in our culture owes much to the notion of romantic or courtly love developed in the twelfth and thirteenth centuries among the nobility of France and later encouraged throughout Europe by the wave of romantic individualism that swept the continent. Romantic love is characterized by total fealty to and idealization of the beloved. While romantic love is totally antithetical to marriage because it cannot withstand the confrontation with reality that day-to-day married life entails, few people in love can be reasoned out of it, no matter how glaring the obstacles are. When people are deeply in love, they forget about the realities of job, money, family ties, religious differences and other "mundane" matters (Strean, 1980).

It should be noted that many of the famous romantic lovers of history never shared a domestic life. Romeo never saw Juliet in curlers and Juliet didn't see Romeo putting out the garbage. Roxanne and Cyrano did not have to quarrel about the family budget, and Tristan and Isolde kept their trysts without being interrupted by a telephone.

From a psychoanalytic perspective, one of the features of romantic love is that the lovers project their "ego ideal" (i.e., their concept of the perfect person and what they wish they themselves could be) onto the loved one. The qualities ascribed to a loved one during the spiritual and aesthetic experience of romantic love are almost always far beyond whatever real qualities the loved one possesses. The dynamically oriented clinician distinguishes between "being in love" which has unrealistic and obsessional characteristics and therefore is a neurotic state, and "loving," which is based on reality and not egocentric (Fine, 1975). Anthropologist Ralph Linton (1936) has contrasted the mature loving individual with the "ecstasy and madness" of the person in love, which he describes as being like an epileptic fit.

Sigmund Freud (1939) likened the romantic lover to the fond parent who projects his own ideal on to his child to substitute for the lost narcissism of his own childhood. He pointed out that what the lover wishes he could have been, he fantasies his beloved as being. To the clinician, the romantic ideal is an irrational, immature, and unrealistic form of love based on the re-awakening of family romances of childhood. The loved one is made into a father or mother figure and becomes the recipient of fantasies that emanate from the lover's childhood.

Although Freud emphasized the importance of the "reality principle," he was unable to practice what he preached in his own courtship with Martha Bernays. His intense overidealization of her is dramatically portrayed in some of his letters to her:

> What I meant to convey was how much the magic of your being expresses itself in your countenance and your body, how much there is visible in your appearance that reveals how sweet, generous, and reasonable you are . . . .
>
> In your face it is the pure noble beauty of your brow and your eyes that shows in almost every picture.

According to his biographer Freud likened Martha "to the fairy princess from whose lips fell roses and pearls, with, however, the doubt whether kindness or good sense came more often from Martha's lips" (Jones, 1953, p. 103).

Although most of us like to conceive of marriage as a result of free, rational choice, writers who have investigated the phenomenon note the strong unconscious determinants in the decision (Blanck & Blanck, 1968; Eisenstein, 1956; Bolton, 1961). According to psychoanalytic theory, mate choice is *never* an accident; the prospective marital partners are always influenced by unconscious and frequently irrational motives. When marriages founder it is usually not because the couple has incompatible interests but because they are ignorant of the unconscious purposes that determined their respective choices.

The psychologist Carl Jung believed that the search for a mate was completely unconscious: "You see that girl. . . . and instantly you get the seizure; you are caught. And afterward you may discover that it was a mistake" (Evans, 1964). Similarly, the philosopher George Santayana described the process of falling in love and wanting to marry as "that deep and dumb instinctive affinity." The ancient Romans described "falling in love" as a form of madness: "Amare et sapere vis deis conceditar" (The ability to maintain one's sanity when in love is not even conceded to the gods).

In order to better understand mate choice, social workers and other helping professionals have utilized the notion of "complimentarity" (Ackerman, 1958). Unconsciously, the hyper-independent person is attracted to the compliant and passive person; the sadistic type enjoys a masochist; and the sexually over-excited man or woman can be drawn to a seemingly inhibited counterpart. What is not always recognized is how each of the partners vicariously enjoys his or her mate's antithetical behavior. The passive husband is unconsciously gratified by his wife's dominance as he identifies with it, while the sexually promiscuous wife can admire her husband's controls. Frequently, a spouse can condemn the partner's overt behavior but on close observation, the critic can be seen to unconsciously appreciate what he or she is criticizing. I recall a wife who daily admonished her husband for watching wrestling matches and severely condemned him for his interest in brutality. One day in anger she bellowed, "Anybody who watches wrestling ought to be shot!"

The notion of complimentarity helps us understand one of the dynamics of some interfaith marriages. An inhibited Catholic woman in treatment vicariously enjoyed the humor and wit at the Seder table of her husband's family and commented that she "loved the Cohens' flexibility." Mr. Cohen was very laudatory of his wife's "controls" and "loved the quietness of the Fitzpatricks." A Jewish husband who was frightened of the symbiotic merging quality of his natural family, extolled the virtues of the autonomy he observed in the Protestant family of his wife.

Very few, if any, people who enter marriage are exempt from childish wishes. All of us have some desire to be dependent on a parental figure. Most of us have not completely relinquished old power-struggles with our fathers and mothers, and only a small minority of married people have completely abandoned family romance fantasies—i.e., the wish to compete with the parent of the same sex for the parent of the opposite sex. In clinically appraising the dynamics of many inter-faith marriages, our knowledge of psychosexual development can help us clarify the unconscious meaning of certain interfaith marital choices. When a man or woman must defend against strong dependency wishes, he or she might say, "I do not need and I do not want to be close to my mother or father. To prove my independence I'll marry a cool, detached partner as different as possible from my parents."

> Joe Abrams told his therapist that he very much resented his "Yiddisheh mommeh." He spent many hours describing how she "made me fat and dependent." He compared his feelings of powerlessness to Portnoy and consistently envisioned his mother as an ogre. What attracted him to Sally Smith, his Protestant wife, was the fact that she was a vegetarian who "always minded her own business." While Joe resented Sally's frequent withdrawals from him, he needed to constantly protect himself from his childlike but unconscious wish to merge with his "Yiddisheh mommeh."

Childhood quarrels do not die easily. Many adults in their twenties, thirties, or forties are still psychologically engaged in parent–child fracases—sometimes in fantasy and occasionally in reality.

> Shirley Bales was the daughter of a Lutheran minister. In treatment she recalled her many battles with her parents who "always stood for law and order." She felt as a child, and as an adolescent as well, that "there was always a noose around my head." To move away from her "uptight" parents, she married Joel Rabinowitz. Joel and his family were described as "loose" people whose "laissez faire" attitude seemed to be such a contrast from her own family's. To protect herself against her own internalized superego commands, her interfaith marriage was a means of escape. While she occasionally resented Joel's "looseness," she needed a marital partner to protect her against the internalized voices of her punitive superego which stood for law and order.

What marriage counselors, social workers and other therapists constantly note is that marriage is frequently used as a means of resolving long-standing, deep-seated, unconscious conflicts. As we have already observed, a marriage may serve as a means for realizing unfulfilled fantasies or forbidden gratifications of childhood. In the last two clinical examples, we saw how marriage can be utilized in the service of righting old wrongs, compensating for old deprivations, exacting vengeance, overcoming humiliations and disappointments, aggrandizing one's self-image or elevating one's self-esteem (Arlow, 1966). What is not realized by many marital partners and even by some therapists is that marriage can *never* cure a neurosis. As already mentioned, it takes two happy people to have a happy marriage and marriage never made an unhappy person become happy. The fate of a marriage is long decided before two people exchange marital vows. Consequently, the childhood wishes and defenses of would-be spouses are more important issues in assessing a prospective marriage than age, interests, occupations, or even religious affiliation (Strean, 1980).

One of the classic explanations for the neurotic evolution of an interfaith marriage is the incest taboo. Many men and women have not fully resolved their unconscious wishes to have sexual contact with the parent of the opposite sex. However, desires to do so usually create anxiety and these individuals are frequently unable to reconcile the tender aspects of love with the sensual ones. In order to avoid feeling sexual feelings toward a Jewish mother, a man can marry somebody who appears very different from her—a shikseh. I recall a client who said, "If Marjorie weren't a shikseh, I'd never be able to go to bed with her. When she mentioned one day that she wanted to convert to Judaism, I started feeling myself becoming impotent."

The splitting of the maternal image into a sexy shikseh and a noble asexual Jewish mother is not without its attendant conflicts.

> As a boy, Harry Caplansky had a close, intense, and erotic relationship with his mother. His mother called him her "prince" and to the exclusion of his father, constantly doted over him. When Harry went to college, he dated only Gentile girls. Although he was consciously unaware of his motives for this, in treatment he learned that he was afraid of his erotic feelings toward his mother, and to deny them he dated only Gentile women. After living with Maggie McCormick for six months, he decided to marry her. The joy of living with Maggie turned into depression when he became a husband and the sexual ecstasy of courtship became routine and boring in marriage. Said Harry after several months of therapy, "I realize that when we got married, I turned Maggie into my Jewish mother. I thought that marrying a Shikseh would save me. But, as long as she's a wife, she's a mother and I must turn myself off."

The more the clinician relates to marital interaction the more he observes how all human beings bring their childhood pasts into the interaction. When childhood conflicts around dependency conflicts, power-struggles, and incestuous fantasies are unresolved, the individual will bring his neurotic difficulties into his or her marital interaction. It is important to reiterate that neurotic conflicts can take many forms in a marriage—e.g. chronic squabbles, avoidance of sex, excessive needs for autonomy, chronic depression, to name just a few. Intermarriage may

be an expression of neurotic conflict as it was in the vignettes w
reviewed. But, as we have already indicated and will demonstra
ther, later in this discussion, intermarriage can take place betwe
relatively mature individuals. Dynamically oriented clinicians w
make inferences from behavior alone. They must be knowled
about their clients' pasts, fantasies, superego injunctions, defens
much more before they can term any form of behavior mat
immature. This same orientation to people is also operative in as
how an individual copes with his religious identification, to wh
shall now turn.

Some Dynamics in Religious Identity

The search for consolation in the face of threatening feelings of
quacy and helplessness to which religion provides an answer is n
new in the life of the person, since everyone has found him
herself in a similar situation of helplessness as a child vis-à-vis his
parents. When young children recognize that they are not omn
and are unable to get everything they want, they unconsciousl
over their omnipotent fantasies to their parents and believe the
are omnipotent. The wish for an omnipotent parent who will lo
protect us, gratify our wishes, and give us strength is not relinq
very easily. The dynamically oriented clinician views the longin
strong parent as closely related to the longing for a father who is l
the Universe. The wisdom and goodness which are attributed
deity reduce our anxiety concerning the dangers of life much l
infant feels protected by the wisdom and goodness of an omnipote
omniscient parent (Freud, 1939; Frenkel-Brunswick, 1974;
1951).

Just as a child who does not get his wishes gratified may learn
his parents, who he believes have it in their power to grant any
an individual may learn to hate his God and his religion when his
and aspirations are unfulfilled in reality. Some individuals who
don their deity and their religion do so out of anger, and n
compared to children or teen-agers who run away from home b
their desires are not being met. Intermarriage for these individua
be viewed as an act of revenge. Just as the obedient child may ra
turn on his parents because they have not gratified him consis
and refuses to do his homework and household chores, a disapp

theist may refuse to obey religious rituals and intermarry because his God has not sufficiently indulged him.

Religious adherence emanates, as we know, from more than a wish to depend on an omnipotent parent. Religion is also regarded as a societal institution which propounds certain ethical and moral values and denounces others. The origin of ethical and moral commitments, the dynamically oriented clinician contends, also emerges from the early parent–child relationship. As Freud (1939) stated: "In the course of an individual's development a portion of the inhibiting forces in the external world are internalized and an agency is constructed in the ego which confronts the rest of the ego in an observing, criticizing, and prohibiting sense. We call this new agency the superego. . . . The superego is the successor and representative of the individual's parents and educators who had supervised his actions in the first period of his life; it carries on their functions almost unchanged" (pp. 116–117).

What is sometimes overlooked about the internal voices of the superego is that they are projected on to other individuals and institutions. For example, frequently the teen-ager who is fighting the rules and regulations of school, home, religion and society in general, is really fighting the voices of his own superego.

Religious rituals can serve as superego protections against forbidden wishes. The "evil eye" in Judaism is viewed by the clinician as an external form of the individual's internal conscience. Religious rituals can placate guilt as is particularly noted on the Day of Atonement.

When an individual has a strong, punitive superego, he can project its voices onto his or her religion and feeling coerced and controlled will take arms against it. Most individuals fail to appreciate the fact that their biggest enemy is themselves and reason that if they get rid of their religious dogma and religious rituals, they will not feel so coerced. They fail to recognize that the coercion comes from within themselves and that by renouncing their religion, they will sooner or later find another external force to inhibit them.

> Doris Diamond was an obedient child and hard-working adolescent who found that when she started to date boys, she felt inhibited and constricted emotionally and sexually. Rather than recognize that her voices from her own prohibitive superego were inhibiting her, she blamed her sexual guilt on her parents and on her religion. So convinced was Doris about her parents' "uptightness" and her religion's "stupid dogma" that she renounced both of them and joined a commune whose religious tenets consisted of free love and few restraints of

any kind. By the time Doris sought out a therapist she was beginning to realize that her inhibitions came from within her and that manipulating her environment could not reduce her discomfort.

The stories of Herman Wouk's *Caine Mutiny* and *Marjorie Morningstar* are excellent examples of superego conflicts. In both of these novels, the main characters spend most of their time and energy fighting authorities—externalized superego figures. As the leading characters' guilt mounts, they beat themselves for their rebellious lives and eventually submit compliantly to their parental figures' edicts. It should be noted that this is also the story of Herman Wouk's marital life. An orthodox Jew, Wouk married a Gentile woman. After a short period of marriage, he insisted that his wife convert and fervently practice all of the Orthodox Jewish rituals.

When a person marries a partner outside of his religious group, he makes a statement about his sense of identity. No matter what the specific context or the individual's background, under most circumstances intermarriage represents a first step in the process of assimilation. Accordingly, intermarriage may mean different things to different people. Much depends upon what being Jewish represents to the individual and what role it plays in his sense of identity (Arlow, 1966).

The attitude of the youngster's parents is, of course, crucial in the development of the child's sense of identity as a Jew. Consciously and unconsciously parents convey to their children how they feel about being Jewish. The growing child quickly learns whether Jewish identity is significant to his parents and what values are attached to the experience of being Jewish. Very often parents subtly encourage their children to abandon Judaism and may even unconsciously encourage them to intermarry. Usually this represents a fulfillment of the parents' adolescent rebellion and they attain a "victory" through their children's intermarriage.

Most individuals view their own religion the way they view themselves. Rarely does a clinician meet a client who likes himself but concomitantly hates his religious identity. Some youngsters grow up with the feeling that being Jewish means that one is not sufficiently masculine. Other youngsters may come to feel that the fact that Jews are often treated as inferiors confirms their feelings of inferiority which they have about themselves.

People can use their religious identity to escape from internalized problems. Clinicians have long recognized that if a man or woman has a low self-image, poor self-esteem, or feels inferior, he may change his

Jewish name, alter his "Jewish nose," and intermarry. However, his low self-image and low self-esteem will not disappear when he manipulates his external environment. The story is told of the Jewish man who had a severe stammering problem but nonetheless applied for a job as a radio announcer. When a friend asked if he got the job, he said he hadn't because the prospective employer suffered from a strong case of anti-Semitism.

Just as a self-hating person will tend to hate his religious identification and may deny it by change of name, religious conversion, or intermarriage, the person with higher self-esteem may enjoy his religious identification. In a note on "The People of Israel" (Freud, 1939), Freud said in describing Jews:

> There is no doubt that they have a particularly high opinion of themselves, that they regard themselves as more distinguished, of higher standing, as superior to other people—from whom they are also distinguished by many of their customs. At the same time they are inspired by a peculiar confidence in life, such as is derived from the secret ownership of some precious possession, a kind of optimism.... We may assert that it was the man Moses who imprinted this trait upon the Jewish people. He raised their self-esteem by assuring them that they were God's chosen people... [Freud, 1939, pp. 105–106].

Although the self-hating person will be inclined to demean his religious identity and the person with high self-esteem will prize it, people are not that simple. It is quite possible for a person with low self-esteem to use his "superior," religious affiliation to compensate for his sense of inferiority.

> Jack Levy acknowledged to his therapist that he always felt very weak next to others when a boy and that his middle name was "loser." He found the synagogue a source of solace and the religious rituals a source of inspiration. "Being Jewish made me feel I was a somebody," Jack pointed out.
> In view of the fact that his Jewish identity seemed to elevate his self-esteem, his therapist was surprised when he learned that Jack had intermarried. When this was subjected to examination in his therapy, Jack reflected: "Judaism is the only thing I have that makes me feel superior. If I am with a non-Jew many hours a day like I am with my Catholic wife, Matilda, I can feel superior several hours a day."

People achieve a sense of identity in countless numbers of subtle ways. One way is what Erik Erikson (1950) has referred to as a "negative

identity." The individual sensitizes himself to what his paren
significant others value and then does the opposite. If parents cha
liberalism, the young person will endorse conservatism, if auth
are Capitalists, the young person might endorse Marxism. It is
possible that intermarriage can be an expression of a negative id
i.e., the young person derives solace from being something and
body if he is very different from his Jewish parents.

Because religious identity is formed early in childhood and c
come an important part of our character structure, it is not aban
very easily. Sigmund Freud is quoted by his biographer, Ernest
(1953) as saying:

> The announcement of my unpleasant findings had the resu
> lost the largest part of my human relations. In this lonelines
> awoke within me the longing for a circle of select, high-mind
> who would accept me in friendship in spite of my daring o|
> B'nai B'rith was pointed out to me as the place where such m
> to be found. The fact that you were Jews could only be desi
> me, for I myself was a Jew and I had always deemed it n
> unworthy, but nonsensical to deny it.

Intermarriage and Maturity

As we have consistently reiterated in this discussion, from a dyna
oriented clinical perspective, behavior cannot be accurately a
unless the person's unconscious motives are exposed and the stor
life is evaluated. Intermarriage can mean different things to d
people. We can never say, at first blush, that an interfaith m
indicative of immaturity. As we have already indicated, it is quit
ble for two members of different religious faiths to genuinely lov
other in a non-defensive, non-childish, non-egocentric way. Tl
nourish each other without feeling eaten-up and do not have to
themselves from old or current power-struggles. A Jew and Gen
love each other and marry without having to ward off incestuou
protect themselves from other sexual anxieties. In this day of c
and freer exchange among people from different denominatic
interfaith marriage does not have to be a neurotic one. As E
Barrett Browning has advised:

> If you must love one another, let it be
> for love's sake only.
> Do not say I love her for her smile—her look—

> Her way of speaking gently—or for trick of
> thought that agrees with me.
> For these things in themselves may be changed
> Or changed for you—and love may be undone.
> Neither love her for pity's sake wiping her
> cheeks dry—
> A creature might forget to weep
> And lose your love thereby.
> But love each other for love's sake, that evermore
> You may love on, through an eternity.

To love another human being regardless of racial or religious extraction was deemed correct by the authors of the Bible. The Hebrew prophet Isaiah expressed the hope of bringing people closer together when he declared, "My House shall be called the House of Worship for all the peoples of the earth." The Psalmist has exclaimed, "Behold how good and how pleasant it is for brethren to dwell together in unity." And in the Bible it is supposed to be God's will that men and women "should beat their swords into plowshares, that they should sit unafraid under their vines and fig trees," and that they should be blessed with peacemaking.

These aforementioned scriptures were not written to justify intermarriage, but it should be said that it is quite possible to conceive of true and genuine love as the capacity to love the other and respect religious differences as well. In a Jewish-Catholic interfaith marriage service at the United Nations, the clergymen read:

> Today, we have standing together at the altar a bride and groom who are of different faiths. They symbolize a lesson in love and brotherhood and harmony, admonishing us to seek and to find the elements that bring us closer to one another. They believe that there is nothing in their faiths which prevents their marriage. They see each other as objects of love and worthy of the sacrament of marriage. This is a concrete expression of that spirit of human unity which we are seeing manifested so much in this part of the twentieth century between whites and blacks, Protestants and Catholics, Jews and Christians, Marxists and believers.

In sum, the central issue of the problem of intermarriage is the goal of preserving Jewish identity. Jewish identity is an important vehicle for transmitting to the next generation the values, ideals, and wisdom which the group has distilled from its history. One's identity as a Jew is inevitably drawn into the conflicts typical for the individual. Intermarriage always raises the problem of the fate of the individual's identity with the group. To some this may be unimportant and not particularly conflictful. In others it may arouse conflict. Intermarriage does not necessarily indicate pathology. Intermarriage is not a disease nor is it a mental health problem. It is a religious and moral problem (Arlow, 1966).

As social workers, we have to face the unique meaning of intermarriage to the unique client. We also have to face what messages they transmit to their children as the family, for example, celebrates both Chanukah and Christmas, Passover and Easter, or ignores these holidays altogether or just observes those of one denomination. Children often use religious differences between parents to disrupt the marital alliance and be part of the scene in which they are not on an equal status. The problem here is not pure religious differences between the parents, but religious differences being used by this child in the service of his or her competition with the parents. If parents from interfaith marriages are confident of their own identities as human beings, interfaith marriages need not be an overwhelming obstacle to the children of mixed marriages.

Interfaith marriages will continue to confront social workers and other helping professionals for some time. Each interfaith marriage is special and the social worker should not be for or against the marriage but try to understand its strengths and limitations, its conflicts and conflict-free areas. It is the clinician's non-judgmental, caring and accepting attitude that will help all clients cope better with their marriages—Jewish marriages, non-Jewish marriages, and interfaith marriages.

REFERENCES

Ackerman, N. *The Psychodynamics of Family Life*. New York: Basic Books, 1958.

Arlow, J. "The Psychological Implications of Intermarriage," *Jewish Journal of Communal Service*, April 1966.

Bettelheim, B. "The Irrational Fear of the 'Goy'," *Commentary*, September, 1951.

Blanck, R., and G. Blanck. *Marriage and Personal Development*. New York: Columbia University Press, 1968.

Bolton, C. "Mate Selection as the Development of a Relationship," *Marriage and Family Living*, vol. 23, no. 4, 1961.

Dean, J. "Jewish Participation in the Life of Middle-Sized American Communities," in *The Jews: Social Patterns of an American Group*, M. Sklare, ed. Glencoe, Ill.: The Free Press, 1960.

Eisenstein, V. *Neurotic Interaction in Marriage*. New York: Basic Books, 1956.

Erikson, E. *Childhood and Society*. New York: W. W. Norton, 1950.

Evans, R. *Conversations with Carl Jung*. Princeton, N.J.: Van Nostrand Reinhold, 1964.

Fine, R. *Psychoanalytic Psychology*. New York: Jason Aronson, 1975.

Freud, S. "An Outline of Psychoanalysis" (1939). *Standard Edition*, vol. 23, London: Hogarth Press, 1964.

————. "Moses and Monotheism" (1939), *Standard Edition*, vol. 23, London: Hogarth Press, 1964.

Frenkel-Brunswick, E. *Selected Papers*, Psychological Monographs, Vol. 31, 1974.

Gover, G. *The American People*. New York: Norton, 1948.

Jones, E. *The Life and Work of Sigmund Freud*, vol. 1. New York: Basic Books, 1953.

Kaye, E. *Cross-Currents: Children, Families and Religion*. New York: Clarkson N. Potter, Inc., 1980.

Linton, R. *The Study of Man*. New York: D. Appleton-Century, 1936.

Myrdal, G. *An American Dilemma*. New York: Harper, 1944.

Polsky, H. "A Study of Orthodoxy in Milwaukee: Social Characteristics, Beliefs, and Observances," in *The Jews: Social Patterns of an American Group*. M. Sklare, ed. Glencoe, Ill.: The Free Press, 1960.

Reik, T. *Dogma and Compulsion*. New York: International Universities Press, 1951.

Rosen, B. "A Minority Group in Transition," in *The Jews: Social Patterns of an American Group*. M. Sklare, ed. Glencoe, Ill.: The Free Press, 1960.

Strean, H. *The Extramarital Affair*. New York: The Free Press, 1980.

DISCUSSANT: LLOYD DEMAUSE

Following Freud,[1] psychohistory views religion as a perversion of the individual's search for love.[2] Therefore, as a psychohistorian, I view Strean's conclusion as to the possibility of the healthy coexistence of love and religion as opposed to my empirical findings: religion stands in the way of love no matter whether the denomination of the partners is similar or different. Since both Strean and I base our conclusions on the same psychoanalytic principles, how can they be so far apart?

Strean's conclusions are also contrary to those of both contemporary sociologists and religious counselors. Most sociological studies find interfaith marriages more unstable than others, including more family strife in the backgrounds of those who intermarry,[3] and most religious advisors who are experienced in intermarriage counseling agree with Rabbi Samuel Silver's blunt advice, "If you're smart, you'll marry someone in your own group."[4]

Yet Strean's vast clinical experience cannot be summarily dismissed: It is a common observation that interfaith marriages like those he focuses on—between modern Jews and non-Jews—*can* be healthy. How can this be, if different religions express deep values reflecting vastly different defenses to childhood wishes?

The answer to this paradox lies in the nature of the audience Strean was addressing in his speech: those who go to Jewish Family Agency conferences, like those who go to Strean to be psychoanalyzed, are generally not strict orthodox "religious" believers. If Strean had addressed a Hassidic Jewish group or a Russian Orthodox group his advice might be closer to Rabbi Silver's to "marry someone in your own group." It can hardly be healthy for a Jew to marry someone who believes Jews are blood-poisoners, nor for a liberated woman to marry a Jewish man who wakes up every morning thanking God for not making him a woman.

What kind of "religion" then is Strean talking about when he says "it is quite possible for two members of different religious faiths to genuinely love each other"? One is tempted to answer: Only if their "religions" are so watered down they don't create conflicts between them. But if in one sense this may be true, still it misses the most important part of the historical relation between love and religion.

rried love once did not exist. It only evolved historically, as the
volution of modes of childrearing over the centuries allowed some
e to have good enough parenting to be able to love their mates
than hate them and cling to them.[5] Romantic love, which Strean
ually calls "neurotic," is an achievement which is not older than
elfth century, and married love the sixteenth. Prior to this, there
nly religious love, only love for gods and divine human beings,
psychotic love, not just neurotic. Until modern times, marriage
mutual clinging to the same delusional object. As childrearing
ved in early modern times, enough cathexis could be withdrawn
gods to begin to create a new kind of marriage, based on love, not
al clinging.[6]

at kind of religion, then, do these "happy intermarriages" prac-
All my psychohistorical evidence points to one conclusion: *both
rs share the same modern religion—nationalism*. They no longer
their lives around religious ritual, they follow national ritual. Not
ass but the *mass media* moves them daily to love, tears, anxiety
ger. Few die for religion any more, only for the nation, and most
ges withstand the long separations of war only because both
rs share the group-fantasy of nationalism.

at is why, when pressed, most of the "happy intermarriage"
es in Strean's audience will reply, "Well, I'm not *really* all that
us—its more of an *ethnic* identification." By "ethnic" they mean
gs like "I only really feel Jewish when I remember the Holocaust"
felt proud when Israel raided Entebbe." These are *nationalist*
-fantasies, not religious.

s group-fantasy of nationalism is a product of modern
earing—that is, of emotional rather than physical manipulation of
en to socialize them into being well-controlled adults.[7] Adults
re products of this "socializing mode" of childrearing are all part
at psychohistorians call the same "psychoclass," whose marital
s, parenting styles, and social behavior are similar enough to avoid
conflict while they spend their lives together.

my answer to Strean's question as to whether intermarriage works
"If you're smart, you'll marry someone in your own group"—only
y "group" I mean "psychoclass," adults who had the same level of
earing. The healthy intermarriages he sees are actually between
of the same psychoclass, both of whom are mature (historically
ologically evolved) enough to have shifted from the "religious
-fantasy" to the "nationalism group-fantasy." The neurotic inter-
ges he sees are between adults who are immature (less historically

evolved) enough to still use both God and spouse as important projective receptacles—idealizing or degrading the other or themselves in a
lifestyle that historically was once common to every human being on
earth.

Finally, the evolution of childhood continues, and a new, *post-
modern* psychoclass is beginning to appear—either as a product of
non-manipulative "helping mode" parenting, or as a result of receiving
very thorough-going psychoanalytic therapy. For those I know who fit
this new psychoclass, religion—whether traditional or "ethnic"—has
simply been dropped, except for remnants like Christmas presents,
Passover dinners or collections of ethnic foods arranged in colorful
cross-cultural confusion. What has replaced religion and other defensive group-fantasies is mature love, which was our real historical goal
all along.

REFERENCES

1. Sigmund Freud. "The Future of an Illusion," *Standard Edition*, vol. 21,
   1927.

2. Lloyd deMause. *Foundations of Psychohistory*. New York: Creative Roots,
   1982.

3. Paul H. Bescenceney. *Interfaith Marriage: Who and Why*. New Haven:
   College and University Press, 1970.

4. Samual Silver. *Mixed Marriages Between Jews and Christians*. New York:
   Arco Publishing, 1977, p. 29.

5. DeMause. *Foundations of Psychohistory*

6. Ibid.

7. Ibid.

DISCUSSANT: MARY L. GOTTESFELD

Many years ago, before my own marriage (inter), I was visiting the
home of a friend. At one point I was alone in the living room with her
elderly grandmother, whom I did not know. For a few minutes we sat in

awkward silence; I wondered if she spoke English since I was not fluent in Italian. Suddenly, she broke into a smile and spoke.

> "You have a boy friend?" she asked.
> "Yes," I replied, a little bemused by her question.
> "Ahhh," she nodded her head, still smiling, "nice Italian boy?"
> "Well, no, he's not."
> "A nice Catholic boy?" still nodding but not smiling.
> "Uh, no. . . "
> "Nice Christian boy?" she said, neither nodding nor smiling.
> "No," and I gasped in desperation, "but he's white!"

For some people, the further away they move from the familiar, the more frightened and disapproving they become.

I do not believe that true interfaith marriages take place at all, because people who are strongly committed to particular religious faiths do not marry out of them. The truly devout Catholic, Jew, Mormon, etc., will either obey religious proscriptions against intermarriage or just naturally seek and want a marriage partner within his or her own faith. Therefore, religious "intermarriage" will take place when one or both partners have some degree of indifference to formal religion, in which case the marriage can hardly be considered a true interfaith marriage where an absence of faith must be presupposed to create the union to begin with.

The question whether intermarriage is pathological deserves little consideration. Obviously, some are and some are not, and this issue is amply addressed in Dr. Strean's paper. I can only add that whatever psychological questions might be raised about intermarriage can also be raised about marriage in general.

More to the point, I believe, is the distinction between a psychological assessment of intermarriage and a value judgment. Dr. Strean says this in regard to the latter: "From the point of view of the organized Jewish community, intermarriage is undesirable for it threatens the perpetuation of the group identity which is an important means of sustaining traditional values, folkways and mores." And so in defense of intermarriage I would like to propose that group identity is not so desirable at all and the human race would do well to have less, not more of it.

The cultural pluralism of America is responsible for the high and increasing rate of interfaith and interethnic marriages. The present interest in ethnic continuity is, to my mind, a backlash to the very decline of ethnicity caused by the American experience. For Jews in particular, victims of an insane search for ethnic purity by Germany most recently, the question of group identity has particular significance.

It is no surprise to me that we have seen a simultaneous rise of both narcissism and ethnocentrism, the latter being the mass version of the former. Ethnocentrism clearly and rigidly distinguishes between "us" and "them," "in-groups" and "out-groups." It must be axiomatic, since it seems almost universal, that love and allegiance to the in-group, creates antipathy to the out-group. In writing about those who are enemies and foreign to us, Kohut says our opponents are a "flaw in a narcissistically perceived reality" (1972). This tells us a great deal about ourselves. Thus while our group identity represents an ego ideal, out-groups represent that which is ego alien to us.

There is a level of mature individuation which seems to be impossible for groups to attain. In an enormously instructive article on the psychohistory of ethnicity, H. Stein (1981) says the following:

> Somehow the group remains elusively beyond the scope of indi-
> vidual psychology. On the one hand, we identify as healthy the dif-
> ferentiation of the individual, and the separation of the self from the
> other. Yet, so the argument goes, when it comes to groups, we would
> deny legitimacy to the separate, autonomous existence of another
> group; we would deny them the right to independence, to their own
> boundary. What is healthy for the individual thus becomes unhealthy
> for the group. If we value *personal* self/other differentiation, what
> justifies our judging as pathological this differentiation between
> *groups?* I think that this distinction is spurious because it fails to
> recognize that *separation-individuation leads to the ability to perceive
> others as no longer extensions of the self*—including members of one's
> own group, and likewise those to whom one has felt heretofore re-
> motely or not at all "related." Genuine differentiation leads neither to
> the insistence on sameness (symbiosis-fusion) nor to the insistence of
> difference (dissociation-projection) [p. 47].

It may well be then that intermarriage represents those beginning steps beyond culture, allowing those who are truly differentiated and emotionally integrated to critically evaluate cultural entanglements, respect those who are different from themselves and avoid the engulfment of group identity.

REFERENCES

Kohut, H. "Thoughts on narcissism and narcissistic rage," *The Psychoanalytic Study of the Child*, 1972, 27:360–400.

Stein, H. "Culture and ethnicity as group fantasies: A psychohistoric paradigm of group identity," *The Journal of Psychohistory*, 1981, 8:1, 21–52.

apter 10

A PSYCHOSOCIAL VIEW OF
SOCIAL DEVIANCY

oncept of "social deviancy," like many psychosocial notions, has
ambiguously defined and many professional experts have contrib-
o the vagueness of the definition. Because the social worker is not
ily professional who works with the social deviant, his perspective
y one of many views of a multifaceted and complex phenomenon.
ittorney, sociologists, psychiatrist, and members of many other
lines are participants in the lives of those that society has labelled
int," e.g., the criminal, the addict, the murderer, etc.
hough this paper will attempt to explicate a clinical view of the
il deviant," concentrating on the diagnosis and treatment of these
duals, it is important first to place our examination into a larger
ogical framework.

ogical Considerations

a societal perspective, social deviancy is any form of behavior
the broader culture or subculture has alleged to be improper
illegal. It is important to recognize that what a significant group
culture at a given time labels as aberrant behavior may be consid-
is quite appropriate by the same group at another time. Murder,
ample, is deemed quite unacceptable by most politicians and they
taken many steps for countless decades to prevent its occurrence in
social sectors. However, the same politicians have also passed
rous bills sanctioning murder. For example, the President and
ress, particularly during the early stages of the Vietnam War, were

Clinical Social Work Journal, vol. 4, no. 3 (September 1976), pp. 187–

sanctioning murder while concomitantly declaring another war to exterminate crime in the streets.

Not only may the same group label the same behavior "deviant" at one time and "healthy" or "appropriate" at another, depending on the behavior's social context, but different social groups take different stances on identical behavior. For example, the behavior of Joan of Arc was defined as not only appropriate in her day, but she was considered a heroine and was hailed as a truly remarkable lady. The same behavior exhibited almost anywhere in the world today would be labelled as paranoid schizophrenia, because Joan of Arc heard voices telling her to save her country.

There are numerous examples which offer much credence to the notion that "social deviancy" is an arbitrary, subjective label that in many ways is defined in a nonscientific manner. Homosexuality was championed in ancient Greece, yet punished severely by the United States Army and other institutions for several decades, has been considered a disease by many psychiatrists and psychoanalysts, upheld by Gay Liberation, and recently, was stricken from the psychiatric nomenclature of the American Psychiatric Association.

Although an adult brutally hitting a child is often considered in a legalistic sense as child abuse and has historically been punishable by the law, Abraham in the Holy Bible is revered to this day as someone who was very pious and far from a criminal for wanting to murder his son Isaac and sacrifice him to God.

Social Deviance and the Audience

Many sociologists do not attach significance to an act of social deviance except as "significant others" react to the commission of the act (Erikson, 1957). To them, deviance is not a quality of an act, but deviance is produced in the interaction between a person who commits an act and those who respond to it (Becker, 1963).

As Kai Erikson has stated:

> Deviance is not a property inherent in certain forms of behavior; it is a property conferred upon these forms by the audiences which directly or indirectly witness them. The critical variable in the study of deviance, then, is the social audience rather than the individual actor, since it is the audience which eventually determines whether or not any episode of behavior or any class of episodes is labelled deviant. [Erikson, 1957, p. 11]

Similarly, the sociologist Becker has opined:

> Social groups create deviance by making rules whose infractions constitute deviance and by applying those rules to particular people and labelling them as outsiders. [Becker, 1963, p. 9]

Sociologists, by and large, do not ascribe any psychological motives to the social deviant. In sharp contrast to the clinician who takes the position that behavior, normal and pathological, is heavily influenced by the individual's unconscious wishes, anxieties, defenses, and internal sanctions, the sociologist looks at inconsistencies in the social structure to explain deviant and "normal" behavior. Consequently, to the latter, delinquency, crime, murder, arson, etc., would be explained by: (1) A person's belonging to a minority group whose values may lead to violations of the rules of the dominant group; (2) the individual may have conflicting responsibilities, and the adequate performance of one role may produce violations in the second role; and (3) the individual may be simply unaware of the rules and violate them unintentionally (Gove, 1970).

A Self-fulfilling Prophecy

Those social scientists who have been interested in labelling theory (Goffman, 1961; Lemert, 1951) have pointed out that deviancy in society is a self-fulfilling prophecy. By this they mean that in every society there are dominant values and norms which particular groups wish to maintain and sustain. Consequently, one way of preserving honesty is to locate those who are dishonest and punish them; one means of sustaining the marital institution is by incarcerating adulterers; and one means of helping children attend school is by referring truants to child guidance clinics and juvenile courts. Thus, deviance cannot be dismissed simply as behavior which disrupts society but is an important condition for preserving stability (Goffman, 1961).

It is not a mystery to even the superficial observer that getting jailed or institutionalized is not a matter of chance. Most children have committed acts which juvenile courts would condemn, yet there is a selection factor by which one child lands in court and another does not. Usually, those children in American society who are members of lower socio-economic classes such as the impoverished Black or lower-class Italian have a better chance of getting caught and thrown in jail than children of higher-ranking socio-economic groups.

Furthermore, similar behavior in an adult of a lower socio-economic class is more readily punished than the identical behavior of a member of a higher status. It did not take much time for Congress to censure the Black politician Adam Clayton Powell but it took much more time to even consider the censuring of the late Senators Joseph McCarthy and Thomas Dodd.

After an individual has been labelled as a deviant, his die is cast! As Goffman and others (Goffman, 1961; Becker, 1963) have pointed out, labelling a person "a patient in a mental hospital" elicits one form of behavior but labelling the same person "President of Citizen Government" in the same hospital yields a different form of behavior, often considered "adaptive" and "healthy."

Once stigmatized, the deviant is typically forced into a deviant group, usually by being placed in an institution (Gove, 1970). Such deviant groups have a common fate, they face the same problems, and because of this they develop a deviant subculture. This subculture combines a perspective on the world with a set of routine activities. According to Becker, "membership in such a group solidifies a deviant identity" and leads to rationalization of their position (Becker, 1963, p. 38).

Once "a patient" or "an offender" has been so labelled, he has enormous difficulty modifying how others view him. He has failed in living and if in an institution such as a prison or a mental hospital, he must, as Lemert notes "give allegiance to an often anomalous conception of himself and the world" (Lemert, 1951, p. 17). Denial of the organizational ideology may lead to the judgment that the "deviant" is unreformed or still sick.

As Gove has summarized:

> The argument of the societal reaction theorists is that persons who have passed through a degradation ceremony and have been forced to become members of a deviant group have experienced a profound and frequently irreversible socialization process. They have acquired an inferiority status and have developed a deviant world view and the knowledge and skill that go with it. [Gove, 1970, p. 875]

The Social Context

Social scientists and some clinicians have noted that differences in psychiatric opinion about diagnosis in individual cases may arise as

from differences in the interaction and context in which the
)sis is made as from differences in the personality structure of the
it. Lennard and Bernstein, pioneers in clinical sociology, a field
never divorces the patient's social context from his internal
nics in diagnosis and treatment, have offered many intriguing
)les that attest to the fact that "patients behave differently with
people than with others and behave differently in some contexts
n others" (Lennard & Bernstein, 1969, p. 31). One example of
orientation is provided in their discussion of Freud's famous
eber Case" (Freud, 1959).

reber's paranoid illness and delusional system became virtually
t when he was in certain social contexts. The following are re-
of Schreber's physician which tend to buttress Lennard and
ein's thesis:

> Since for the last nine months Herr President Schreber has taken his
> meals daily at my family board, I have had the most ample opportu-
> nity of conversing with him upon every imaginable topic. . . . In his
> lighter talk with the ladies of the party, he was both courteous and
> affable . . . . Never once during those innocent talks around the dining
> table, did he introduce subjects which should more properly have
> been raised at a medical consultation. [Freud, 1959, p. 394]

Deviancy, Civil Rights, and Mental Health

ccept the premise that "social deviancy" and "aberrant behavior"
many ways arbitrarily defined and, in many ways, subjective
is, our next step is to evaluate the position of the social worker and
helping professionals vis-à-vis the norm setters of society. Those
ave researched the subject (Riessman, Cohen, & Pearl, 1964;
1958; Hollingshead & Redlich, 1958) almost unanimously con-
that those who are in the mental health profession tend to equate
al health" with the dominant norms of society. As Davis (1958)
ncluded, many of the persistent refrains emanating from mental
ists are quite consistent with the Protestant ethic—work, disci-
introspection, etc.
quite easy, furthermore, to not only document the affinity be-
the Protestant ethic and the concept of mental health as found in
and other works dealing with mental hygiene (Davis, 1958), but
ch tends to reveal that virtually 70 percent of the material in
l hygiene literature contains statements which can be identified as

falling within the middle-class cultural mold—statements about middle-class households, executives at work, etc. (Davis, 1958).

Because the mental health movement contributes to the maintenance and persistence of the middle-class sociocultural structure by providing authoritative "scientific" support to middle-class values, it should not come as a surprise that there is a peculiar collusion between mental hygienists and the major upholders of middle-class norms. Recently, a head of the Gay Teachers Caucus of the National Education Association received public attention because the school authorities wanted to turn him over to a psychiatrist (*The Bergen* [N.J.] *Record*, October 1, 1973). The man refused examination, and if he had consented and had been adjudged as "emotionally disturbed" by a psychiatrist, he probably would have lost his job. It was clearly documented in this particular case that his superiors did not devote much thought to the man's abilities, skills, and knowledge as a teacher. His alleged "psychiatric disturbance" was decisive. Because of the teacher's refusal to see a psychiatrist, he was suspended from his job anyway.

The aforementioned case is not unique. It is well known that individuals labelled as deviant such as the homosexual, transsexual, gambler, fetishist, alcoholic, etc. can easily lose jobs and other privileges simply because of their deviant status. All too frequently a psychiatrist or other mental hygienist has participated in discharging "the deviant" from his job by labelling him as "emotionally disturbed."

As will be demonstrated later, from a psychosocial perspective it is quite clear that homosexuality, bisexuality, and the addictions are indicative of maturational lags and of emotional conflict. However, as analysts and social workers can avow, there is no direct correlation between maturational impoverishment and poor job performance. The modern therapist has often observed that certain types of maturational fixations may even make one a better soldier, a better teacher, and even a better psychotherapist, at least at certain times.

In considering diagnosis and disposition of an individual labelled "deviant," the social worker recognizes that there is a huge range of possible behavior within one given psychiatric category. For example, a person who chooses as sexual partners members of his or her own sex exclusively, may be aggressive or passive, very egocentric or quite altruistic, impulsive or controlled, intelligent or unintelligent. The same can be said about an individual suffering from gambling addiction or alcoholism.

Because the label "deviant" or the psychiatric categories "sexual dysfunction," "perversion," "antisocial character," and "sociopath" do not fully describe an individual but categorize and stereotype him, they offer little predictive power in fully determining personality functioning. Furthermore, many forms of behavior which are considered antisocial or illegal may be *less* psychologically debilitating than emotional aberrations that are tolerated by society. For example, religious zeal may be a manifestation of severe neurotic conflicts but rare is the zealot who is referred for psychiatric consultation because his religious preoccupations might interfere with his job performance.

The infringement by psychiatry and the mental health professions on the civil rights of individuals is quite pervasive in our courts and penal systems. Frequently an individual who is a skyjacker can have his incarceration changed from a few years imprisonment to a life term because a psychiatric expert will state that the individual is a "psychopath" and not "psychotic." The label determines the man's fate—not the crime, the court proceedings, a comprehensive personality evaluation, or the rehabilitation program.

Psychiatry often obfuscates the disposition of a deviant person when knowledge of unconscious motivation is applied. Motives, the clinician recognizes, are both conscious and unconscious. The latter influence behavior much more. Consequently, if an individual harbors unconscious guilt feelings and to ease his anxiety about them commits a felony so that the anticipated punishment will relieve him, is he less guilty of a crime than the individual who commits the same felony because he felt deprived by the recent death of his sister? Guilt or innocence in a court is a legal matter—not the domain of a psychotherapist.

In dealing with problems of social deviancy, legal or not, three issues must be clearly separated: the individual's civil rights, the individual's mental health, and the protection of society. To ensure an individual's civil rights, his emotional health should never be a factor in determining the adequacy of his job performance or guilt or innocence in court. If a man or woman's emotional pathology invades his or her occupational functioning, it is the latter that should be the focus of attention, not the emotional factors that contribute to it. If a teacher hits children or seduces them, the school authorities must decide on how "appropriate" or "inappropriate" this behavior is and make a disposition that is administrative and legal. The social worker or therapist's job is not an administrative or legal one but is to help those who wish to do something about their own emotional maladaptations.

The role of the modern psychotherapist in dealing with social deviations is limited, therefore, to the consultation room. In my opinion he should have no role in administering justice; his role is in the diagnosis and therapy of those who wish to understand the unconscious nature of their motives, symptoms, and character problems.

Some Diagnostic Considerations in the Treatment of Social Deviancy

Recognizing that the definition of "deviant" is somewhat arbitrary, varies from social context to social context, and is further modified by historical, military, political, and other social and economic factors, we are now in a position to discuss the therapist's role in understanding and working with the social deviant in treatment.

The clinician is much more interested in the person with a deviant label than he is in the deviancy per se. He looks at homosexuality, bisexuality, drug addictions, etc., as symptoms of internal stress. Rather than using the master label, "deviant," the modern therapist is interested in understanding what propels the individual's *total* behavior, not just his "deviant" or "acting out" behavior.

The Social Deviant and Self-Destructiveness

The reason the clinical social worker regards much of deviant behavior as self-destructive is because the individual often suffers external and internal punishment after participating in it. He has noted the gambler's self-torture when omnipotent "lady luck" has not brought him fortune; he has observed the alcoholic's self-recriminations after the latter has been through a binge; and he has empathized with the self-hatred of a parent who has sadistically beaten his child.

The modern therapist is interested in understanding better the dynamics of the deviant's self-destructiveness. He asks the questions, "Why does the patient compulsively engage in self-destructive behavior?" "Why does he arrange to live a life that brings so much pain?"

From a clinical perspective, much of the self-destructive behavior that can be noted in individuals who participate in deviant behavior can be attributed to the patient's faulty handling of the aggressive drive (Spotnitz, 1967). Therapists who have worked with the addict, alcoholic, and other deviants have been impressed with the fact that these

duals as children have suffered acute frustration and deprivation.
xperience then forces these individuals to harbor huge quantities
ression within themselves. However, because children need the
arents and "significant others" who have administered the frustra-
they often cannot feel free to put into words how angry and
erous they feel. It is not at all uncommon to hear from deprived
en in reformatories and adults in penal institutions how "wonder-
eir parents were! These children, adolescents, and adults often
ze the frustrating parents, repress their murderous impulses towards
and go on hoping that if they keep their hate to themselves, some
r or father will eventually love them (Spotnitz, 1967; Nelson,
Nagelberg & Spotnitz, 1958).

aforementioned phenomenon is readily verified when one reads,
newspapers, reports about assassins and other murderers. They
en described by their neighbors as "good" children (or adults)—
withdrawn, and seemingly harmless. What is not so manifestly
arent is that their reclusive, seclusive, withdrawn schizoid state is
ase against their murderous drive. This is why Spotnitz (1967) and
(Nelson, 1968; Nagelberg & Spotnitz, 1958) have viewed schizo-
ia and other schizoid states as a defense against murder. When the
or "the child" in the adult patient can no longer protect himself
his own murderous thoughts and/or his fears that his parent or
s may murder him we then can expect homicide, suicide, or
hing akin to these phenomena.

poor handling of aggressive impulses is also observed in other
-situation constellations that have been labelled "socially de-
' The alcoholic, for example, who is frequently enraged by the
eprivation that he has experienced can be viewed psychologically
hild who is saying: "Mother, so you won't feed me or nurse me
ly! Then, I'll take my own bottle and suck on it!" After experienc-
elated manic feeling from alcohol, the patient gets his just
t, namely, punishment for his oral sadism. By suffering from
overs" and other unpleasant sensations, he can genuinely accuse
f of being the bad boy he feels he is; "bad" because he is full of
nd it is "wrong" to hate.

same sado-masochistic sequellae can be observed in the drug
and in many homosexuals. The drug addict, like the alcoholic,
cutely murderous because of his past and present deprivations and
tion. Since he is not and/or has not been "given to," he gives
f doses of drugs. Angrily taking in drugs is the equivalent of

feeding himself and then, like the alcoholic, he suffers acutely from the after-effects of the drug. He shivers, cannot judge properly, feels nauseous and vulnerable. The "bad" after-effects are again experienced as appropriate punishment for the patient's "bad" murderous feelings.

The homosexual, who often has strong angry feelings toward the parent of the same sex and who fears the parent's retaliation, submits to the parent of the same sex and, therefore, avoids a mutually hostile explosion (Strean, 1972). In his submission to his sexual partner, like towards the parent of the same sex, the homosexual defends against his (or her) murderous wishes; that is why homosexuals are known to beat each other up after a sexual experience.

The defense against murder appears to be a theme in most antisocial behavior. When the defense breaks down, the observer can then see the aggressive excitement of the arsonist, the sadistic satisfaction of the child abuser, and the sexual joy of the rapist. From a clinical perspective, the social deviant is often one who has experienced acute deprivation and frustration. His "deviation" is a manifestation of his inability to come to terms with huge amounts of undischarged rage and aggression.

The Social Deviant and Psychosexual Development

As has already been indicated, the modern therapist, when meeting with an individual who has been labelled as a deviant, is concerned with the individual's complete metapsychology. To understand his patient's behavior the therapist relates to how the patient experiences himself and others; what the patient's dominant fantasies are; what are the salient aspects of the patient's history—particularly how he, the patient, has experienced them; the patient's major defenses; his ego ideals, internal sanctions, and many other variables. The therapist is interested, in other words, in studying the patient from several perspectives— dynamic, economic, genetic, topographic, and structural (Fine, 1962).

One means of appreciating and understanding the deviant's metapsychology is to determine where he is in his maturational development. For example, the social work clinician is not content to merely say that "alcoholism is an oral problem." Rather, he wonders whether the orality represents a maturational *fixation* of the patient's wherein he is still angrily struggling to get nourishment from a withholding mother. Or, does the oral problem of alcoholism represent a *regression*, due to the patient's inability to cope with maturational tasks of a higher level of development? An example of the latter case might be a man who has acute hostile feelings towards a father whom he regards as an oedipal rival. Because the aggressive feelings and murderous thoughts of the patient towards his father are unacceptable to the patient, he submits to father. However, for many men, homosexual fantasies are very difficult to acknowledge. One means of "drowning out" homosexual fantasies is to resort to alcoholism.

The determination of where the patient's struggle is, i.e., at what level of maturational development, has extremely important implications for treatment. If the patient is fixated at an oral level of development, he will probably need an experience with the therapist wherein he can express his oral aggression and mistrust towards maternal figures, including the therapist and then move up the psychosexual ladder, with the therapist serving as maturational agent. However, if the patient's alcoholism is a regression serving to protect him against oedipal anxiety, the therapeutic task will be to help the patient feel more comfortable with his phallic aggression in and out of the therapy.

The social work clinician is not satisfied with just "feeding" the alcoholic. He wants to know the nature of his patient's conflict. Is the patient's struggle primarily at the oral level, anal, phallic-oedipal or, just where? Furthermore, the therapist is not only eager to establish in his mind what stage of development the patient's conflict is at, but perhaps of more importance, he wants to know how significant others have responded to the patient's needs at the particular stage of development. An alcoholic and a drug addict may both be suffering from anxieties emanating from the oral period. However, in one case the patient may have been underfed and in the other instance, may have been overfed and indulged. In the latter situation, the patient will need an experience in the therapy where he can learn to take on some frustration, develop controls, and defer gratification, i.e., be weaned. In the former case, the therapist will attempt to create an atmosphere in the therapy such that aggression can be expressed and oral wishes can eventually be considered more acceptable to the patient.

As has already been implied, knowledge of the patient's maturational deficits not only helps the clinician understand the patient's maladaptive behavior with more certainty, but appreciation of the patient's maturational conflicts provides guides for treatment. Is the homosexual defending against an oedipal conflict or is he identifying with an oral mother so that by feeding his sexual partner, he is vicariously feeding his own oral hunger? Is the gambler storing up "gold" in his fantasies, i.e.,

an anal problem, or is he omnipotently striving to be an empe
conflict deriving from the early oral phase when the baby wants t
narcissistic King or "His Majesty, the Prince" (Freud, 1938, p. ?
the addict pricking himself in a phallic manner or is he feeding h
in an oral manner?

In some cases of deviancy the therapist recognizes that the pa
symptoms may emanate from more than one maturational dysfun
i.e., be overdetermined. Gambling may express both oral and
fantasies; homosexuality may derive from oral and phallic conflict:
addictions may be in the service of phallic, anal, and oral fantas

Maturational difficulties and the level or levels of development
which they derive can not only be determined from the story of tl
tient's life, his fantasies and dreams, but can also be ascertained b
the patient experiences the therapist, i.e., the transference. Is the
pist experienced as the oral mother (frustrating or indulgent); tl
limiting anal parent; the not sufficiently restrictive parent? Is h
tyrannical parent; or perhaps the seductive parent? In sum, the tra
ence reactions to the therapist provide an excellent guide to whe
patient is maturationally and also indicate how the therapist s
conduct himself in the therapy. For the indulged, he provides lim
the hungry, he provides an atmosphere to express his wishes and ̄
them with less self-hate; and for the too dependent, he provides
ture (Strean, 1972).

The Deviant and His Ego Functions

To understand the deviant patient's complex metapsychology, an
feature of the personality that should be studied comprehensively
patient's ego functions. Particularly, ego functions such as judg
reality testing, defensive arrangements, self-image, and object rel
are quite pertinent (Strean, 1972). If the patient's ego functior
quite weak and his self-image is fragile, his deviant behavior ma
well represent a defense against an underlying psychosis. The m
social work clinician, therefore, would not attempt to enlist a
fragile ego to overcome a protective and needed symptom. Rath
would join the patient in keeping this symptom as long as he ne
(Strean, 1972; Nagelberg & Spotnitz, 1958; Nelson, 1968; Sp
1967).

In contrast to the patient whose ego functions are weak, some n
tic individuals have a good observing ego which can be enlisted i

treatment. Such an individual might very well look at his deviant behavior as ego dystonic, seek to understand its causes, and recognize its disadvantageous consequences.

The strength or weakness of ego functions not only speaks to the prognosis of the therapy, and not only to how much the patient's cooperation can be enlisted in studying his problems, but his ego strength or weakness will also serve as a predictor in determining how the patient will view the therapist. Usually, patients with limited and weak ego functions have suffered trauma during the first year or two of life, harbor much distrust, and may have to try to defeat the therapist's efforts. The patient with stronger ego functions may be able to view the therapist more realistically and patient and therapist can be in many ways allies in the treatment encounter.

A very useful ego function to observe carefully in the treatment of deviants is the patient's capacity for object relations. Some deviant patients such as the psychopath and sociopath are so narcissistic that they have little remorse about how often or how much they harm other human beings. In addition to their manipulative and exploitative manner, often carried out with a charming facade, they have a weak superego and little sense of guilt. Obviously, they will use the therapist only if they believe the latter can help them rob without getting caught, rape with no penalties, or steal without having to pay too heavy a price for it. This kind of patient has an extremely guarded prognosis.

On the other hand, there are neurotic individuals plagued by irrational, yet real guilt, who often commit criminal acts so that by landing in jail, they can feel a reduction in anxiety. These individuals often have the capacity to form genuine object relations, have too strong a superego, and can more easily than the psychopath enter into a cooperative therapeutic relationship; this kind of a patient has a better prognosis.

In sum, by understanding the strength of the patient's ego functions, we can assess how "necessary" the deviant behavior is for his psychic equilibrium. Furthermore, the prognosis of the patient can be more easily determined with accurate knowledge of his ego functions and the patient's therapeutic cooperativeness can be assessed, as well.

Treatment of the Social Deviant

As was stated earlier, the main consideration in the treatment of the patient with deviant behavior is the complex metapsychology of the complex patient. The clinician is not particularly interested in "getting rid" of the patient's aberrant behavior, but is concerned with the study of his personality. This approach is particularly helpful to most individuals coming for treatment because they usually want genuine understanding of their total being, and it appears to be the treatment of choice for the social deviant. The latter, when he is referred for therapy, rarely wants to get rid of his deviant behavior, despite his conscious protests to the contrary. The therapist, by genuinely conveying the message that symptom removal is not his goal, but empathic understanding is, meets the patient where he is.

> Mr. A., a 30-year-old man, who practiced homosexuality exclusively, sought psychotherapy not for his homosexuality, but for depression, loneliness, and many psychosomatic complaints. He became emotionally involved quite early in the treatment when he "liked the idea of just talking about whatever comes to my mind." The sheer ventilation of aggression towards his parents, complaints about the therapist for not loving him enough, and "the attention I get sometimes," reduced his sense of loneliness, depression, and psychosomatic complaints after just a couple of months of twice-a-week therapy.
>
> When the patient's wishes to have a homosexual "affair" with the therapist became the focus of treatment, and the therapist explored the why's and wherefore's of the patient's fantasies towards him (rather than gratifying them) the patient told the therapist that he abhorred him, similar to the way he abhorred both his parents. The therapist, like Mr. A.'s parents, never fondled him, fed him, or "tickled" him and this proved that they hated him.
>
> With the release of bottled-up aggression, the patient's ego functions began to emerge in a more mature fashion. After a year of treatment, referring to his homosexuality, Mr. A. remarked, "Isn't it crazy to want to punish my parents by being a pervert?"
>
> As Mr. A. psychologically gained some separation from his introjected parents, he felt less afraid of his assertiveness. As he needed to be less of an angry child and developed more autonomy and maturity as a person, only then could he even consider what heterosexual relationships were all about.

In the above example, it can be noted that the therapist did not particularly relate to the patient's deviancy, per se. Rather, he was more interested in helping the patient resolve some of his resistances towards expressing his murderous fantasies. As the patient could enjoy hating the therapist, his depression lifted, his psychosomatic complaints diminished, and he could then begin to explore with the therapist some of the dynamics of his "perversion" (Strean, 1973).

Very often the person labelled as "socially deviant" does not come for help voluntarily; he resists the therapist and therapy. To try to convince the patient that he needs therapy only compounds his resistance to it, makes him feel more attacked, and causes him to flee from the therapist.

The clinical social worker, as has been repeatedly implied, recognizes that resistances are like skin; they are designed to protect the individual. Consequently, to help the patient maintain his precarious equilibrium, the therapist often supports and reinforces resistances. With this experience, self-esteem rises and the therapist is not experienced as too threatening and forbidding an object.

> Steve, age 15, was picked up by police authorities several times after he had been found truanting from school. He hated school and all that it implied—"horrible teachers, dumb kids, and dull subjects. Why the heck should I go there? There are better things to do."
>
> When Steve met his therapist, he very quickly transferred to him all the qualities of a strict school disciplinarian. "What the heck do I want to do with you? There's nothing wrong with my head, Doc! I bet you work for the school, anyway, and you only want to get me back there. You are a head shrinker and you know it!" he dogmatically asserted.
>
> On being told by the therapist that he had no interest in getting him back to school, "because that would be a pretty dull job for a head doctor and I have better things to do anyway," Steve responded, "So what the heck do you want with me?" The therapist responded, "Not a darn thing!"
>
> Steve then tried to cover up an anxious smile by saying, "You're pretty wacky, aren't you? Are you some kind of fairy?" The therapist responded, "Maybe I am. Sometimes it is hard for me to understand myself." To this Steve managed a mild giggle and exclaimed, "You must have been an interesting jerk in your day." He speculated that the therapist was a criminal "let loose from a booby hatch" and was never caught and that he had changed his name from Stinkweed to Strean. Furthermore, the therapist smoked a pipe because underneath he was a "cock sucker." He wondered if the therapist had ever gone to college. "You mean with horrible professors and stupid college students?" the therapist queried.
>
> Steve went on to say that this conversation was "O.K." but he didn't think he'd want to visit the therapist again. Then after a long pause, he said very quietly that maybe he'd come back in three weeks if he had nothing else to do. "Three weeks," the therapist exclaimed, "why not six months?" The remainder of the interview consisted of an attempt on Steve's part to convince the therapist that maybe another "bull" session was in order.

While the events of the above interview are rather dramatic and the movement somewhat rapid, the interaction tends to demonstrate a de-

linquent youngster's struggle in meeting a therapist for the first tir
it does suggest some means of helping him cope with the burde
situation (Strean, 1970).

When the patient arrived at the therapist's office he was ready t
somebody who would be exactly like a police officer. He atte
immediately to knock the therapist's authority and to indu
therapist to respond with anger and perhaps react punitively. Wh
therapist told Steve that he was not interested in sending the wa
youth back to school, he was able to accomplish two things. Fi
patient could begin to believe that he was not being forced inte
ment, and secondly, Steve could become a little intrigued with
body who appeared like himself, a rebellious deceiver.

Sometimes the degree of individual and social pathology of
cially deviant patient is so great, and the difficulties that are appar
so pervasive, that actual demonstrations of concern are necessar
ticularly for patients whose difficulties emanate from a preverbal
some noninterpretive work is necessary (Spotnitz, 1967). The fo
case is taken from a social agency.

> Miss C., a young Black woman of 32, had five illegitimate p
> cies. Living in a housing project and on welfare, she was fre
> drunk, often depressed, and managed her home and childr
> extremely limited care and discipline. The management of the
> sent a female social worker to her home to "see what could be
> before processing an eviction.
>
> The social worker found Miss C.'s house extremely unti
> children poorly cared for, and Miss C. in her third month
> nancy. When the social worker, at her first home visit, told I
> that the management of the project had suggested that she b
> before the social worker could finish her opening remarks, th
> bellowed, "Oh, they want to throw me out because they don't
> way I keep the house!" The social worker looked around a
> calmly: "I'm sure things are very difficult for you. You must
> very rough!" The client spent the next half hour talking about I
> children were a burden to her, that meeting their physical ne
> impossible, how difficult it was to make ends meet financial
> that the only pleasure she got once in a while was "a little se
> little drink." The social worker remarked that she could und
> that sex and drinking were the only pleasures available to Miss
> wondered if she, the social worker, could bring Miss C. son
> sure. Miss C. pointed to the children's clothes, her poor fu
> and stressed that she had limited time for herself.
>
> The social worker quickly arranged with the Department of
> and other agencies to supply Miss C. with some of the tangib

she requested. Clothes were gotten for Miss C. and her children, mattresses and a bed were also located for her, and a volunteer was located to do some babysitting.

By the second and third interviews, Miss C. was talking about her current pregnancy and previous ones. She mentioned also that she knew "damn well that I don't appeal to men" and that all of her sexual affairs were one-night stands. The social worker took note of her client's feelings of depreciation vis-à-vis men and said, "You hate yourself and get men to hate you, too. A man only has something to do with you in bed, right?"

The treatment had begun. Miss C. in succeeding interviews could report on how she remembered wishing that a boy friend of her mother's who visited occasionally would be her father. She talked about her strong wish for a father "who could like me as a girl" but "how her mother just didn't meet up with one."

In the case above, Miss C.'s preverbal and preoedipal needs were so strong that before any verbal treatment could take place, the therapist had to show some tangible evidence of real empathy. Sometimes with the social deviant the therapist may have to lend money or call a judge, the police department, or some community agency—not so much because he can or should influence the latter but so the client or patient can experience him as an object who is at least trying to be of some help (Strean, 1970).

Conclusion

"Social deviancy" is part of the web of any culture. By offering negative sanctions for certain types of behavior, a society preserves its stability and reaffirms its norms. What is labelled as deviant behavior varies from social context to social context.

The modern therapist is not preoccupied with deviant or acting-out behavior per se, but he is very much interested in the individual with the deviant label. The modern therapist treats the "social deviant" within the same metapsychological perspective that he utilizes for the treatment of any patient. He studies the patient's conflicts, fantasies, dreams, and life story; he particularly focuses on where in his patient's psychosexual development has maturation been halted. Treatment of the deviant patient within a solid social work perspective seeks to offer an appropriate maturational experience based on the patient's maturational needs (Strean, 1973).

REFERENCES

Aichorn, A. *Wayward Youth*. New York: Viking Press, 1948.

Becker, H. *Outsiders: Studies in the Sociology of Deviance*. New York: The Free Press, 1963.

Blos, P. *The Adolescent Personality*. New York: Appleton-Century-Crofts, 1941.

Davis, K. "Mental hygiene and the class structure," in H. Stein and R. Cloward (eds.), *Social Perspectives on Behavior*. New York: Free Press, 1958.

Erikson, K. "Notes on the Sociology of Deviance," 9–21, in Howard Becker, *The Other Side*. New York: Free Press, 1964.

Fine, R. *Freud: A Critical Re-evaluation of His Theories*. New York: David McKay Company, 1962.

Freud, S. "Psychoanalytic notes on a autobiographical account of a case of paranoia," in *Collected Papers of Sigmund Freud, Vol. 3*. New York: Basic Books, 1959. Originally published 1911.

_____. *The Basic Writings of Sigmund Freud*. New York: Random House, 1938.

Goffman, E. *Asylums*. Garden City, N.Y.: Anchor Books, 1961.

Gove, W. "Societal reaction as an explanation of mental illness: An evaluation," *American Sociological Review*, 1970, 35(5), 873–883.

Hoffer, W. "Deceiving the deceiver," in K. R. Eissler (ed.), *Searchlights on Delinquency*. New York: International Universities Press, 1949.

Hollingshead, A., and Redlich, F. "Social stratification and psychiatric disorders," in H. Stein and R. Cloward (eds.), *Social Perspectives on Behavior*. New York: Free Press, 1958.

Lemert, E. *Social Pathology*. New York: McGraw-Hill, 1951.

Lennard, H., and Bernstein, A. *Patterns in Human Interaction*. San Francisco: Jossey-Bass, Inc., 1969.

Nagelberg, L., and Spotnitz, H. "Strengthening the ego through the release of frustration-aggression," *American Journal of Orthopsychiatry*, 1958, 28, 794–801.

Nelson, M.; Nelson, B.; Sherman, M.; and Strean, H. *Roles and Paradigms in Psychotherapy.* New York: Grune & Stratton, 1968.

Riessman, F.; Cohen, J.; and Pearl, A. *Mental Health of the Poor.* New York: The Free Press, 1964.

Spotnitz, H. *Modern Psychoanalysis of the Schizophrenic Patient.* New York: Grune & Stratton, 1967.

————. "Techniques for the resolution of the narcissistic defense," in B. Wolman (ed.), *Psychoanalytic Techniques.* New York: Basic Books, 1967.

Strean, H. "Psychoanalytically oriented casework versus behavior modification therapy," *Clinical Social Work Journal,* 1973, *1*(3), 143–160.

————. *The Experience of Psychotherapy.* Metuchen, N.J.: Scarecrow Press, 1972.

————. *New Approaches in Child Guidance.* Metuchen, N.J.: Scarecrow Press, 1970.

DISCUSSANT: PAUL LERMAN

According to Strean, the definition of deviance is not only "arbitrary," but "varies from social context to social context," and can be modified by "historical, military, political, and other social and economic factors" (p. 234). Given this relativistic approach to the topic, therapists can also offer a viewpoint—a "psychosocial view" of social deviancy and its treatment. This approach to the problem avoids concern about the deviant or "acting out" behavior per se; instead, the modern therapist is interested in the individual who is associated with the deviant label. The individual's deviancy can therefore, be best understood by employing "the same metapsychological perspective that he utilizes for the treatment of *any* patient" (emphasis added).

In the discussion that follows, I would like to re-examine Strean's perceptions about the relativity of societal reactions to deviant behavior. On the basis of this re-examination, I would like to offer an alternative view about the critical roles that clinical therapists can perform for the larger society. This discussion will rely on a different reading of sociological theories, as well as inferences stemming from empirical research.

The idea that societal reactions to deviant behavior can vary according to social context was first systematically presented by Edwin M. Lemert in *Social Pathology* (New York: McGraw-Hill, 1951). The notion that deviance was a form of societal-imposed pathology—and that deviance did not reside within the actor, but was imposed by "labelling agents"—appeared provocative to many. It also appeared to offer a social, rather than a psychological, view about "pathology." As the labelling perspective gained both respectability and adherents within academic departments of sociology, attention turned towards the process whereby people became labelled as deviant. Theories about the labelling process were deemed to be more important, theoretically and strategically, than theories about deviant behavior per se. One theorist even offered the view that "mental illness" was a "residual" conceptual category for labelling types of deviants whose behavior appeared not to fit other proscribed classifications.

The labelling perspective about deviance (it never really advanced to a systematic theoretical stage) relied on a variety of assumptions. One critical assumption was that modern societies do not possess a shared system of norms and values. Instead of a societal consensus about right and wrong, good and bad, appropriate and inappropriate, there existed group, community, and societal conflicts. Traditional sociologists, often termed the structuralist–functional school, were accused of projecting ideal, middle-class, standards onto American society. Our pluralistic society was marked by inter-groups competition and conflict—not Merton's assertions of consensus about common "goals of success," legitimate means for attaining prized values, and patterned deviant responses to the discrepancy between means and ends.

I think it is fair to infer that Strean's discussion of the sociological view of deviance is strongly influenced by the labelling perspective. I believe the world is more complex and that both the structuralist–functional and conflict modes of sociological perception, imagination, and theorizing are useful in understanding and formulating policies concerning deviant behaviors. The intellectual challenge is to attempt to understand when consensus *or* conflict about norms appears to be a reasonable conceptual stance. I believe this challenge is more than an intellectual exercise sponsored by academics to sponsor their interest in specifying ideas. Rather, I believe that the societal role of clinical therapists shifts according to whether a consensus or conflict view actually exists within a community. But first, it is appropriate to provide the empirical basis for asserting that *both* views about sociocultural reality are accurate—but not about the same types of deviance or societal responses to deviance.

Contrary to the views of the labelling theorists, there is strong evidence that there is broad agreement within American society that most acts proscribed by the criminal laws of the 50 states are indeed wrongful actions by individuals. Not only is there agreement about these acts, but American police and students, as well as judges and citizens, agree quite strongly about the relative seriousness of criminal acts—their rankings from most to least serious are similar to an unusually high degree of concurrence. These findings were first reported by Sellin and Wolfgang in 1964 (see *The Measurement of Delinquency*. New York: John Wiley). A recent study of a random sample of urban households, using a different research instrument, corroborated these original findings. As Rossi, Waite, et al., found out in their 1972 study, "norms concerning crime seriousness are widely diffused throughout subgroups of our society" ("The Seriousness of Crime: Normative Structure and Individual Differences," *American Sociological Review*, 1974, 39, 224–237). Any differences between individuals were largely accounted for by differences in formal educational attainment, suggesting that increased exposure to a consensually validated normative structure and language would lead to greater agreement. In addition, it is instructive to note the reports of consensus about crime and the ranking of seriousness in French- and English-speaking parts of Canada, as well as in Puerto Rico. It appears that some norms may, in fact, even be shared *across* societies, as well as within societies.

Though there is sufficiently strong evidence to believe that a broad consensus exists about crimes, there is not the same agreement about other forms of deviance. For example, a doctoral dissertation by Norma Weiss presented vignette descriptions about deviant behaviors to a random sample of households in a suburban, middle-income, community in New Jersey. A vignette describing homicide and paranoid schizophrenic behaviors were recognized and reacted to as very serious behaviors, but there was a great deal of disagreement (or dissensus) about family desertion, alcoholism, anxiety-depression, and prostitution. Respondents were unsure whether to view these behaviors as "mad" or "bad." Not only was there disagreement about the seriousness of the behaviors, respondents were also uncertain whether these deviant behaviors should be responded to as a criminal, mental health, or as a nonformal family or community problem.

It appears that a broad agreement exists about "extreme" "mad" or "bad" behaviors, and for many traditional common law crimes. In areas where deviance is less serious or criminal, responses to deviancy are indeed quite varied; virtually all of Strean's assertions about deviant behaviors might apply. As Weiss noted in her study of "mad" and "bad" behaviors, it appears that a "situational approach toward deviancy emerges" as a significant perspective regarding a diverse array of activities (Weiss, *Mad or Bad*, unpublished doctoral dissertation, Rutgers University, 1979).

Given these kinds of findings, it is clear that the therapist can perform at least two types of societal roles. Where there is consensus, she/he can argue for understanding the individual deviant as a person, but the larger community will continue to provide labels based on their shared norms about "mad" and "bad" behaviors. Where there is a lack of consensus, and neighbors, police, and family members disagree about the social meaning of the deviant behaviors, mental health professionals can provide the basis for a new moral ideology—one that transforms ambiguity about personal responsibility and free will of the actor into a moderately "mad" category. Uncertain about whether to criminalize many "bad" behaviors a pluralistic society may be willing to permit therapists to impose "acting out" categorizations—and, thereby, legitimate the suspension of a moral judgment. Whether Strean and other clinical therapists (and teachers) are comfortable with this kind of "moral" role is uncertain.

DISCUSSANT: MAX SIPORIN

This comment is not just a reaction to Herb Strean's paper on "A Psychosocial View of Social Deviancy." It should be considered also in the context of Strean's many other papers and books. In addition, consideration will be given to the two levels of meaning that can be identified here. As in all communication, there are a level of substantive content and a level of metacommunication that offer a message as to the meaning of this content. Fortunately, Strean's metacommunications are characteristically explicit, clear, and congruent with the substantive content. I will discuss this latter metastatement first.

Strean's article is representative of his heroic efforts during these past fifteen years to maintain social work's continued concern for the welfare of the individual human being. As a national leader of clinical social workers, he has given a great deal of his energies to fight for the social work client as a person. He has campaigned for the need to recognize the personality of clients, and of the person's capacities and potentialities for rational as well as for irrational, motives, desires, fantasies, feelings, and actions. In this way, he has served important functions and carried out major responsibilities for the social work profession in helping it through a very troubled and difficult period.

During the recent social reform era, many social workers became politically radicalized and subscribed to a social determinism and a social reform ideology that views the person as a helpless victim of an oppressive social order. Many social workers also rebelled against the dominant psychoanalytic model of therapy, and advanced themselves by espousing "more effective and scientific" behavior modification types of therapy. Such views rob people of their humanity and of their personhood. Herb stood against such trends, and spoke out for the significance of the inner person, and of the inner phenomenological, psychodynamic world. It is this inner world of the personality that mediates the perception and understanding of reality, and the person's actions and relation to it. He also spoke out for the validity of the psychoanalytic theories and procedures to which he is committed and through which he believes the person is best comprehended and helped.

At the same time, Strean responded to the temper and the needs of the time (the social unrest and the rights revolution of the late 1960s and early 1970s) by attempting to integrate certain social science theories into his psychoanalytic conceptual framework and practice. Many of these ideas be absorbed during his doctoral studies at Columbia, and are part of his identification as a social worker. Two major contributions came out of this effort: the well known paper on role theory and this paper on deviancy. The concepts and theories of social role and of deviant behavior are central ideas in sociological thought, and very challenging to a lively and adventurous mind. Along with the effort at theoretical clarification and integration, Herb chose to demonstrate that the psychoanalytic concepts and casework procedures are very helpful. And he presented ideas and case illustrations to show how they are helpful in casework with the poor, with ethnic minorities, and also with socially deviant as well as mentally deviant people.

In this paper on social deviancy, we can observe these varied intentions and metamessages. There is an expository section on the meaning of deviance which gives selective emphasis to certain aspects of the subject. Thus, deviance is declared to be "in many ways arbitrarily defined," and a subjective notion, which stigmatizes and stereotypes the person, results in self-fulfilling prophecies and deprives the deviant person of his civil rights.

The net effect of this exposition of deviance theory is to indicate that the deviant behavior is not as important as the personality of the actor. The label of "deviant," and the psychiatric personality classifications are said "to offer little predictive power in fully determining personality functioning." The clinician is said to be "more interested in the person with a deviant label than he is in the deviancy per se," which is to be understood as "symptoms of internal stress." There follows a set of interpretations of the deviant person as "often one who has experienced acute deprivation and frustrations. His 'deviation' is a manifestation of his inability to come to terms with huge amounts of undischarged rage and aggression." These are attributed to a lack of psychosexual maturation and developmental fixation, with resulting impairment of ego functions. Therapy is therefore to be directed to establishing a therapeutic relationship, not removing ego defenses or symptomatic behavior where there is a "weak ego," and providing a maturational helping experience.

The case examples are of great interest, and show Strean to be an experienced, sophisticated, and effective therapist at work. Here is one of his great strengths as a teacher and writer. He tells fine stories of his encounters with his clients, and of those made by other therapists. These vignettes and anecdotes are vivid, alive, and effective illustrations of the insights concerning personality and the assessment and interventive procedures that he is teaching. They validate for the reader the psychoanalytic theories and the psychoanalytic techniques and helping principles as they apply and are applied with these clients.

But I am bothered by the segmented, partial view of people and of the helping process that is presented here, and in Strean's body of work. And I also miss the interpersonal, social situations and processes, which not only provide a context for the personalities of clients, but which give them a full-blooded character and really make them persons. There is some mention in this paper of the interrelation of deviant behavior and its social context. But this is really given short shrift in this paper and elsewhere. The Schreber case, for example, is used to show that the social context of other people influences Schreber not to verbalize his psychotic ideas. But there is no dialogical relationship or transactional process reported between Schreber and these people in this incident.

The therapeutic relationship is the one in which dialogue and encounter between people takes place. What happens in the real world, and the need for situational interventions by the social work therapist, seem of little importance. Strean is well versed in family and marital therapies, and in their processes. But even in this regard, it is what happens in the therapy sessions that are of engrossing interest. One can respond to this observation by pointing out that the major purposes of Herb's writings is to help the student and the social work practitioner with what is directly relevant to the therapist's activities, which largely is in the office. Yet his image and description of what the social work therapist thinks and does in regard to the world outside of the office seems incomplete.

In this discussion of social deviancy, there is a characteristic overriding concern with the personality of the client, and with the psychotherapeutic process, presented from what is essentially a psychological, rather than a psychosocial perspective. We can identify what is missing here by comparing this paper with other discussions of this subject in the social work literature.[1] We discover aspects of social symbolic interactional and intersubjective processes that are of crucial importance for a fuller understanding of this subject. They are of major importance also for the more accurate assessment of the client's behavior and life situations, as well as of his or her personality, and also for a more effective intervention to influence constructive and lasting change.

There is a need, for example, to understand the constructive meanings of much deviant behavior, as influences not only for social control, but also for innovative social change. Many people deviate because of social influences that meet normal human needs, for membership, affection, identity, status, etc. The interrelation of sociodynamics and psychodynamics, of social and self identities, of social and self-typing, of reference group supports for deviant careers, of situational and cultural reinforcement for behavior and interaction patterns—these are concepts and processes that need attention in assessment and intervention procedures. Studies of homosexually active persons find many of them to be quite "normal," or "mature," in mental health, psychiatric terms. There may be question as to the price many of them have to pay for this kind of adjustment. One can recognize that many homosexuals have not been socialized to accept, or to find satisfaction and fulfillment in, stable, intimate, heterosexual relationships. But it is an excessive statement, and an inaccurate generalization, to declare that all homosexuals or deviants act out in their deviant, anti-social behavior "murderous feelings" and "undischarged rage and aggression."

The above observations need to be entered in this kind of inventory book. It should also be observed that there are times when excessive and zealous statements are needed, to counteract unhelpful and self-destructive trends. Strean has been the great spokesman for a very much needed point of view, at a time when it was, and in many places still is, derided and unpopular. At this present time, we are entering a different and more difficult kind of era, of increasing mechanization and bureaucratization of our life, of a culture that gives prime value to modernism, conservatism, and conformity. His voice and his messages continue to be very much needed, in the fight for social work humanistic values, and for the welfare of the individual human being, as well as the welfare of the family and community. Strean's voice and his distinguished body of work have contributed and will contribute greatly in this cause.

REFERENCE

1. Max Siporin, "Deviant Behavior Theory in Social Work: Diagnosis and Treatment," *Social Work* 10 (July 1965): 59–67. Roger M. Nooe, "A Model for Integrating Theoretical Approaches to Deviance," *Social Work* 25 (September 1980): 366–370.

Chapter 11

THE PSYCHOPATH REVISITED: SOME RECONSIDERATIONS IN DIAGNOSIS AND TREATMENT

Psychopathy is one of the most baffling problems in therapeutic work. A substantial number of psychoanalysts have alleged that the condition does not exist and in the index of Freud's *Collected Papers* there are no references to the "psychopath" or to the "antisocial personality." The psychopathic group has been regarded by many clinicians as a meaningless "dumping ground for unclassified disorders" (Glover, 1960).

Among those psychoanalysts who do utilize the clinical label of "psychopath" in their therapeutic work, few have enhanced dynamic understanding of this patient by reporting some of his fantasies, dreams, historical events in his life, transference responses, common resistances and defenses, ego functions and ego dysfunctions, and other dimensions of his unique metapsychology. Furthermore, there is a paucity of material in the psychoanalytic literature which discusses in depth a psychopathic patient's response to psychoanalytic treatment.

One of the explanations offered for the clinical neglect of psychopathic patients is that few of them seek out a therapist, and therefore only a limited number of clinicians have had an opportunity to work intensively with them (Freedman, Kaplan, Sadock, 1976). However, Glover has advised that when psychopathic individuals do come to the psychoanalytic consulting room, "their successful analysis is not easily achieved" (Glover, 1960). Many analytic and non-analytic clinicians have averred that the psychopath is untreatable because he is "too infantile," "much too narcissistic," "has limited if any anxiety," and has "severe superego lacunae" (Davies, 1955; Cleckley, 1959; McCord and McCord, 1956; Newkirk, 1957). Yet, as Lindner has pointed out, "here we encounter the most expensive and most destructive of all known forms of aberrant behavior" (Lindner, 1948), and in a recent book, *Violence: Perspectives on Murder and Aggression,* Kutash and his colleagues refer to psychopathy as "the psychosis psychoanalysis and psychiatry refuse to face" (Kutash, Kutash, and Schlesinger, 1979).

What is Psychopathy?

According to the second edition of the American Psychiatric Association's *Diagnostic and Statistical Manual of Mental Disorders* (DSM, II), the term "psychopath" or "antisocial personality" is "reserved for individuals who are basically unsocialized and whose behavior pattern brings them repeatedly into conflict with society. They are incapable of significant loyalty to individuals, groups, or social values. They are grossly selfish, callous, irresponsible, impulsive, and unable to feel guilt or to learn from experience and punishment. Frustration tolerance is low. They tend to blame others or offer plausible rationalizations for their behavior" (DSM, II, 1964).

Of those psychoanalytic writers who have attempted to define psychopathy most do agree that the psychopath is an asocial, aggressive, highly impulsive individual who feels little or no remorse and is unable to form lasting bonds of affection with other human beings (McCord and McCord, 1956; Glover, 1949; Fenichel, 1945). The individual diagnosed as psychopathic frequently demonstrates superior intelligence and succeeds brilliantly for a while in work, in studies, and in human relationships. However, inevitably and repeatedly, he fails by losing his job, alienating his spouse, or provoking his family or friends. Seldom does the person find adequate motivation to explain why in the midst of success he grossly shirks his responsibilities and abandons his work at the behest of impulses that seem no more compelling than a trivial whim (Cleckley, 1959). Unreliability, untruthfulness and insincerity are his distinguishing defenses. When the psychopath demonstrates no remorse or guilt and is confronted with the facts of his behavior, he is usually quite skillful at projecting blame on others (Freedman, Kaplan, Sadock, 1976; Fenichel, 1945; Glover, 1949).

The psychopath has been described as one who exhibits a love of prestige and limelight which he gratifies on the shallowest of grounds. He manifests a tendency to crude gratification of primitive forms of instinct. Sexual attachments are fleeting but he tends to be promiscuous (Fenichel, 1945). Behind an apparently friendly facade, the psychopath is aggressive in reaction to minor frustrations.

Glover in 1960 summarized the major writings on psychopathy and concluded that the psychopath is:

> a constitutionally sensitive person, peculiarly intolerant of frustration; inclined to sexual excess; deeply aggressive and openly negativistic; selfish and egotistical, with an immediately ineffective reality sense; incapable of sustained effort; callous, inconsiderate, unprincipled and lacking in moral sense; incapable of deep attachments; recidivist and refractory to punishment. His psychopathic outbursts are irregular in incidence, stereotyped and on the whole compulsive but even in quiescent periods his character is disharmonious and often eccentric. At the same time he wears the mask of friendly normality. [Glover, 1960, p. 128]

The Psychopath's Absence of a Superego?

Virtually every psychoanalytic writer who has explored the problem of psychopathy has referred to the patient's lack of remorse and guilt and has emphasized the apparent lacunae in the psychopath's superego. Glover has described the psychopath as "inconsiderate, thoughtless, *without conscience or sense of guilt*" (Glover, 1960). Fenichel has discussed the psychopath's "*lack of guilt feelings* since (he) readily yields to impulses, the suppression of which is customary for normal persons" (Fenichel, 1945). Freedman, et al. (1976), in referring to the psychopath's "charming and ingratiating quality," have pointed out that he "*shows no remorse or guilt over his misbehavior.*" Gaylin in his review of studies on maternal deprivation concluded: "Early deprivation of such socialization is considered one of the strongest factors responsible for the unfeeling conscienceless *individual known as a psychopath*" (Gaylin, 1976).

Although there is much unanimity among writers that the psychopath is devoid of guilt feelings and has a weak, fragmented superego at best, certain phenomena that the typical psychopath exhibits make this inference a questionable one.

An early discovery of Freud's that has been continually reaffirmed is that we can never rely on manifest behavior alone if we are to assess the human being thoroughly (Freud, 1900). Although the patient diagnosed as psychopathic is usually callous, hedonistic, and impulsive, his manifest behavior should not necessarily imply that only instinctual drives are being expressed. The psychopathic gambler may eventually be ruined; the arsonist, caught; and the thief, incarcerated (Fenichel, 1945).

One of the dynamics that has been consistently observed in patients who have been assessed as "criminal psychopaths" is their feeling of relief when they are caught and punished. As an example of this, Freud described the "criminal out of a sense of guilt" (Freud, 1916). This is an individual who is so oppressed by a tyrannical superego that by becoming involved in provocative and illegal acts, he finds comfort in being incarcerated. His punishment dissipates his guilt which almost always has an unconscious origin.

An example of a guilt ridden criminal psychopath may be seen in the following case illustration:

> Mr. Saul A., aged 30, was referred for analytic therapy by a criminal court judge who felt that Mr. A.'s constant thefts, illegal manipulations, and sadistic assaults reflected "deep psychological problems." Mr. A., an attorney, initially showed no remorse when he discussed the fact that he had stolen money from his clients, was promiscuous and sadistic with women, made false promises to colleagues and friends and neglected his children. However, after fifteen sessions with the therapist, he asked, "Aren't you ready to throw me out for my 'lousy' behavior?" When the meaning of the patient's question was explored, Mr. A. pointed out that "in some peculiar way, I'd feel better if you thought little of me and punished me for *my sins. When I am not punished I feel a sense of uncertainty."*
>
> Later in Mr. A.'s treatment he was able to identify the feelng of "constant guilt" for "gypping my brothers and father and being my mother's favorite"; "seducing teachers and fooling the other children"; and "being number one in my crowd, without deserving it." As Mr. A. became aware of his oppressive superego which he was using to punish himself for childhood fantasies and childhood deeds, he realized "how guilty I feel and have to do things to relieve it."

Recent psychobiographers, particularly those who are psychoanalytically oriented, have agreed that many well known public figures in history who have been described as brutally dishonest, callous and ruthless, have also harbored a strong sense of guilt. In the case of former President Nixon, he, himself, acknowledged that the death of his brothers during his childhood left him with a strong sense of guilt and an attendant need to punish himself for harboring hostile and rivalrous feelings towards his brothers (Johnson, 1979). In Nixon's book, *Six Crises*, he describes how he felt after incriminating Alger Hiss, a member of the United States State Department.

> I should have been elated.... However, I experienced a sense of
> let-down which is difficult to describe or even to understand.... There
> was also a sense of shock and sadness that a man like Hiss could have
> fallen so low. I imagined myself in his place.... I realized that Hiss
> stood before us completely unmasked—our hearing had saved one
> life, but had ruined another. [Nixon, 1962, p. 37]

The quotation above seems to refer to Nixon's feelings of sadness,
depression, and guilt after exposing Hiss. Some twenty-five years later,
Mr. Nixon was to stand "unmasked" and "ruined" after he unconsciously arranged to expose his own guilt by producing tapes that revealed his own illegal activities. In Nixon's 1974 State of the Union
Message, he asked Congress to "join me in mounting a new effort to
replace the *discredited President*—discredited present welfare system"
(*New York Times*, Nov. 18, 1973).

The existence of a superego in Adolph Hitler's psychic structure may
be inferred from reviewing some of the work of his biographers.
Psychoanalyst Gertrude M. Kurth implies the presence of a superego in
Hitler when she notes that his father's death (when Hitler was thirteen
years old) plunged Adolph into "a guilty sense of despair" (Kurth, 1947).

It should also be noted that one of Hitler's ideals was a religious
figure. Leon Saul in *Psychodynamics of Hostility* quotes Hitler as saying, "Again and again I enjoyed the best possibility of intoxicating
myself with the solemn splendor of the dazzling festivals of the
church.... It seemed to me perfectly natural to regard the Abbot as the
highest and most desirable ideal, just as my father regarded the village
priest as his ideal" (Saul, 1976, p. 169).

In analyzing Hitler's character, Robert Payne has said:

> If he resembled anyone at all, it was Dostoevsky's ill-tempered "un-
> derground man," the man who comes out from under the floor
> boards, who thirsts for power and is powerless, desires to torture and
> be tortured, to debase himself and to debase others, to be proud and to
> humble himself. [Payne, 1973, p. 172]

Supporting Payne's thesis is the fact that Hitler in his sexual activities
with his mistress enjoyed being whipped by her (Kurth, 1947).

It would appear that the presence of guilt and the existence of a
punitive superego has been overlooked and/or underestimated in the
diagnosis and treatment of psychopathic personalities. In a recent report
on ten thieves who robbed banks during one week in New York City, all

of them arranged to be caught and punished within a few days after they committed the robberies. Furthermore, most of them in due course acknowledged their guilt (*New York Times*, August 23, 1979).

In his summary of the fate of scientific ideas, Loewald (Panel, 1976) cited one reason for complacency among analysts—if a theory has served well as a convincing explanation for a body of material, over time its users tend to blur distinctions between theoretical concepts and observational data. In this manner, novel configurations may easily be overlooked (Gedo, 1979). In this context, Charcot's famous aphorism, which he delivered to Freud, may be noted: "La theorie c'est bon, mais ca n'empeche pas d'exister!" (Theory is good, but it doesn't prevent things from existing. Quoted in Gedo, 1979).

Although traditional theory states that the patient diagnosed as psychopathic has a very weak superego, cannot experience much guilt, and therefore is a poor candidate for psychoanalytic therapy, the main purpose of this paper is to demonstrate that the psychopath is in fact, fighting a harsh superego, and that treatment with him may be helpful to him if this important dynamic is taken into account.

The Role of the Superego in the Psychopath

Those psychoanalysts and psychotherapists who have investigated the problem of psychopathy have concurred that the psychopath has, in most instances, been deprived of a warm, empathic relationship with a mother and in many cases has never had a father (Aichorn, 1935; Glover, 1960; Gaylin, 1976). When the child who is to become a psychopath feels emotionally neglected and abandoned, his initial reaction is usually protest and hostility (Bowlby, 1951). However, he cannot freely discharge his angry feelings. Like most children, he anticipates hostile retaliation for his aggressive wishes and therefore he represses his desires (Freud, 1909).

Because the "would-be psychopath" usually experiences his parents as sadistic and brutal, rather than oppose them, he introjects their punitive voices into his conscience. The more hatred he feels, the more retaliation he expects, and the more he becomes subject to a punitive, primitive, and sadistic superego.

> The child, projecting his hostile fantasies on to the imagos of the parents, creates imagos that are more powerful and draconic in morality than the parents actually are. . . . As he continued to intro-

> ject parental imagos, the child introjects these distorted elements also, with the result that his unconscious conscience can be more severe (sadistic). . .than are the realistic inferences of the parents. [Glover, 1960, p. 142]

In contrast to the child that has had empathic parents who have been able to provide optimal maturational experiences which have yielded what Schafer (1960) has called "the loving and beloved superego," the psychopath has a sadistic superego which constantly condemns him.

The psychopath may be described as an individual who is at war with a strong, sadistic, primitive superego that constantly dominates him. He is similar to the child who feels overpowered by aggressively demanding parents and wants to rebel against their strict and punitive controls. His asocial, aggressive, callous and impulsive behavior may be viewed as a defensive operation, i.e., a rebellion against his punitive superego which he projects onto spouse, family, colleagues, and society in general. Because the psychopath has an unloving superego, he feels that he must be punished for his rebellious antisocial activity and that is why he inevitably leaves traces of his misdeeds available for others to see.

Some day we may discover that many of the individuals incarcerated in prisons are men and women who have strong, primitive, and punitive superegos and who have landed in prison because they have been rebelling against their own internal sadistic voices. We may also discover that these individuals feel gratified by being in prison because incarceration placates that punitive superego. Finally, we may discover that the reason many convicts become recidivists is that they cannot cope with their overwhelming guilt. When they are granted the freedom to leave prison they have to arrange unconsciously to be imprisoned again.

For those clinicians who are or have been engaged in the practice of child therapy and child analysis, the presence of a strict superego in a youngster diagnosed as psychopathic, seems quite evident.

> Joe B., age ten, was referred to me for psychotherapy because he had physically assaulted other children, sexually molested young girls, stole goods from stores and sold them at enormously high prices, defied authorities, and seemed to feel unperturbed by his behavior.
>
> In the therapeutic situation, Joe at first denied that he was involved in any antisocial activity. When his defense of denial was not challenged, in his tenth session he pointed out that he had, in fact, participated in some of the illegal acts that he was accused of, but he was merely "protecting myself." First, he accused teachers, and then later his peers of "picking on me." "They are all unfair people," he

bellowed. His injustice collecting embraced "unfair" acts on the part of almost every citizen in his community.

In Joe's fortieth session, he was asked by his therapist if his parents ever treated him unfairly. In contrast to his response to teachers, peers and others, Joe made several idealizing statements about both of his parents. Although he rarely saw his alcoholic father, and felt very vulnerable next to his neglectful mother who was a prostitute, he told the therapist that his "biggest wish is to please both of my parents." When the therapist asked Joe how he was progressing in this effort, he described himself as "a failure." He "could not memorize everything in the magazines that my mother leaves me when she goes out, nor can I make everything spick and span like she wants it." Joe also mentioned that he could not hit home-runs like his father wanted him to hit.

As Joe continued in his therapy, he began to realize that he was trying to be an omnipotent giant to please his parents. When he couldn't succeed, he "had to lie," and "when lying doesn't work," Joe pointed out, "all hell breaks loose and I want to hurt everybody."

Although Joe was labelled a psychopath by several professionals, it was clear that his punitive superego exerted a powerful effect on him. Guilty and vulnerable when he could not please his internalized parental introjects, he defied their voices by becoming impulsive, hostile, callous and destructive.

It would appear that the psychopath experiences his superego as having an omnipotent power that threatens his obliteration. Therefore, he needs to reassure himself of his survival by what he considers to be an omnipotent act of equal proportion. In vigorously asserting his defiance of his forbidding, condemning superego, he defends against feelings of vulnerability and weakness. By declaring through his antisocial behavior that he will *not* submit to the dictates of his superego, he feels the momentary triumph of a rebellious child (Glasser, 1978). As one notes the sexual excitement of the arsonist, thief, rapist, or legal manipulator, one also senses a forceful aggression against an *internal* prohibition.

One of the central themes of the psychopath's dynamics seems to be revenge. He moves from the position of victim to that of victor; from passive object of his superego's hostile dictates to a powerful director. His tormentors become his victims. Rather than feel threatened by punitive forces, the psychopath threatens others by becoming very sadistic. When he acts out his hostility by hurting others, he momentarily experiences a sense of grandiosity and no longer feels castrated and humiliated (Stoller, 1975).

To recapitulate, the psychopath is an individual who has murderous wishes that emanate from the severe neglect and frustration that he experienced as a child. To cope with his strong hatred, the child who is destined to be a psychopath internalizes his hatred and forms a primitive punitive, sadistic and omnipotent superego. Projecting the dictates of his superego onto others (parents, teachers, peers, and society in general), the child feels tormented and oppressed by the world. His antisocial behavior that is directed at others is his expression of rebellion against the dictates of his own punitive superego—i.e. a defense. Because the psychopath is basically a guilty person, he has to arrange unconsciously to be caught and punished for his transgressions.

It would appear that the "psychopathic syndrome" that we have just outlined exists to a small or large extent in many different types of patients—psychotic, neurotic, character disorders, etc. While there are patients whose "modus vivendi" consists largely of coping with a tyrannical superego by becoming involved in antisocial activity, we can probably see this dynamic to some extent in almost every patient who is in analysis and perhaps it exists in every human being in small or large doses.

Psychopathy and the Therapist's Countertransference

It is extremely rare that the term, "psychopath" is used benignly. Usually the antisocial characteristics of the psychopath are described in derogatory terms. The following are descriptions by dynamically oriented therapists and psychoanalysts which are intended to illuminate the dynamics of the psychopath—"irresponsible"; "absence of anxiety"; "inability to distinguish between truth and falsehood"; "inability to accept blame"; "failure to learn by experience"; "incapacity for love"; "lack of insight" and "shallow interpersonal responses to sex."

The derogatory and pejorative inferences in the above descriptions are quite obvious and are suggestive of what Erikson (1964) has called "diagnostic name-calling." It would appear that many therapists and analysts feel a sense of indignation when confronted with a patient's abusive antisocial behavior. Rather than noting that it is a defense against a punitive superego which is being projected onto the therapist and others, they condemn the antisocial behavior of the individual exhibiting it and label him a psychopath who is "untreatable."

Inasmuch as the person who manifests antisocial behavior can tax the analyst or therapist's patience and self-esteem, it is not difficult to understand that the clinician, to cope with his own vulnerability and anger, hostilely labels the patient "a psychopath whose prognosis is extremely guarded." However, when the term "psychopath" is used without a full discussion of the patient's metapsychology—psychic structure, history, dynamics, etc. and the patient is declared untreatable, this can usually be regarded as an expression of a negative countertransference (Fine, 1971).

As was suggested earlier in this paper, we can never rely on manifest behavior alone to fully understand an individual. In assessing antisocial behavior, it is necessary to observe the patient in depth and not just comment on some of his overt defensive maneuvers (Gedo, 1979; Stoller, 1975).

Some Considerations in the Treatment of the Psychopath

As has already been implied, many clinicians question the usefulness of analytic psychotherapy for the psychopath. Freedman, et al. (1976) declared: "The usefulness of outpatient psychotherapy along traditional lines (for the psychopath) is highly questionable. Phyllis Greenacre (1947) has pointed out that favorable changes are often illusory and quickly vanish, "leaving the fundamentally unsound organization of the personality of the psychopath. . .not. . . much influenced." On the basis of many years of experience with psychopathic patients Cleckley (1959) concluded that "analytic treatment of the psychopath has proven a failure."

However, the successful treatment by Freudian psychoanalysis of patients regarded as psychopaths has occasionally been reported (Schmideberg, 1947). Karpman (1948) has expressed optimism about the beneficial effects of prolonged psychotherapy on the majority of those classified as psychopaths, who, he maintained were actually neurotic. The work of Aichorn (1935) and Redl (1954) who combined analytically oriented therapy with milieu therapy seemed quite successful.

One of the reasons that may account for some of the pessimism about analytically oriented therapy for the psychopath is a partial misunderstanding of his dynamics and a partial misunderstanding of his transference reactions. Many analysts have regarded the psychopath as one with superego deficiencies who needs "an educative behavior to make up for omissions of the original education, until the readiness for cooperation is attained" (Fenichel, 1945). This therapeutic orientation, which is popular, is destined to fail because the psychopath does have a strong sense of right and wrong and resents the therapist if he becomes a superego figure who teaches him what he already knows. Furthermore, the psychopathic patient usually projects his tyrannical, sadistic, and punitive superego onto the analyst. If the analyst tries to educate this patient, he appears too much like the introjected parental figure who is always critical and dominating and who eventually must be defeated.

Although the psychopath characteristically enters the treatment situation in a state of defiance, this defiance has to be well understood by the analyst and related to empathically. As already suggested, the defiance is almost always an expression of rebellion against the analyst, who is experienced as a tyrannical superego. If the analyst does not take the patient's provocative remarks too literally or defensively, but helps the patient see how he is asking for punishment, the patient eventually becomes more involved in the treatment and slowly begins to examine the meaning of his superego mandates. Although the psychopath will eventually look at his own sadism that gives rise to his sadistic superego, he tries to test repeatedly the analyst's capacity to relate to him therapeutically and not get involved in a sado-masochistic power struggle.

When the patient has tested the analyst many times and learns that a sado-masochistic power struggle is not easy to achieve, he then usually moves to a regressed transference where he feels his painful affects, recalls being and feeling neglected as a child, gets in touch with his infantile murderous feelings and reviews his life much like any patient in any classical analysis.

> Mr. Leon C., aged 45 and divorced, was referred to me for analysis by his physician because of many psychosomatic complaints—migraine headaches, peptic ulcers, asthma, and hypertension. A business man, Mr. C. during the course of one year could be a millionaire three or four times and be unemployed as many times. The product of a broken home, he described his mother as "a good woman who had to work hard as a waitress because my old man was off drinking and screwing all of the time." Although he described the world as "a jungle" composed mainly of ruthless people, he did not speak too negatively about his parents.
>
> In Mr. C.'s first consultation interview, he mentioned that he had "been through six analysts and they all were jerks." He pointed out that several of them were "stupid Freudians" and could easily be

"outfoxed." When the analyst asked Mr. C. what he thought would happen with him inasmuch as all of his previous therapeutic experiences were so disappointing, Mr. C. remarked, "You're a smart guy. You won that round but I'll get you yet!"

Mr. C. missed his next two scheduled appointments without notifying the analyst. When he called him on the phone after the missed sessions he stated, "I think I should drop in to help you out. You must miss me!" On coming in for his second session, Mr. C. told the analyst that he, the analyst, was feeling like a loser but did not want to admit it. He went on to say that not only did the analyst look like a loser but that he was probably a latent homosexual who could never take on a tough guy like Mr. C. Mr. C. then reported a dream in which he was in a boxing ring with the analyst and was "ready to pound the living daylights out of you!. . . But, I felt sorry for you and woke up instead!"

During Mr. C.'s next several sessions he continued to make constant derogatory remarks about the analyst—his lack of skills, lack of virility, lack of knowledge, etc. When the analyst listened attentively without making any comments Mr. C. belligerently asked in his twelfth session, "When are you going to be a man and fight back?" Here the analyst asked, "What does fighting with me do for you?" After burlesquing the analyst's voice and then telling him that he asked a stupid question, Mr. C. began to recall many childhood episodes in which he was in brutal fist-fights. Although it was obvious that he derived some exhibitionistic gratification in boasting about his boxing prowess, Mr. C. did acknowledge that "as a child I sometimes doubted myself, felt a bit small, and boxing was a way of proving myself."

After revealing some of his castration anxiety and feelings of weakness as a child, Mr. C. missed four appointments. (He was being seen three times a week.) He did call the analyst to say that he would be out of town, but when he returned for a session he confessed that he was not out of town, but just "needed a rest from treatment." When the analyst did not respond to the patient's provocativeness Mr. C. said, "I've decided to stop this treatment. I need somebody stronger and you are a weakling. As I look at you, I can tell you have a lot of self-doubt." He then reported a dream. "I was leaving your office and you were crying. I felt sorry for you but I had to leave!" Mr. C. had no associations to the dream but continued to point out, "I've made a decision. This is my last session!" When the analyst mentioned that Mr. C. wanted to place the analyst in a weak position and make him cry, much like Mr. C. felt when he was a boy, Mr. C. said, "Don't try that wise guy shit! You can't beat me with that Freudian stuff! You are a schmuck and accept it!" After a long silence Mr. C. rather meekly asked, "Can't I get you upset?" When the analyst smiled and said, "You are trying awfully hard to do so!" Mr. C. retorted, "I think you like me and I'll stay for a while."

When Mr. C. after about six months of treatment recognized that it was somewhat difficult to provoke the analyst to fight with him and/or reject him, he entered into a cooperative phase of analysis. He took the couch and examined homosexual fantasies toward the analyst, had many oedipal dreams which he could analyze quite well by himself, began to be quite productive in his work, his somatic symptoms disappeared, and he became involved in a reasonably mature relationship with a woman. For about two months Mr. C. described a feeling of well-being that he "never had before in my life."

Although Mr. C. enjoyed his "honeymoon" with the analyst, his dreams and fantasies started to reveal a wish to be punished. In one dream, he told the analyst that he was making a lot of analytic progress and the analyst disagreed. In another dream, he was being sadistically raped by the analyst. When Mr. C. was asked to freely associate to his wish to be demeaned and raped, he brought out many fantasies of being beaten up by his father. These sado-masochistic fantasies all ended on the theme of "kissing and making up" with his father, and in several fantasies Mr. C. became his father's wife.

Mr. C. had to defend against his deep homosexual yearning for a father by once again trying to fight with the analyst. He started to miss appointments again and threatened to leave treatment altogether. When his defense against the wish for a father was interpreted to him, Mr. C. first fought the interpretation and the analyst. On seeing once more that he could not easily provoke the analyst to be rejected, Mr. C. slowly began to examine his wish for a father. In looking at his wish for a father, Mr. C. alternated between expressions of grief and hatred and had many fantasies of being reunited with his father.

Mr. C. who is now in his fourth year of analysis has been focusing more on his pre-oedipal and oedipal relationship with his mother. As with his father, he has wept bitterly on recalling being and feeling rejected by her and has expressed deep yearnings for "a loving mother."

As Mr. C. has worked through some of his rage, his superego is not as forceful and punitive. Consequently, he has not demonstrated for some time his erratic behavior, provocative attacks and other forms of antisocial behavior.

Mr. C. is quite typical of how a psychopathic patient responds to analytic treatment. At first, the patient experiences the analyst as his own sadistic superego and wants to obliterate him. When the analyst is not provoked by the patient's "antisocial transference," the latter attempts to cooperate with the analyst, and usually falls in love with him. However, warm, erotic feelings become threatening to the patient and again he makes bids to leave treatment. Having weathered many analytic storms by now, the patient can usually accept the interpretation that he is fighting his libidinal yearnings and move on to an examination of his own sadism and his own tyrannical superego.

When analyst and patient are of different sexes, one of the initial resistances that the psychopathic analysand can express is an active attempt to sexually seduce the analyst.

Sally D., age 30 and married, came for analysis because of severe marital problems, sexual promiscuity, difficulties with her children, constant arguments with parents, friends, and colleagues, stealing in stores, frigidity, obesity, and hay fever. In her initial consultation interview, she told her male analyst that she had been sexually seduced by three of her former therapists. "I really try to do the therapeutic work. But, something happens and they want me sexually. I know it's of no help to screw your analyst, but they get to me," Mrs. D. lamented.

For her first six sessions Mrs. D. seemed to take her therapy seriously. She examined fantasies, dreams and history but with no references made to the analyst. In her seventh session, she told the analyst that she experienced him as cold, "just like my father." She asked, "Couldn't you be a little warmer? Couldn't you show some love? When the analyst asked Mrs. D. what she was feeling now, that made her want some warmth from the analyst, Mrs. D. broke out into a rage. "That is a stupid question. It's like asking somebody who is thirsty why he wants water. You are a cold potato," she bellowed, and walked out of the office.

In her next session, Mrs. D. apologized for her "performance" and "realized that you want to help me." She went on for several sessions to talk about how she always missed approval and warmth from her father "who was always out with the boys." In her thirteenth session, after telling the analyst how she still yearned for a father, she asked the analyst to hold her for a brief moment "for some reassurance." On the analyst's asking Mrs. D. what she was feeling and thinking that made her want some physical reassurance, Mrs. D. got off the couch, and said, "I'm leaving for ever."

Mrs. D. did not come for her next three sessions but did call the analyst's office and cursed him on the phone machine. During one of these calls, the analyst picked up the phone and after a silence, Mrs. D. asked, "Will you still see me?" The analyst responded that he had been keeping her hours open and would see her.

Mrs. D. came for her next session with a proposal. She would like to stop the treatment with the analyst because she was not ripe for psychoanalysis. She will go into group therapy with another therapist and become the analyst's friend. On being asked by the analyst what bothered her about being in analysis with him, Mrs. D. commented, "I feel so beneath you as a patient. I can't stand your power over me. You seem like a big prick and I feel like a nothing that has been wiped out."

As Mrs. D. began to see how she was projecting her own ego ideal—an omnipotent phallus on to the analyst and hating him for it—her sexual provocativeness decreased and she began to examine her rivalry with men and her feelings of low self-worth as a woman. Her own sadistic superego became obvious and some of her own murderous feelings were eventually discharged. Though still in treatment and still occasionally testing the analyst, as Mrs. D. has been working through her own sadism, her superego mandates are less severe, and she has little desire to resume her antisocial activities.

Summary

The psychopathic personality is one who has murderous wishes that emanate from severe neglect and frustration that he experienced as a child. To cope with his strong hatred, the child who is destined to be a psychopath internalizes his hatred and forms a primitive, sadistic, and omnipotent superego. Projecting the voices of his tyrannical superego on to others, he hates the world for controlling him and abusing him. Tormented and oppressed, the psychopath's antisocial behavior should be regarded as a rebellion against his own superego. Although not often recognized as such, the psychopath is a very guilty person who wants to be punished.

The psychopath often induces a negative countertransference in the analyst by becoming "antisocial" and provocative with "the analyst–superego." If the analyst understands the patient's wish to fight and be rejected as a function of his punitive superego and helps the patient recognize this, analytic treatment with a psychopathic personality can be quite helpful.

REFERENCES

Aichorn, A. *Wayward Youth*. New York: Viking Press, 1935.

Bowlby, J. *Maternal Care and Mental Health*. Geneva: World Health Organization, 1951.

Cleckley, H. "Psychopathic States," in *American Handbook of Psychiatry*, Vol. 1, S. Ariebi, ed. New York: Basic Books, 1959.

Davies, J. *Phrenology: Fad and Science*. New Haven, Conn.: Yale University Press, 1955.

"Diagnostic and Statistical Manual." *Mental Disorders*, Vol. II, Washington, D.C.: American Psychiatric Association, 1964.

Fenichel, O. *Psychoanalytic Theory of Neuroses*. New York: Norton, 1945.

Fine, R. *The Healing of the Mind*. New York: David McKay, 1971.

Freedman, A.; H. Kaplan; B. Sadock. *Modern Synopsis of Psychiatry*, Vol. II. Baltimore, Md.: The Williams and Wilkins Co., 1976.

Freud, S. "The Interpretation of Dreams." (1900) *Standard Edition*, Vols. 4 and 5. London: Hogarth, 1953.

_____. "Analysis of a Phobia in a Five-Year Old Boy" (1909), *Standard Edition*, Vol. 10. London: Hogarth, 1955.

_____. "Some Analytic Character-Types Met in Psychoanalytic Work." (1916), *Standard Edition*, Vol. 14. London: Hogarth, 1957.

Gaylin, W. *Caring*. New York: Alfred A. Knopf, 1976.

Gedo, J. *Beyond Interpretation*. New York: International Universities Press, 1979.

Glasser, M. "The Role of the Superego in Exhibitionism," in *International Journal of Psychoanalytic Psychotherapy*, Vol. 7, R. Langs, ed. New York: Jason Aronson, 1978.

Glover, E. *Psychoanalysis*. London: Staples Press, 1949.

_____. *The Roots of Crime*. New York: International Universities Press, 1960.

Greenacre, P. "Problems of Patient-Therapist Relationship in the Treatment of Psychopaths," in *Handbook of Correctional Psychology*. R. Lindner and R. Seliger, eds. New York: Philosophical Library, 1947.

Johnson, J. "Nixon's Use of Metaphor: The Real Nixon Tapes," *Psychoanalytic Review*, Vol. 66, No. 2, 1979.

Karpman, B. "Myth of Psychopathic Personality," *American Journal of Psychiatry*, Vol. 104, 1948.

Kurth, G. "The Jew and Adolph Hitler," *Psychoanalytic Quarterly*, Vol. 16, 1947.

Kutash, S.; I. Kutash; and L. Schlesinger. *Violence: Perspectives on Murder and Aggression*. San Jose, California: Jossey-Bass, 1979.

Lindner, R. "Psychopathy as a Psychological Problem," in *Encyclopedia of Psychology*, P. L. Harriman, ed. New York: Philosophy Library, 1948.

Loewald, H. *Panel:* "New Horizons in Metapsychology," *Journal of the American Psychoanalytic Association*, Vol. 24, 1976.

McCord, W., and J. McCord. *Psychopathy and Delinquency*. New York: Grune and Stratton, 1956.

Newkirk, P. "Psychopathic Traits are Inheritable," *Journal of Nervous Diseases*, Vol. 18, 1957.

New York Times, November 18, 1973.

New York Times, August 23, 1979.

Nixon, R. *Six Crises*. New York: Doubleday and Company, 1962.

Payne, R. *The Life and Death of Adolph Hitler*. New York: Praeger, 1973.

Redl, F. *Controls from Within: Techniques for the Treatment of the Aggressive Child*. Glencoe, Ill.: The Free Press, 1954.

Saul, L. *Psychodynamics of Hostility*. New York: Jason Aronson, 1976.

Schafer, R. "The Loving and Beloved Superego in Freud's Structural Theory," *Psychoanalytic Study of the Child*, Vol. 15. New York: International Universities Press, 1960.

Schmideberg, M. "The Analytic Treatment of Major Criminals: Therapeutic Results and Technical Problems," in *Searchlights on Delinquency*. New York: International Universities Press, 1949.

Stoller, R. *Perversion: The Erotic Form of Hatred*. New York: Pantheon Books, 1975.

DISCUSSANT: SANDA BRAGMAN LEWIS

The psychopathic patient has long been considered most refractory to psychotherapeutic treatment. As Dr. Strean notes in his paper, most clinicians declare such patients untreatable, and avoid them in their practice. Others take these patients on, while feeling little hope that their efforts will be effective. When the treatment ends in failure, no one is surprised.

What is so remarkable about Dr. Strean's paper is that he has approached the phenomena of the psychopath with fresh eyes. He has taken what has been considered one of the hallmarks of the psychopathic personality—the absence of guilt—and turned it on its head. In the best tradition of the most original thinkers of our field, he has looked at his patients, looked at the accepted ideas about what makes them tick, compared the two, and been able to say in a clear, stimulating, thought-provoking way, that the two do not fit. That is, the psychopathic patient, who is usually thought to have an insufficiently developed superego, and thus suffers no guilt, is actually someone suffering from a most severe and punitive superego. Further, the superego is so unrelenting, that the psychopathic individual, in order to survive psychically, projects this harsh force onto others around him, and then does battle with what now appears to the patient to be an outside opponent. In this battle, the individual alternates between seeking to provoke punishment, and getting revenge.

One of the elements that makes this formulation so exciting is that it helps to explain the difficulty of doing treatment with such patients. For when the psychopath enters treatment, he brings his battle into the transference, projecting onto the therapist his own very harsh superego. Once the therapist can see that the patient is trying to get the therapist to punish him, the patient's provocative behavior takes on new meaning. This perspective offers the clinician a tremendously valuable handle for understanding his patient. My own experience with patients definitely bears out Dr. Strean's formulations. I have long observed that once the initial attempts of the patient to establish a sado-masochistic power struggle with the analyst have been explored as to their dynamic meaning, these patients then exhibit pervasive feelings of guilt and very low self-esteem. Since their guilt is so extreme, they tend to need to try to battle in the transference until the severity of the superego has been reduced. As treatment continues, the acting-out behavior in the outside world, and the provocations in the transference, diminish, if not disappear entirely.

In reading Dr. Strean's paper, I was struck by the language, very familiar to me, used by clinicians to describe the psychopath: "callous," "selfish," "without remorse," "incapable of deep attachments," etc. The highly judgmental nature of these descriptions is startling, particularly when compared to that of other diagnostic categories, except those that also involve a great deal of acting-out. To me, these descriptions signal the presence of intense countertransference feelings in the clinician. Calling the patient selfish, unprincipled, and irresponsible serves to mask the despair, helplessness, and rage these patients provoke in the therapist. Not being able to see, prior to Dr. Strean's formulations, the meaningfulness of the patient's provocative behavior, the therapist has been left to feel confused and hopeless. One of the factors making it difficult for clinicians to see the superego struggles of the patient involves the need to keep an emotional distance from people who engage in activities which are in opposition to our own standards. For, to view the patient as guilt-ridden would lead to empathy, and this could arouse a great deal of anxiety in the therapist when dealing with someone whose behavior and attitudes offend our personal sensibilities. The more usual response in working with these patients is for the therapist to feel outrage and anger, often denied, and because of this, attack the patient in the guise of interpretations or dismiss them altogether.

Another possible countertransference reaction in working with the psychopath is the tendency to unconsciously identify with the patient in his battles with seemingly outside forces. Sometimes these people carry out in action impulses that the therapist shares but cannot, for various reasons, put into action himself. The patient's feeling of being a victim, his urgent wish to break the rules, may stir up similar feelings in the therapist, who then unconsciously encourages the patient in his acting-out. Identification with the wish to break the rules may also lead the therapist to break the analytic rules and socialize with the patient, have sex with him, or otherwise be too involved. Often these activities are rationalized by the therapist as necessary given the desperate nature of the patient's problem. I also agree with Dr. Strean's finding that these patients actually have a highly developed sense of right and wrong. Because of this, the therapist's efforts to educate them are experienced as attacks and tend to exascerbate their need to battle and also their feeling that they are being misunderstood.

In reading this paper, I found Dr. Strean's case illustrations to be clear, informative, and compelling. The course of treatment he describes—projecting the superego onto the therapist, testing the therapist repeatedly, and then movement to a regressed transference—is confirmed in my experience with patients. In two of his cases, Dr. Strean describes the patient's idealization of his parents. I have found this also to be so, with the patient seeing the parents in a golden light.

Often the patient will describe lives filled with terrible neglect and/or abuse, yet feel very "understanding" of the parents. Parents are described as "doing the best they could," "under a lot of pressure," or "unaware of what they were doing." The only exception to this would be two patients who fit this description, but who are largely amnesic about their early lives. With both, this amnesia seems to protect them from the pain and anger they would feel if they could connect more with their childhood experiences. In these cases, in addition to the superego struggle that Dr. Strean describes, acting does stand in place of memory.

Something that Dr. Strean mentioned in his case discussions and which I would like to emphasize, are the other defensive factors involved in the patient's need to battle. In addition to guilt, the psychopathic person is struggling against overwhelming feelings of anxiety. These patients will do anything not to feel anxiety, not because they are incapable of it, but because it is so terribly threatening. In line with Dr. Strean's view, it seems to me that too much of the psychopath's behavior has been seen as involving direct instinctual discharge. In my experience, there is tremendous compulsivity involved in their acting-out, and often little actual pleasure.

The other defensive aspects to the patient's aggression appear later on in treatment. Dr. Strean describes a process in which a regressed, cooperative phase follows the initial period (which may take months or years) of testing and provocation. This cooperative phase is generally blown apart by the patient's resumption, in the transference, of his battling position. Dr. Strean describes his patient, Mr. C., as wanting to fight with him again as his homosexual yearnings were becoming conscious. I want to confirm this finding from my own practice. That is, as the treatment proceeds, the patient tends to try to start battling again within the transference as a defense against very frightening feelings and longings. To these patients, the most frightening feelings are love, dependency, and erotic feelings, both homosexual and heterosexual. For them, experiencing these kinds of longings leads to a tremendous sense of vulnerability and weakness. This is usually accompanied by very powerful feelings of humiliation, and the conviction that they will be rejected. For some, the experience of love, sexuality and/or dependency can induce terrible fears of annihilation as well. Since the patients have already experienced progress in their lives through working out the early storms of the treatment, they tend to be willing to stay and work on these later battles, although doing so involves a great deal of internal suffering for them. If the therapist can keep the defensive aspects of these battles in mind, the results, in terms of positive changes in a patient's internal structure and external life, can be most gratifying.

Dr. Strean's formulation of a psychopathic syndrome which could exist in patients of other diagnostic categories, offers a valuable tool for understanding behavior, either in the transference or outside, that would appear to be otherwise puzzling. I can confirm the presence of this kind of syndrome in patients who vary from neurotic, through character disordered, to schizophrenic.

As I see it, the value of Dr. Strean's paper goes beyond his reformulation of our understanding of the psychopathic personality, something that in itself is a major achievement. For what he has done is to bring our attention back to one of the most important elements of psychic structure, the superego. In recent years, as our interest has focused on elucidating the dynamics of the infant's first two years, the superego as an important concept in psychological development and in treatment has fallen into a state of neglect. Dr. Strean's work goes a long way toward rectifying that imbalance.

DISCUSSANT: NORMAN SHELLY

Before focusing on a specific clinical example I would like to address myself to some of the main issues in Strean's reconsideration in the treatment or lack of treatment of the "psychopath." 1) Why do some workers in the field latch on to the idea that a person who is repetitively "antisocial" is unable to feel guilt? 2) Why use diagnostic labeling rather than treatment? 3) What is this idea of a "weak" superego? 4) Why has the "psychopath" with many psychoanalysts (not to mention those who are not analysts) taken on the complexion and therefore the unretrievable position of being different from other patients? I believe, in agreement with Strean, that the answer, whether institutionally augmented or in a clinical setting, is primarily a negative superego countertransference reaction or defense. As I go along I will try to clarify what must be presumed to be an unconcious defense.

Freud looks to Shakespeare to substantiate some of his observations on "The Exceptions" (1916). In the opening soliloquy of *Richard III*, Gloucester says:

> But I that am not shaped for sportive tricks
> Nor made to court an amorous looking glass;
> • • •
> Deformed, unfinished, sent before my time
> Into this breathing world scarce half made up,
> • • •
> And therefore, since I cannot prove a lover,
> To entertain these fair well spoken days,
> I am determined to prove a villain,
> And hate the idle pleasures of these days.

Freud then tells us that this embittered speech has more meaning than meets the eye. "Nature has done me a grievous wrong in denying me the beauty of form which wins human love. Life owes me reparation for this, and I will see that I get it. I have a right to be an exception, to disregard the scruples by which others let themselves be held back. *I may do wrong myself, since wrong has been done me*" (emphasis added). Those who have never been given love are emotionally crippled and therefore cannot give love. This inability to love creates a weak ego and this weak ego structure is the result of the destructiveness of contact with the mother (Jones *Collected Papers on Psychoanalysis*. 5th ed. London: Bailliere, Tindall and Zox). Fine, in *Psychoanalytic Vision* (1980), writes in reference to pathology, "... the effect that is most strongly brought to the fore in pathology is hostility. Thus all emotional disturbance involves a fixation at, or a regression to, the early infantile states of rage. This rage may be directed at other people or inward, at oneself." He further states, "All severe mental disturbance involves a harsh superego."

Strean, in his paper, helps us understand the dynamic defense in the psychopathy of the "anti-social" character by demonstrating how the harsh superego is projected onto the analyst. As a result of this projection, the analyst is the object of pugnacious attacks. This is a last ditch effort to ward off forbidden wishes. As the analytic work proceeds the patient may project these forbidden wishes onto the analyst. During this development of the transference, Strean is quite right in pointing to the danger of the analyst being drawn into a power struggle. When eventually the unconscious fantasies are uncovered and explored, very often desperately defended against, the guilt that was contained in the projections can be seen as the motivating need for punishment. What is baffling to many analysts, as born out by Strean's review of the literature, is the absence of conscious guilt and in its stead a "devil may care" posture. This brings me to the issue of negative countertransference.

The "devil may care" attitude of the patients is aimed at weakening the analyst. Very often this impervious response of the patients must be endured for long periods of time. Every effort of the analyst is met with various constellations of the same resistance. The patient appears to be unreachable and the analyst may experience much despair. The treatment may very well depend on how the therapist resolves his own countertransference.

It has been my experience in my own practice and in supervising others, that if countertransference issues do not hinder the work with the "anti-social" character, what slowly is uncovered is an underlying well of despair and hopelessness. I agree with Strean that the superego must be analyzed in all patients. When the patient contains the punitive introjects he must be relieved of his "hair shirt." When the patient projects the harsh superego onto the therapist without experiencing conscious guilt, the therapist must gingerly work towards making the guilt conscious. This is the case when working with the "psychopath." I believe it is more helpful to view the superego as loving or unloving and all that entails in the transference and resistance. I would reserve the weakness or strong description to the psycho-sexual development of the ego.

Strean tells us that it is extremely rare that the term "psychopath" is used benignly. In fact, in most instances, the label "psychopath" coupled with a diagnostic description has become generic in its meaning and virtually amounts to a "character assassination." This I believe is mostly due to the negative countertransference and is related to the unconscious superego and the infantile wishes of the therapist. This could be extended to the whole of society. These forbidden wishes are connected to unconscious feelings of envy and admiration for the "anti-social" acting out. What the analyst must repress, the "psychopath" acts out. This brings to mind the many instances when analysts cannot tolerate the restraints of their profession and seek libidinal and aggressive gratification by turning to other modalities and therapies. The type of patient we are presented with by Strean suffers from the same restraints and must rebel in an anti-social way. I cannot stress strongly enough that the use of diagnostic labeling has very little clinical application and serves primarily to separate those who do the treating and those who are treated. The concept of normality is a fiction and most normal persons have egos that range from the normal to the psychotic (*Analysis Terminable and Interminable*, Freud, 1937). Sullivan stated it most succinctly when he said that we are all more human than otherwise.

What follows is a condensed version of a case in which the transference developed primarily around the defense of projecting the critical, withholding, and punitive superego onto the analyst. The countertransference developed around my own self-critical superego.

> Carrie, age 32 and divorced, came to therapy because of her difficulties with authority figures in work situations. Her relationships with men would begin with high hopes, but would eventually deteriorate to an angry hostile relationship. She would then question what she had ever seen in these men. They were "pip-squeaks," intellectually inferior, and socially beneath her. She fantasied that she would one day meet a man that was at least her intellectual equal and strong. She longed for someone to protect her. She had been in many different kinds of therapy, including marriage counseling. She hadn't been able to change, because she hadn't been ready. She was now ready. She was attractive, intelligent, and somewhat feisty. She had learned a certain amount of "psychological jargon" in her previous therapy and told me that she sometimes saw herself as "borderline" or perhaps "pathological." (Very often patients will put diagnostic labels on themselves in an effort to avoid real feelings of guilt). She felt she had been stymied by her parents her whole life. She had been very rebellious as an adolescent.
>
> In the first session she told me that I had the same name as her father. The therapy proceeded in a somewhat "honeymoon" state. She increased her sessions. At this point a certain amount of ambivalence became evident. She felt I gave her space and that I could tolerate her feelings, but she wanted more feedback. She wasn't sure this was the "right" therapy for her. It wasn't long before she was demanding to have her appointments changed. She would call on the phone and tell me she was going out of town and could she make up the hour. When I didn't change her hour she became enraged. I was one of those rigid "Freudians." I was "tight assed" and she followed this by a litany of accusations and ended with the remark that I didn't understand her needs or her pain. Confronted, she admitted that she had fought with all the therapists she had seen. Interpretations were greeted with "so what." She saw me as the depriving parent. She was unrelentless in her attacks. At the same time she was fearful that I would end the treatment. It had crossed my mind. My countertransference was ambivalent and I had to deal with my "psychoanalytic superego" whose command was to be benign, understanding, be in touch with the patient's pain, give interpretations that would dilute the negative transference while at the same time avoid getting into a power struggle with her. Very often she would call to tell me she was quitting therapy and then show up for her session. At times she would be seductive, somewhat the same as one of Strean's patients. Asked what would happen if she seduced me she answered, "I'd fuck you and leave." At other times she would weep and then return to the

attack. She could not tolerate her desire to be close to me as it made her feel vulnerable. What she longed for she had to fight with. She was warding off her unconscious guilt.

She then began to bounce checks. At first I accepted her excuses which were given in a fashion that to her seemed perfectly acceptable. I had nothing to worry about. She always paid her bills eventually. Her bookkeeping was never very good. We live in a credit society. Her rationalizations were endless. The "devil may care attitude" coupled with the need to be special became an additional demand. When I told her that she would have to pay by cash or money order she became enraged and threatened to walk out. She said I was only interested in money. Despite this reaction she decided to continue the sessions. There was some indication that she was beginning to experience a tinge of guilt. Unless the reader be misled this was not the end of her "acting out."

I have tried to convey in this case, in a telescopic manner, some of the elements involved in the transference and countertransference where the emphasis on the projection of the superego is so prevalent. The "anti-social" activities of these patients can run the gamut from serious criminal acts to diluted manifest provocations whose meaning is revealed when we can uncover the unconscious fantasies.

In reconsidering the treatment of the "psychopath," Strean brings into focus the dynamics of the superego in the transference. By taking a hard look at the negative countertransference we can see how it interferes with the "anti-social" character receiving adequate help. I agree with Strean that diagnostic labeling is part of the negative countertransference. This negative countertransference becomes part of the learning experience of students who may never test the non-validity of diagnosis. There is a marked difference between condoning anti-social behavior and understanding the meaning of such behavior. Strean points the way to further understanding.

ABOUT THE DISCUSSANTS

ARTHUR BLATT, Ph.D., a psychologist and psychoanalyst in private practice in New York, has been on the faculty of several psychoanalytic training institutes and has published articles in psychoanalytic and psychotherapeutic journals on group therapy, mental retardation, the dynamics of referrals, long term vs. short term therapy and other issues in psychotherapy.

MARGARET BONNEFIL, M.S.W., a social worker, has specialized in short-term treatment and is an ardent spokesperson for it. She is Director of Education and Training, Didi Hirch Community Mental Health Center in California.

POLLY CONDIT, M.S.W., a psychoanalyst and social worker, is on the faculties of the New York Center for Psychoanalytic Training and Fordham University in New York. An analyst who works with children, adolescents, and adults, Ms. Condit divides her time between doing psychotherapy and training social workers and psychoanalysts.

ABRAHAM DAVIS, M.S.W., a clinical social worker in New Jersey, is Executive Director of the Jewish Family Service of Northern New Jersey. In addition to administering a social agency and his own private practice, Mr. Davis is a national leader in social work. Among his many responsibilities, he is on the editorial board of *Social Casework*.

LLOYD DEMAUSE, M.A., one of the world's best known psychohistorians, is also a prolific writer, having written on the psychological and social dynamics of political events and political leaders, child abuse, the history of childhood, and applied psychoanalysis. He is Director of the Institute for Psychohistory in New York.

DAVID EDWARDS, M.S.W., a social worker practicing in California, is Director of the San Benito County Mental Health Services. He is a strong proponent of the encounter and sensitivity movements and has written extensively on the subject.

JUDITH FELTON, M.S.W., a psychoanalyst in Princeton, New Jersey, is a member of the Society for Psychoanalytic Training in New York. She is currently completing her doctorate at Rutgers University. A supervisor of therapists, Ms. Felton is also active with the Clinical Society of Social Workers in New Jersey. She is on the faculty of Bryn Mawr Graduate School of Social Work.

REUBEN FINE, Ph.D., a psychoanalyst and psychologist in New York, is Director of the New York Center for Psychoanalytic Training. He has written over 40 books and 100 professional articles. Among some of his well-known books are A *History of Psychoanalysis, The Psychoanalytic Vision, The Healing of the Mind,* and *Freud: A Reevaluation of His Theories.* Internationally recognized as an outstanding psychoanalytic theoretician, educator, and practitioner, one of Dr. Fine's major interests is bringing psychoanalysis into the academic setting.

MARGARET FRANK, M.S.W., until very recently, a professor in charge of the Treatment Sequence at Smith College School of Social Work, is also a nationally renowned child therapist. An expert in ego psychology, Professor Frank has written extensively in social work, group therapy, and many psychotherapeutic journals. A past president of the American Orthopsychiatric Association, she has been on the faculties of Columbia University, Simmons College, New York University, and Rutgers University.

LAURA FUERSTEIN, M.S.W., divides her time doing psychotherapy and psychoanalysis in New York City and Highland Park, New Jersey. Associated with the New York Center for Psychoanalytic Training and the East Side Consultation Center in New York, Ms. Fuerstein is one of the leaders of the Clinical Society of Social Workers in New Jersey.

MARY GOTTESFELD, M.S.W., a psychotherapist in private practice in New York, has been editor of *Clinical Social Work* for the past ten years. A creative writer, her articles have appeared in several prominent psychoanalytic and psychotherapeutic journals.

MARTIN GREENE, D.S.W., a professor of social work at Adelphi University, is also a psychoanalyst in private practice in New York. Among his written contributions are articles in the *International Jour-*

nal of Psychoanalysis and *Clinical Social Work*. He is also on the faculty of the New York Center for Psychoanalytic Training and the Lenox Hill Hospital Psychotherapy Program.

ANN HARTMAN, D.S.W., a professor of social work at University of Michigan, is also a family therapist in private practice in Ann Arbor, Michigan. Dr. Hartman is a prominent leader in social work education. Her many articles have appeared in *Social Casework*, *Social Work* and other prominent journals.

RALPH KOLODNY, M.A., M.S.S.S., professor of social work at Boston University, is an internationally known expert in social group work. His text on the subject is used worldwide. Professor Kolodny is also a frequent contributor to social work journals.

ARTHUR LEADER, M.S.W., is Associate Director of the Jewish Board of Family Guardians in New York. A renowned family therapist, Mr. Leader has been on the faculties of Columbia University, New York University, and Adelphi University. His many publications have appeared in *Social Casework*, *Social Work*, and journals in social work education.

PAUL LERMAN, D.S.W., is Distinguished Professor at Rutgers University where he teaches sociology and social work. Chairman of the doctoral program at Rutgers Graduate School of Social Work, Dr. Lerman is an internationally renowned expert on juvenile delinquency. He has written several articles and books on juvenile delinquency; a widely used text is his *Juvenile Delinquency and Social Policy*. Dr. Lerman is also a consultant on delinquency and mental health to the National Institute of Mental Health.

SANDA LEWIS, M.S.W., is a psychoanalyst in private practice in New York. She is on the faculties of Fordham University and the New York Center for Psychoanalytic Training and is a supervisor for the East Side Consultation Center.

SHERMAN MERLE, Ph.D., is Dean of the Graduate School of Social Work at Sir Wilfred Laurier University in Waterloo, Ontario. Prior to his current position, he was Dean of the Graduate School of

Social Work at the State University of New York at Buffalo. A prominent social work educator and practicing clinician, Dean Merle has written on the sociology of private practice in social work, organizational theory, undergraduate education in social work, and other educational and clinical subjects.

JEROME ROSEN practices psychotherapy and psychoanalysis in New York City. He is affiliated with the East Side Consultation Center and the New York Center for Psychoanalytic Training. Among Mr. Rosen's articles is a study of the high-school drop-out.

LESLIE ROSENTHAL, Ph.D., is a psychoanalyst and group therapist in New York City. For many years, he was Director of the Group Therapy Department of the Jewish Board of Guardians and is currently Director of the Group Therapy Department of the Center for Modern Psychoanalysis in New York. Group Therapy Consultant to many social agencies and clinics in New York and New Jersey, Dr. Rosenthal's many articles have appeared in the *International Journal of Group Psychotherapy, The Psychoanalytic Review, Social Casework* and *The Jewish Journal for Communal Service.*

NORMAN SHELLY is a psychoanalyst in private practice in New York City. Director of Clinical Services at the East Side Consultation Service in New York, Mr. Shelly is also on the faculty of the New York Center for Psychoanalytic Training.

MAX SIPORIN, D.S.W., is Professor of Social Work at the Graduate School of Social Work at the State University of New York in Albany. An internationally prominent social work educator, Dr. Siporin is the author of many articles in all of the major social work journals. In addition, his text *Introduction to Social Work Practice* is widely used all over the world.

RONALD SUNSHINE, M.S.W., is a psychoanalyst in private practice in New York City. He is Chairman of the Training Program at the New York Center for Psychoanalytic Training where he is on the faculty of the Training Institute. A contributor to *The International Journal of Psychoanalysis*, Mr. Sunshine has been on the faculties of Rutgers and Fordham Universities.

JOHN WODARSKI, Ph.D., is Professor of Social Work at the Graduate School of Social Work at the University of Georgia. A prominent researcher in social work and in charge of research at the University of Georgia, Dr. Wodarski is one of the country's leading exponents of learning theory and behavior modification therapy. His many articles have appeared in *Clinical Social Work* and other clinical journals.

INDEX